THE GREAT SOUTHWEST

The sunset-tinted buttes of
Oak Creek Canyon are reflected
in a pool of quiet water
where the stream slows and widens
at Red Rock Crossing.

3

*Montezuma's Castle (with which
the Aztec chief had
no connection) dates to
about A.D. 1100. The superbly
situated ruin is preserved
today as a national monument.*

*Overleaf: Monument Valley,
a Navajo tribal park, sits
astride the Arizona-Utah border.
Its formations mark the
partnership of erosion and time.*

THE GREAT SOUTHWEST

The Story of a Land and Its People

By
Elna Bakker
and
Richard G. Lillard

The Great West Series

AMERICAN WEST PUBLISHING COMPANY
PALO ALTO, CALIFORNIA

Yucca at sunset in southern Arizona.

Library of Congress Card Number 72-75554

ISBN 0-910118-26-4

CONTENTS

INTRODUCTION

THE DESERT REGION, the geographic province, the whole balanced environment once lay wholly within what is now the Estados Unidos Mexicanos. For well over a century the great desert has been shared by the United States of America, for it includes the spacious Southwest, now homeland of a people who call themselves Americans and whom Mexicans call North Americans. The desert subcontinent extends from the abrupt Tehachapi and San Bernardino mountains to the rolling plains east of the Sangre de Cristo Mountains and the red waters of the Pecos River, from the plateau country north of the Colorado River to the tropical southern edge of the Chihuahuan Desert, from below sea level at Bad Water in Death Valley to the snow-topped ridges of the Sierra Occidental, that rugged barrier between Sonora and Chihuahua.

Though interspersed by peaks and by patches or even stretches of grass and forest lands, the region is essentially a desert, high or low, an expanse of surface that is sunlit geology by day and starlit astronomy by night. It is unified by climate, ecological homogeneity, economics, and history. Its one disunity is political—the arbitrary boundary line, an extraordinary imposition that slits in two the weaving waters of the Rio Grande, breeds international cities by the pair, spawns vice and smuggling rackets on a grand scale, and engenders both pacifying treaties and armed surveillance.

It is a land of deserts, flat or rumpled, of monumental ranges, or stupendous canyons, that encompass all the known eras of geologic time, of blowing sand dunes, of narrow valleys green with cottonwoods and cultivated crops, and of occasional irrigated plains. It seems vast because of wide visible distances and because the places people want to reach are far apart. Like many other deserts it is naturally rich in plants and wildlife, and it holds stark evidence of human activity older than written record—dwellings under sandstone cliffs and many-storied pueblos, now ruins among the brush and grass. It is a modern urban and technological scene as well. The buildings of the biggest towns—Phoenix, Juárez, Mexicali, El Paso, Tucson, Chihuahua, Albuquerque, and Las Vegas—thrust up into machine-age air near mountains rising from plains that disappear around earth's curvature.

It is a provincial empire, sometimes charming, sometimes overwhelming, and sometimes ugly, cut off from the sea except at the small gulf ports of Sonora and Baja California. It is ever enticing to exploiters of natural resources and nowadays also to tourists, artists, scientists, archaeologists, and affluent pleasure-seekers, young and old. No other area in the United States exhibits more evidence of civilizations that long preceded Iberian explorers. As Harvey Fergusson says, the area as a whole is "a living museum of its own history." Nowhere else in the two nations have older ways of living persisted more vitally and steadily than along the upper waters of the Rio Grande (called Río Bravo in Mexico) and on the slopes of the Sierra Madre Occidental, as among the Tarahumaras, those amazing long-distance walkers who tread in breech clouts along the streets of Chihuahua with as much dignity and confidence as did any emissary sent by the viceroy of Spain.

No other regions of the United States and Mexico hold more surviving ruins of activity by non-Indians—of missions, haciendas, forts, mining operations, and mining towns. Nowhere are there longer distances without people and greater, more surprising, sudden contrasts of desolate space and crowded, teeming towns—Las Vegas, San Luis Río Colorado, Hermosillo, Bisbee, Sante Fe.

The region includes the driest parts of California and Texas; southern Nevada, driest part of the driest state; and the most arid Mexican states, which are also Mexico's largest in area, first Chihuahua and then Sonora, Coahuila, and the length of Baja California, which Mexicans call the fleshless arm of Mexico. Larger in area than Chihuahua is each of the five southwestern states: Texas, California, New Mexico, Arizona, and Nevada.

Desert states, like desert ranches and counties, tend to be large in size with relatively few people per square mile, as population figures for Arizona or Sonora illustrate. California's San Bernardino County, which is mostly desert, is the largest county in the nation.

The politics of boundaries in several arid states have produced too many big counties with too few people. New Mexico has huge counties that some legislators would like to combine into viable super-counties. De Baca County has 2,547 persons; Harding County, 1,348. In the far-western prong of Texas, a state of small counties, Loving County is the least populated county in the nation. Its population fell by 27.4 percent from 1960 to 1970, to a total of 164 residents. There are more oil wells than persons in Loving County. No babies are born there—they are born in the next county, for it has a hospital.

Whether the area is Loving County, Bernalillo County (with Albuquerque and a total of more than 316,000 persons) or Maricopa County (with Phoenix, the twentieth-largest United States city, and a total of more than 963,000 persons), the population, though far too secular to worship the sun, is ever conscious of it. Every day the *El Paso Herald-Post* prints a box called "El Paso Sunshine." One August 18 it read: "The sun shone today for the 174th consecutive day. The sun has failed to shine only 7 of the last 3,236 days." The next January 12: "The sun shone today for the 87th consecutive day. The sun has failed to shine only 9 of the last 3,391 days."

The retirement community called Sun City, west of Phoenix in the "Valley of the Sun," averages 220 clear days a year and "has more sunshine than any other part of the country," its spokesmen say, calling it "the driest, sunniest, clearest resort area in the U.S." Tucson claims that the sun appears 3,800 hours a year. Even Douglas, Arizona, mottled at times by the sulphurous plumes from the stacks of nearby copper smelters, claims the same 3,800 hours—"an average of 10 hours of sunshine every day in the year," which means "over 300 days a year for outdoor sports." In the days of travel by train, the Southern Pacific Hotel in Yuma had a long sign out in front: "Free Meals Every Day the Sun Doesn't Shine."

Whether north or south of the political border, the region is a land where native creatures, including fishes, have evolved to survive with little water and much drought, where Indians long ago intelligently adjusted to scanty water and lived confidently as a biologically balanced, relatively static part of the total environment. The invading Spaniards and Mexicans recognized the climate and topography but introduced change, sometimes to the point of violent disruption—war, mayhem, genocide. Then came the trespasses and assaults by United States citizens and other immigrants, who progressively unbalanced the lives of native and resident peoples, wild animals, and even the stability of the inorganic setting.

The story of ecological destruction moves on ever faster in the name of development and progress. In the Mexicans' Northwest and the North Americans' Southwest, the push is on to obliterate any remaining corner of this desert Eden. A mechanized citizenry with trucks, motorcycles, dune buggies, and automobiles seeks easy profit or superficial pleasure, even if their wasted fumes and gases blot out the commanding feature, the sun above. A citizen asked the editor of *The Arizona Republic:* "I can remember blue sky. Can you?"

The overt regional wars of man against man are over, together with the paradoxes they enacted, as when barbarous whites killed civilized redskins in the name of civilization, but the campaign of man against nature is in full momentum. Glories remain—the Grand Canyon, the Big Bend gorges of the Rio Grande, Carlsbad Caverns, Barranca del Cobre, a few watery oases, and a thousand unpopulated desert vistas. But striking anomalies are everywhere that the booming new alien populations accumulate: Indian pueblos so crowded on festival days that it is hard to see an Indian; Los Alamos, a community devoted to the technology of modern war, situated in a verdant, idyllic setting near peaceful pueblos; engineering projects that save water by damming it—and vastly increasing the amount of evaporation and the degree of salinity; promoters who advertise regional charm and allure but steadily destroy the old and indigenous in order to commercialize on the new and phony; four-lane highways slashing across the scenery they lead people in to view. Growth, over-population, and heavy capitalization are turning the Land of Enchantment into a technological complex of harsh realities.

The Great Southwest dedicates itself to several ideas. Self-renewing nature is an indispensable adjunct to human survival. Unspoiled nature scenery can inspire human beings and provide them with heartfelt happiness. History provides explanation of the present and a guide to future action. The desert scenery of the Southwest constitutes a marvelous part of man's heritage. It merits a deeper understanding and an increase in efforts to preserve it.

Our opening chapters cover the climate, the geologic events, the topography, the special adaptations of plants and animals that all combine to make the American and Mexican deserts special and extraordinary portions of the earth's surface. Central chapters trace the activities of the first human beings in the area, and the final dozen chapters sample the events from Cabeza de Vaca and Coronado to the present. A historic span of more than four hundred fifty years involves the peoples of the deserts—Indians, Spaniards, Mexicans, and Americans. These all play roles in the long tale of settlement, war, mining, ranching, water litigation, artistic creation, and scientific achievement.

The desert is a world unto itself. Time, climate, and geologic and biologic forces have made it what it is. And for thousands of years men and women have made their mark on it, giving it a rich human history, a tumultuous present scene, and a portentous future.

ELNA BAKKER

RICHARD G. LILLARD

PART ONE

LAND OF SPACE AND SUN

The vast arid reaches along the Mexican-American border offer, as no other place on the North American continent, the true experience of desert. (Photographed in the Organ Mountains, New Mexico.)

15

CHAPTER 1

THE ANCIENT CROSSROADS

Where cultures meet and species mingle, giving the vast
Mexican–American borderlands a character all their own

POISED BETWEEN THE ARCTIC and the tropics, between the grassy plains and the Pacific Coast, lies the great desert heartland of the continent. Americans chauvinistically call it "the Southwest," but in fact it transcends the political boundary and stretches deep into the Mexican Northwest as well. The very binational character of the area is symbolic of its ancient role as crossroads and meeting grounds for diverse species and cultures.

In many ways and through many ages, this cluster of deserts has supported living things on the move—southbound, northbound, from the east, from the west. Thousands of migratory birds in their twice-yearly exodus fly over these basins and hills. Slow tides of vegetation types have ebbed and flowed in rhythm with changes in climate and topography. People, from the primitive breakers of giant-sloth bones to the hopefuls headed for gaming tables in Las Vegas, have struck across these challenging stretches.

Not only are the deserts a huge intersection where traffic has crossed and recrossed, but they are also a terminus where a motley aggregation of living things have wandered in from surrounding regions to stay—to mingle and settle down in a rich assortment of environments.

One of the most significant features of the Mexican-American deserts is that they are encircled by widely differing biotic regions. Far in the evolutionary past, before the desert was desert, firs and other plants typical of more northerly latitudes moved in. In later eras the climate became slowly warmer and drier, and moun-

tains began to build. The firs and their companions found sanctuary on the moist, cool slopes while other species came from the south to occupy the desert floor.

And so, settling down beside neighbors whose ancestral roots had long been in the area, the successful immigrants began to evolve their own ways of survival in an increasingly dry environment. Each species added a bit to the rich mosaic of desert plant life. From the Great Plains, next door to the east, came species of short grass now common over parts of the Colorado Plateau. Great forests to the north had contributed cone-bearers for higher elevations, while trees of the subtropical thorn forest of southern Sonora and Sinaloa moved up to mingle with northern varieties on the desert floor. Joshua trees met coastal valley oaks as unlikely companions on the desert side of California's mountains.

Today, the desert West offers a generous variety of homesites for living things: sand dunes for dune dwellers; rocky cliffs for those adapted to live on them; oases and streamcourses for species that need abundant water; cold winters for those that prefer chill; heat aplenty for those that do not.

These eras saw animals entering from other places in the same way, drawn partly by the same forces that had influenced the plants, and partly by the very presence of those plants. Animals, too, had to adapt to increasing drought or perish. Soon the desert species had acquired characteristics that clearly distinguished them from their cousins who had never left home.

While species have proliferated, very few biological types have developed in these deserts at what biologists

In an Anglo Southwest, Tumacácori Mission stands as a reminder of earlier cultures
—the Spanish who built it and the Indians they came to "save."

The banded armadillo looks like a prototype of an armored tank. It is unique among mammals, being the only species whose litters of four are either all female or all male.

call the family or even the genus level. There has not yet been time—by evolutionary reckoning, these are young landscapes. But evolution goes on. Given another several million years and freedom from man's interference, the deserts will develop a whole new assortment of organisms.

Thus the desert has evolved a diversity of life forms to match the diversity of land forms and climatic features bestowed by the earth itself. Nowhere else on the continent can one find such extremes of biting cold and dizzying heat, flash floods and merciless drought, icicles dripping into hot springs, lush forests of yellow pine looking down on cactus-dotted plains, aspens and cottonwoods tossing their golden doubloons of autumn into streams that will eventually flush them out onto a burning desert floor.

As wildlife traffic had made use of hospitable routes, so the earliest human hunters followed the animal herds into the Southwest. Primitive though they were, mere shadows moving through the dark of prehistory, the Ancient Ones brought with them one great ad-

vantage in the ordeal of desert survival—conscious adaptability. Unlike other animal and plant species, whose continued existence was at the mercy of impersonal processes of gene mutation, natural selection, and chance, man could think and plan; he could make tools, cook his meat, cooperate with his fellows. In time, he learned to build permanent homes, grow a food supply more dependable than the elusive herds, even harness the precious waters of the desert streams.

The native Indian cultures were already highly developed when the first Spaniards headed northward across the desert in search of gold. Like the tropical coral-bean and the armadillo before them, the human newcomers from the south settled down in desert communities, though in less harmony with their neighbors than had the simpler species that preceded them.

There seems to be an accelerated rhythm in the waves of immigrants to the desert. Plant migrations may be reckoned in millions of years, primitive tribes' in millennia. But scarcely three centures after the first white men from New Spain headed north across the

From Zabriskie Point, a great panorama of eroded, richly colored siltstone stretches away to Death Valley, with the Panamint Range beyond.

desert, another culture, the Anglos from the North Atlantic seaboard, began to leave new footprints on the desert sands. As Spaniard had clashed with Indian, Anglo clashed with Spaniard and later Mexican. But whether in ascendancy or decline, each culture left a permanent legacy to the place and the mystique that are called "Southwest."

Indian raids, seasonal heat, and the distance between watering places slowed modern man's development of major transportation routes across the desert, but only for a while. In time, stage roads followed the forty-niners' trails, and freeways followed the stage roads. As one civilization builds on the ruins of an earlier one—a fact found to be literally true at many an archaeological site—so the migrations of plants and animals and successive human cultures have traced overlapping trafficways through the passes and stream courses of the Mexican-American desert.

Dwellers of the desert plains and plateaus—man included—find their existence dominated by the urgent quest for water. Deserts, by definition arid, nevertheless have a spectrum of water availability, depending on place and season. Saline lakes, while often ephemeral, are common features, and even permanent fresh water is not totally absent. Happy are the dry lands bordered or islanded with high mountain ranges, as the Mexican-American deserts are, for rainfall is more generous, and perennial streams flow from the melting snows. Eventually these streams disappear into the thirsty alluvium skirting the mountains, only to be tapped by wells that recover their precious contents. Springs occur, too, where underground water is thrust to the surface by peculiarities of the bedrock. Accompanied by the typically green and water-extravagant plants of such oases, they are among the most delightful places on the desert scene. Their clustered foliage casts welcome shadows, offering a dramatic contrast between the sere distance and this lush immediacy.

Much of the Southwest has an average annual rainfall of at least five inches; in certain places it exceeds ten inches. Some of this moisture is unfortunately lost to local vegetation because it falls in sudden, torrential downpours, resulting in flash floods and rapid drainoff.

When a violent summer thunderstorm strikes the desert, visitors from town and city usually flee to shelter, startled by the dangerous drama of elemental nature. Men have forgotten how to huddle, backs against the wind, vital organs protected against what the skies can hurl at them. When the crash and brilliance of the storm passes, when tranquility returns and visitors venture out again, the desert has a drenched, almost sodden look.

There are no permanent natural lakes of any size in Arizona or New Mexico, but Nevada, Utah, and California boast several rather large bodies of water, some saline, some fresh. All are fed by streams originating in places of higher rainfall. Some, like the Great Salt Lake, are remnants of ancient, much larger lakes common to the region in the Ice Age. In recent years, great reservoirs have been impounded behind dams on the desert rivers. Fluctuating shorelines, unfortunately, preclude the growth of vegetation, which along natural lakes and streams gives such delightful relief to the parched-earth tones of the landscape.

Of all the water resources in the desert Southwest, it is the rivers that have most affected the face of the land and the movement and survival of living things. Through geological time, they have carved some of the deepest and most spectacular canyons on earth. As plant life evolved, some species followed the stream courses into the far reaches of an otherwise forbidding territory. And animals in turn followed both water and forage along the riverbeds. In his own time, man—the hunter, farmer, explorer, road builder—has kept his steps as close as possible to the riverbanks. The Ancient Ones, in their wanderings from hunting site to water hole, presaged the day when the desert would provide the most feasible route for cross-continental traffic of more complex human societies.

The two major streams of the Southwest are the Colorado and the Rio Grande. Like those other historic desert waterways, the Nile and the Tigris-Euphrates, these rivers hold great significance for the present and future of the arid country they drain.

Hidden Springs oasis holds a delightful surprise for those energetic enough to negotiate the narrow, winding gorges that drain the Mecca Hills in the California desert.

CHAPTER 2

THE MANY FACES OF DESERT

Differences in geology and climate that make the Southwest's chain
of deserts a kaleidoscope of scenery and life forms

CERTAINLY THE DOMINANT LANDSCAPE in southwestern United States and northern Mexico is desert. Though there are forested slopes and green mountain meadows, too, they are but islands in a vast sea of desert. It would be more accurate to say "deserts," for the arid lands of the North American continent display a fascinating variety of topography and life forms if their differences are recognized.

Physiographers divide the Southwest into provinces, as shown on the map on page 25. (Two of these provinces will be discussed in detail in chapters 4 and 5.) Extending across the province boundaries is a wide swath of desert "heartland"—the epicenter of the great climatic changes and attendant geological forces that have created it. The heartland encompasses several adjacent deserts: the Mojave, the Sonoran—including the Western Sonoran, Eastern Sonoran, and Arizona Upland—and the Chihuahuan. Beyond the heartland lie the Great Basin and the Gulf and Interior subdivisions of the Sonoran Desert in Mexico, which will be treated here peripherally, and the Navajoan Desert, which is of such interest that it will be given somewhat more attention.

The names given to these regional deserts and the exact areas they cover vary from one authority to another. A botanist will divide them differently from, say, a geologist, and even two geologists may not quite agree. The names and boundaries used in this book are indicated on the map on pages 284–85.

To the casual visitor from Ohio or New Hampshire, these deserts may all seem alike, barren and unproductive except where irrigation is used for the growth of cotton, alfalfa, and other crops. Why such academic fussiness in separating these sere reaches of the continent? Who cares whether the geographers want certain portions to be called the Mojave Desert and others the Arizona Upland? The answer, of course, is that these differences *are* important when one learns their meaning. They indicate differences of rainfall, seasonality, geology, and even paleohistory. They have been separated in many ways for millions of years, as plant distributions testify. For example, creosote bush, ocotillo (coachwhip), and mesquite characterize the lower, warmer deserts; sagebrush and scattered woodlands of piñon-juniper typify the higher, more northern desert lands. Palo verde does not appear north of Kingman, Arizona, yet saltbush is found throughout the deserts if soil conditions are suitable.

For the most part, definite topographical boundaries can be described for each desert or subdivision. The *Western Sonoran* is fenced on the west by the Peninsular Range, a spinal column turning south around Mount San Jacinto. It is lavish with yellow pines, black oaks and odd types of cypress in the back country of San Diego, and becomes the San Pedro Martir Range in northern Baja California. The mountains that connect this geographic backbone to the Coast Ranges are the Transverse Ranges, one of the few east-west trending mountain complexes on the continent. The two major ranges, the San Gabriel and the San Bernardino, form the familiar rugged background of the Los Angeles basin—when they are visible on a smogless day. Recent evidence points out that the unusual trend of the Transverse Ranges is the

Ocotillo and three types of cactus—organ pipe, saguaro, and cholla—make hiking
in parts of Organ Pipe National Monument a real adventure.

result of the San Andreas Fault, which makes a major turn to the east in the vicinity of Santa Barbara.

An eastern extension of the Transverse Ranges, the Little San Bernardinos, is more or less the delineation between the Mojave Desert to the north and the Western Sonoran to the south. The two deserts overlap as the elevation drops toward the Colorado River. Only the absence of certain vegetation types distinguishes one desert from the other in this region; to the lay visitor the two become one. The town of Needles on the river is arbitrarily considered the northernmost point of the Western Sonoran.

East of the Colorado River the desert is known as the *Eastern Sonoran*. The river is not the reason these two Sonoran deserts are different, but merely a convenient landmark at about the spot where the differences become visible. Soil, relief features, rainfall seasonality, and average rainfall are primarily responsible for these variations.

After one crosses the Colorado at Yuma or Blythe, there is at once a pronounced change in scenery: the sudden and dramatic appearance of saguaro cactus, a large, multibranched form of one of the Western Hemisphere's most interesting floral families. As the saguaros become larger and more concentrated, other forms of vegetation begin to appear, including many small trees—palo verde, ironwood, desert willow, mesquite, catclaw, and others. For this reason the Eastern Sonoran has often been referred to as an *arboreal* desert. Though most of the tree species on these arid hills and plains also occur in California, they seldom dominate the landscape as they do in certain areas of Arizona, New Mexico, and western Texas. The vegetation in this area might be described as woodland rather than scrub.

Within this immense and striking country of the Sonoran Desert are several noteworthy landform features. One is the series of sand dunes paralleling the Colorado River north and west of Yuma. Another is the Salton Sea, created early in this century when the Colorado River washed high flood waters into the Salton Sink. This trough, according to the latest theory, had dropped between two branches of the San Andreas Fault, creating what is technically called a *graben*. The Salton Sea serves as a major recreation resource for water sports, but its increasing salinity and fluctuating water levels have produced problems for developers and dwellers in the Imperial and Coachella valleys, which bound the sea on its northern and southern shores.

Just to the west of the Salton Sea is a chopped-up embayment of colorful badlands, the location of the Anza-Borrego State Park. A number of canyons have been carved into the flanks of the fencing range to the west, many graced with wild palms, cottonwoods, and other types of oasis plant life.

Across both Eastern and Western Sonoran, roughly sculptured ranges and peaks rise from the desert floor, landmarks since man began using the desert as a crossroads. Two peaks, both called Picacho, guard routes in central Arizona and southeastern California. Other important recognition ranges are the Superstition Mountains, east of Phoenix; the Chuckawalla, to the south on the main road to Blythe; the Kofa, with its solitary palm oasis; and the Harquahala, whose Eagle Eye, a natural hole in the crest, has been a favorite landmark since traffic has become heavy between Phoenix and Los Angeles.

In less comfortable days the Eagle Eye signaled the approach to Aguila ("Eagle") Junction, a turn-off point to a road that soon leads the hot and weary traveler up Yarnell Grade to the wonderful relief of a five-thousand-foot elevation. The deserts of the North American continent are indeed fortunate in having such high "islands"—places of green serenity where one can escape the sea of heat surrounding them. They have also provided refuges for animal and plant life accustomed to cooler temperatures.

The two major tributaries of the lower Colorado River, the Salt and the Gila, are like gigantic fingers holding the Eastern Sonoran and Arizona Upland deserts in their grasp. Looking down from a jetliner at thirty-two thousand feet, one can trace the drainage ways, the washes and gorges, for the most part dry, that fan out into this great system of interlocking handholds. They secure these subdivisions of the desert in what amounts to an anomalous partnership: the desert is carved by water, but water is scarce.

The other great feature of the Sonoran Desert is that enchanting body of water, the Sea of Cortez, or Gulf of California. Scientists have long suspected that

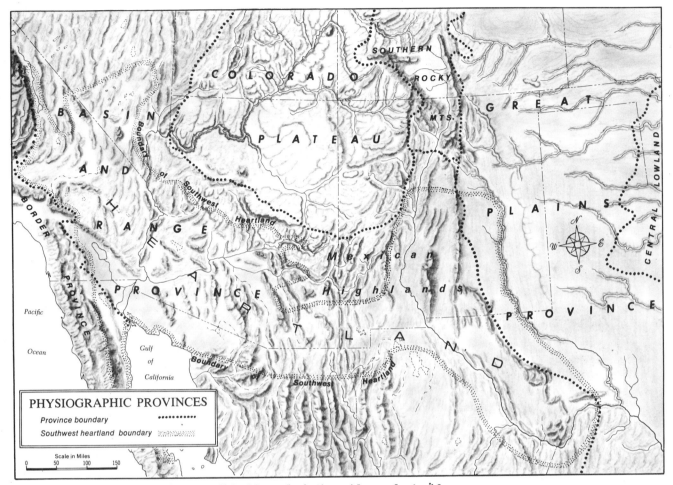

Cutting across physiographic and political boundaries is a wide swath of arid heartland, where landforms and life-forms most clearly say desert.

it must have some relationship to the San Andreas Fault—a spectacular rupture in the earth's surface, entering California north of Point Reyes, trending southeast, and slipping under the waters of the gulf. Most geologists now agree that the gulf is indeed a manifestation of the rubbing together of the huge plates into which the earth's surface is divided. The fault system apparently extends out under the gulf, continuing the graben which accounts for the Salton Sink. Here, however, the subsidence was great enough for an intrusion of the Pacific Ocean. There seems to be evidence as well that the gulf is slowly widening, as molten rock upwells under the earth's surface, pushing the two opposing shores apart.

Visitors to points along both sides of the gulf acclaim its spectacular beauty. When the Baja Highway is finished, however, this lonely but magnificent landscape may one day be cluttered with the same type of resort development now blighting much of the rest of the desert.

To those familiar with the often monotonous landscapes of the Eastern and Western Sonoran deserts, the *Arizona Upland* is refreshing. Here, for example, is famed Sabino Canyon, gouged into the side of one of the many highland islands that vary the scenery of southern Arizona. The meandering road, narrow in places where it fords the stream, carries pockets of saguaro cactus, palo verde trees, and other desert species up into the sides of washes, where they mingle with cottonwoods and other riparian trees. Pools

mirror both the austere charm of giant cacti and the lush, inviting shadows of box elder and willow. Cave Creek; the San Pedro River; Madera Canyon; Sonoita Creek, home of many tropical bird species; Aravaipa Canyon, a new sanctuary of the Nature Conservancy—all reflect the profligacy of the desert when fed with water, permanent, dependable water. In this more generous upland country, summer rains and catchment areas enrich the desert scene to the point where some of it can no longer be classified as true desert.

From Phoenix, the Arizona Upland spreads east and south to include the rough country broken by the gorges and valleys of the Salt, Gila, San Pedro, and Santa Cruz rivers and their many contributing creeks and washes. The elevation of the desert floor varies from about two to four thousand feet, with numerous isolated ranges scattered about. The uplands continue south of the border for some distance.

ONE OF THE OTHER TWO DESERTS included in the heartland section is the *Mojave,* the smallest and in some ways the least distinctive of all arid landscapes on the continent. It has the typical basin-and-range topography, but it lacks, with two exceptions, the spectacular scenery we have come to expect from the desert region as a whole.

The first exception is the magnificent Owens Valley, another graben between two towering ranges: the Sierra Nevada to the west and the Inyo-White complex to the east. On a morning in late May or early June, when large masses of snow, like cake frosting, decorate the creamy granite beneath, and the rising sun strikes the eastern face of the great Sierran scarp, the visitor can see the valley in its full glory. The southern end of Owens Valley is very much a part of the Mojave Desert. Joshua trees, one of the "indicator plants" of this particular slice of the arid Southwest, advance about as far north as Owens Lake. The northern end of the valley, on the other hand, has plants more characteristic of the Great Basin. The floor of the valley is covered with small, sparse scrub of various species, except where interrupted by irrigated

Cotton-white clouds over Canyonlands National Park are a foil for statuesque cliffs of the Wingate formation.

fields and streamside growth along what is left of the Owens River and its tributaries.

Several other valleys—including the Saline and Panamint—are separated by scarred mountains intervening between the Owens Valley and that other great depression of the eastern Mojave, Death Valley. Its depth below sea level, its harsh human history, its exquisitely tinted badlands, its soaring summer temperatures, and its strange beauty have given Death Valley a special fascination.

The Mojave bites into quite a chunk of southern Nevada, crosses the Colorado River north of Needles, and traces a narrow transition zone in northern Arizona between the Arizona Upland and the Colorado Plateau to the north, locale of the Navajoan Desert.

The other desert included in the heartland is the *Chihuahuan,* but only portions of it are in this region. The westernmost extension is a small area around the town of Tombstone in southeastern Arizona. A tongue of this typically Mexican desert thrusts up along the Rio Grande River about as far north as Albuquerque. To the east is the famous valley containing White Sands National Monument, the nearby testing grounds at Alamagordo, and the desiccated plain known as the Jornada del Muerto, whose alkali flats meant death for many early travelers. The welter of basin and range east of the Arizona Upland is the Mexican Highlands portion of the Chihuahuan Desert. Its eastern section of this region, just west of the beginning of the Great Plains, is termed the Sacramento Highlands. They include what the lay visitor might consider bits and pieces of the southern Rocky Mountains, but geologic differences apparently provide sufficient reason to consider them a separate province.

Between the scattered ranges—many of them high enough to encourage "island hopping" of typically northern, cone-bearing trees and aspens—are basins containing typical Chihuahuan desert plant life. In Texas, the whole of what is called the Trans-Pecos—the region west of the Pecos River—is desert of this nature. The southern part of the Sacramento Highlands is dominated by the Guadalupe Mountains, whose northern half is in New Mexico and whose southern half is in Texas. The southernmost promontory, El Capitan, is the highest point in Texas.

Among the numerous ranges in the Trans-Pecos is

Overleaf: A northerly arm of the Mojave Desert meets a southerly arm of the Great Basin in Owens Valley.

the Davis Mountain complex, a pleasing country in late August, when the grasses are long and lush in this land of summer rain. The undulating floor of the Chihuahuan Desert continues south to the Big Bend country with its deeply dissected Chisos Mountains, home of a number of tropical plants that have found their way this far north. The Chihuahuan Desert dominates the lower elevation of central Mexico as far south as San Luis Potosí and parts of Hidalgo.

TWO OTHER DESERTS will be treated with somewhat less detail and attention: the *Great Basin* and the *Navajoan*. They are far from the central core of least rainfall, and their vegetation is distinctly different from that of the other deserts, with the exception of stream-course plants and those adapted to saline or alkaline conditions. Both of these peripheral deserts are largely dominated by Great Basin sagebrush. This ubiquitous, aromatic shrub, though present at certain elevations in the western California desert, is missing throughout most of the southern deserts. Conversely, creosote bush, the major matrix plant for the Sonoran, Mojave, and Chihuahuan deserts, is absent from these higher, cooler, and more northerly arid areas.

The Great Basin covers most of Nevada, creeps into the western edge of Utah, and drifts as far north as central Oregon and southern Idaho. The basin is not actually a depression, in the sense of being an area of low elevation, as a number of mountain ranges vary the relief. The word "basin" refers rather to the fact that it is landlocked—it has internal drainage, with no substantial outlet to the sea. Runoff collects in basins separated from each other by numerous ranges, large and small. The Navajoan Desert, on the other hand, is located on the huge Colorado Plateau. Though there are places where local runoff "stays put," almost the entire tableland is drained by the Colorado River. Some drainage escapes into the Rio Grande on the eastern edge of the plateau.

The scenic contrast between the Great Basin and Navajoan Deserts could not be more dramatic. Much of Nevada north of the creosote-bush zone is rather monotonous. A few ranges, some as high as Wheeler Peak in the eastern part of the state, provide occasional variation, but the miles between Reno and the Utah border are a seemingly endless expanse of rolling scrub.

Once at the foot of the Wasatch Mountains—a mirror image of the Sierra in their geologic history and impressiveness—one enters a different world, that of the Colorado Plateau. East of the range anywhere in Utah, one is bombarded with fantastic scenery, brilliant in color, magnificent in proportion, immense in confusing topography, broken, desolate, and luridly beautiful. What can match the Mittens of Monument Valley, the overwhelming view from Dead Horse Point in the Canyonlands country, the sculptured perfection of Delicate Arch, or the colors in Cedar Breaks?

Pink cliffs sheltering grottos with minute waterfalls and maidenhair fern; eyeball-searing white beds of alkali that often contain commercially valuable minerals; rolling hills graciously decked in summer's green; forest-fringed canyons, large enough to hold a mountain range; sandy wash floors covered with spring's floral wealth; lakes where water skiers are as numerous as the cacti on their rims; below sea level, above timberline—the Southwest's deserts offer a varied menu. There *is* something for everyone.

Habitat variety in the arid West is encapsulated in Big Bend National Park
as mountains, washes, canyons, and rivers merge in a typical mosaic.

CHAPTER 3

DISPATCHERS OF THE RAIN

*Forces that make the Southwest climate unique on this continent
—global wind patterns, mountain barriers, and the ever-present sun*

ONE OF THE MORE intriguing features of our planet's climate is the fact that it is not completely dry. As far as we can tell, the earth is the only planet in the solar system that has a large amount of water. Theoretically, it should not have such an abundance, for early in its history the earth lost most substances that are as heavy as water. The precipitation cycle is operating on relatively small amounts of water from several sources, such as the so-called "young" water from volcanic activity.

Nevertheless, there is an impressive amount of water on the surface of the planet; indeed, more water than land. The question has been raised: why doesn't daily solar heating (in warmer regions and seasons) turn the liquid surface water into vapor, which at night would reach dew point and return to the ocean in liquid form? In other words, one might expect a kind of steady-state equilibrium—an endless cycle of evaporation and condensation confined to the ocean surface, never involving land at all.

The answer includes a number of factors: winds that carry moisture from the oceans to and across land masses, a physical circumstance known as "adiabatic cooling," and the peculiar properties of water itself.

Though many onshore winds are local in nature, there are four great global airstreams: the southern trade winds, the northern trade winds, the southern stormy westerlies, and the northern stormy westerlies. The former two wind systems are dry when they begin their journey toward the equator; they pick up moisture as they travel over large bodies of water. The latter two are notorious for the amounts of water that they

dump on the lands they journey across.

Another source of precipitation is the monsoon airflow patterns that develop when continental heartlands are heated during the warm season. They create large areas of low barometric pressure, sucking up moisture from neighboring oceans and seas. Local wind-moisture disturbances—hurricanes and typhoons—violently throw quantities of water drawn from these ocean surfaces onto adjacent land.

Moisture-full winds might, of course, scud across the whole North American continent carrying nothing but sterile fog-type clouds, much like those prevalent along the California coast during the summer. They are wet but useless, except for some condensation when reaching dew point, causing what is called "fog drip" from leaves and other surfaces.

Something must push these moisture masses high enough to cool, condense, and produce true rain. Mountains are the prime source of uplift. Storms obviously cannot go through mountain ranges but must rise over them. Adiabatic cooling occurs at the rate of roughly a four-degree drop in temperature for every thousand feet gained in altitude—the higher, the colder. This does not mean, however, that the tallest peaks and crests receive the most rain. There is a leveling off at about eight thousand feet, and above this elevation rainfall tends to decrease. A vegetation type known as "mist forest" depends upon fog-type condensation from clouds perpetually hanging around the tops of many tropical mountain ranges.

Warm, moist air may be lifted by updrafts to altitudes necessary for rain-producing condensation. Such "con-

*When rain comes to the desert, it may come
suddenly and with destructive force.*

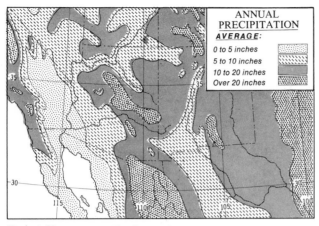

Rainfall patterns play key roles in forming most landscapes. They are even more significant in arid regions where relief features are complex.

vection currents," are responsible for the towering thunderheads typical of summer weather in many parts of the earth.

Mountain barrier or updraft, there still would be no precipitation if it were not for the nature of water itself. Unlike most substances in vapor form, it need not be compressed for condensation to occur. Something *is* necessary, however: there must be minute particles in the atmosphere around which drops can build. Luckily, the atmosphere usually contains enough of these mote-sized dust grains for vapor to liquefy. Scientists have discovered that "seeding" likely-looking clouds with particles of silver iodide can induce them to give up additional moisture. It is like a pregnant mother having triplets instead of the expected single child.

WITH ALL OF THESE WINDS rushing back and forth, updrafts mounting swiftly from warm land surfaces, why do we have deserts, occupying roughly 30 percent of terrestrial surfaces? Before entering a discussion of the reasons for deserts and examples of various types, it might be helpful to define just what the characteristics of a desert are, keeping in mind that there is some disagreement among geographers and other scientists regarding the following terms: *true desert, extreme desert, desert, semidesert,* and *steppe.*

One well-known definition of desert begins with the assumption that rainfall does not exceed ten inches. Other authorities would lower the total annual rain-

fall to perhaps five inches. There are some universally accepted criteria for deserts, however. Rainfall is scarce and undependable; it may not fall in some areas for several years. Other deserts can expect some precipitation annually, but the amount may vary considerably.

Low atmospheric humidity is the general rule, with local modifications. Wind is frequent and accentuates climatic drought. Shrubby, scattered vegetation — in many places missing altogether or so ephemeral in nature that it is inconsequential—does little to protect the ground surface from intense solar radiation. Surface soils of sand and gravel on a hot day are very high— 160 degrees is normal. It has been pointed out that the major reason for the extreme air temperatures of the desert summer is contact with hot ground surfaces. They absorb solar heat and in return radiate warmth to the air above.

Temperatures in the lower mid-latitude, subtropical, and tropical deserts are high in summer, with warm-season averages in the nineties. Cool-season temperatures, below two thousand feet, rarely drop below freezing. Cold air draining down from higher altitudes tends to modify this rule somewhat, but exceptions are local. In some deserts, though not all, day-night temperature ranges are wide. Drops and rises of fifty degrees in one twenty-four hour period are not uncommon.

The temperature-rainfall relationship is very important in evaluating a desert's plant production potential. This is often described in terms of the evaporation-precipitation ratio: deserts occur where evaporation from soil and plant life exceeds rainfall.

Many of the world's desert patterns result from a feature of global climatic pressure systems: the so-called "horse latitudes." Subtropical deserts, vast areas of smoldering aridity, encircle the earth just north of the Tropic of Cancer and south of the Tropic of Capricorn.

To understand why these particular latitudes are so devoid of moisture, one must begin at the equator. The year-round warmth of the lowland equatorial zone produces great quantities of rising, and therefore cooling, air. In consequence, the equatorial regions are drenched throughout the year by heavy rainfall resulting from convectional updrafts. Tropical rain forest, with all of its prodigality and richness of plant life, is the offspring of the happy union of warmth and moisture.

Once aloft, these now drying air masses spread north

and south. In the latitudes of the two tropics—the points most distant from the equator where the sun is directly overhead—they begin to fall, building up huge high-pressure cells of stable air. These are the famous horse latitudes, dreaded by sailors when wind was the only propellent force for their ships. They are belts of comparative calm with little or no consistent wind direction.

These masses of sinking, dry, warm air are drought makers in themselves. Moreover, they are often augmented by two other aridity-producing features: rain shadow and distance from moisture source. The first is the direct result of adiabatic cooling. Moisture-bearing winds sweep up a mountain slope, chilling as they travel upward; consequently, rain falls on the windward slope. By the time the storms have topped the crest of the range, they have lost much of the water vapor with which they began. They dissipate, their moisture used up, and the lee side is usually much drier than the slopes that face storm-laden winds.

One of the most interesting types of desert is the so-called coastal fog desert, such as is found along the central Pacific coast of Baja California. It parallels upwelling currents of cold water, which chill onshore winds as they pass over. Atmospheric moisture condenses to fog, but no further. Some of these fog deserts are among the most rainless in the world, but they support unusual, often bizarre types of vegetation adapted to and dependent on air humidity—up to 100-percent saturation—instead of soil moisture.

One authority, Dr. Richard Logan of UCLA, has pointed out that these concentrations of dry climate extend far to the west of continental edges. In some instances the centers of high-pressure cells of the subtropics are out over oceans. Their eastern edges seem to be drier than those on the west. This accounts for the fact that western shores of North America and other continents are arid, while the eastern coasts enjoy plentiful rainfall. For example, contrast Florida and Baja California.

THE CLIMATES of the Mexican-American deserts are as varied as their landscapes. It has been a long-standing joke among meteorologists that the daily summer high temperature record is not at Blythe, Needles, El Centro, or any of the other often-named stations in the Western Sonoran Desert. It is invariably,

without exception, at Death Valley. But that statistic would become so monotonous that it is politely forgotten. Death Valley swelters along in its 120-degree temperatures while Needles, with its comparatively low reading of 108 degrees, gets credit for being the nation's hot spot. In contrast, one of the favorite postcard scenes of Southern California is a Joshua tree, symbol of the Mojave Desert, whose blossoms are sprinkled with fresh snow. Diversity, hallmark of the North American deserts, is the child of many parents: latitude, altitude, distance from moisture sources, pressure systems, and global wind patterns.

The Western Sonoran, the Gran Desierto of Sonora, low basins such as Death Valley in the Mojave, and the Viscaino in Baja California are the driest areas in the North American arid zone. Rainfall ranges from two inches yearly at Yuma, on the lower Colorado River, to twelve and fifteen inches in the uplands around Tucson. About the only climatic generalization one can make for the entire desert area is that precipitation is both scanty and irregular. Each desert has its particular pattern of climate.

The Western Sonoran Desert is subtropical and is also in the rain shadow cast by the Peninsular Range to the west. What rain it does get arrives in winter, in

Windward mountain slopes usually have heavier rainfall than leeward slopes because masses of moist air, pushed aloft by storm-burdened winds, become cooler as they rise, and much of the water vapor they carry condenses before it reaches the crest.

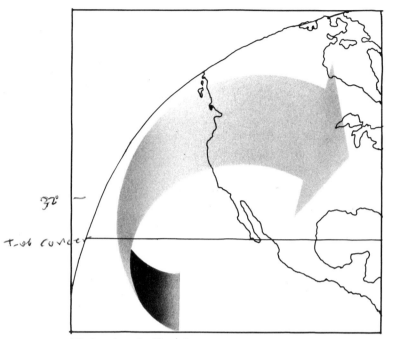

Moist air spiraling above steamy equatorial regions rises, travels north or south, and then descends, becoming drier and heavier. Settling in huge high-pressure cells, it blocks storms and local updrafts that could otherwise have induced rainfall.

contrast to the summer precipitation peak typical of desert lands to the east. Why this is so requires discussion of another feature of the world's geography.

Latitudes 30° to 38° are in a transition zone of major importance. Two factors are at work: the earth tilts on its axis, and the planet's climate is divided into broad belts. Beginning at the equator and going toward both poles, they are as follows:

(1) *Equatorial calms.* The "doldrums" of sailing days. They have inconsistent winds, heavy convectional-type rainfall, and year-round warmth.

(2) *Trade wind belt.* The trades blow toward the equator from about latitudes 20° north and south. Influenced by the Coriolus Effect, the northeast trades flow southwest; the southeast trades sweep to the northwest. (Remember, the name of a wind indicates where it comes from, not where it is going.) The trade winds begin at the dry edges of the horse latitudes but gather moisture as they flow over oceans, gulfs, and seas. Mountain barriers facing the trades after their moisture-

collecting journeys are frequently drenched by heavy, though short-lived downpours. Even lowland tropics are comfortable where the trades are constant. These are the tropical paradises of travel brochures—Bora-Bora, Bali, Martinique, and a host of other palm-strewn islands and sea coasts where the snorkeling is good and the seafood delicious.

The trade latitudes usually have two well-defined seasons: wet and dry—or, in some areas, wet and less wet. This seasonality has a profound effect on the vegetation. Deciduous forest and woodland are characteristic. The new leaves appear just prior to or at the beginning of the wet season.

(3) *Subtropical belt.* This zone has already been discussed in detail: dry, warm, settling air with little chance of picking up moisture on the arid edges of high pressure cells; moist unstable air within the western peripheral area.

(4) *Stormy Westerlies belt.* This zone is a broad band of turbulence between the fortieth and sixtieth parallels. They enclose the "roaring forties," storm-lashed pathways encircling both the Southern and Northern hemispheres. For instance, cold "fronts" are constantly being spawned in the Gulf of Alaska, traveling southeast across the continent, and often grabbing up more moisture from vapor-bearing air masses moving north from the Gulf of Mexico.

(5) There are two polar belts, but they need not concern us here.

The lands between the thirtieth and thirty-eighth parallels mentioned previously are influenced by both the horse latitudes and the stormy westerlies. A simple way to understand this is to imagine that, contrary to reality, the sun travels around the earth. Because of the tilting of the planet on its axis, the sun's most powerful, most direct rays cross the equator twice a year—the spring and fall equinoxes. They reach the Tropic of Cancer on June 21, start of the northern summer, and travel across the equator to arrive at the Tropic of Capricorn on its first summer day, December 21, only to return north again in an eternal journey back and forth between the two tropics. This is perpendicular radiation, with the sun straight overhead. It has much more intensity than solar radiation which strikes the earth at a more oblique angle.

The effect is this: the warm equatorial zone tends to

move north, following the sun's best efforts, as it were, during the northern hemisphere's summer, bringing its typical rainstorms to drier areas along its edge. The trade winds travel north as well. The subtropics with their high pressure areas also move north, accounting for the summer drought along the coast of California as far north as Oregon. The stormy westerlies retreat poleward in cooperation with this annual climatic migration.

During the winter season of the northern hemisphere, the opposite occurs. The sun's strongest rays move south, accompanied by all the belts between the equator and the poles. The stormy westerlies push aside vast humps of dry subtropical air down into lower latitudes. Rain returns to coastal California.

The wet-dry seasonal pattern of the subtropics and the lower mid-latitudes is enhanced by the monsoon effect. Continental interiors heat up in summer, pulling in masses of water vapor from ocean and sea. In winter, these heartlands build up huge cold cores, fending off moisture sources from nearby warm seas. In the mid-latitudes this is offset by the southward trend of storms brought by the westerlies, which by now have moved on to the south.

Thus the climates of the Mexican-American deserts are influenced by several controls: dry, high-pressure units that travel north and south "with the sun"; winter storms when the westerlies come south; the summer monsoon, which hauls in moisture from the Gulf of Mexico; and occasional hurricane-type disturbances moving north along the tropical reaches of both Atlantic and Pacific coasts.

THE WESTERN SONORAN DESERT, though it belongs in the dry subtropics, is influenced by rain shadow. Occasional winter storms leak through the passes and over the crest of the Peninsular Range. Wildflower enthusiasts in Southern California watch desert rainfall statistics with much interest. If Indio, center of the Coachella Valley, receives an inch of rain in November, a half an inch in December, and several inches in January and February, other factors being cooperative, such as cool but not freezing nights and minimum wind—it's a bonanza year!

Loaded with cameras, wildflower guidebooks stowed in the map compartment, and picnic lunch in hand,

nature lovers head for blooming desert. On a cool, breezy day in March during full flower season, one could not wish for a more wonderful "day in the sun." Rosy sand verbena lies like a Persian rug. Desert dandelion nods over this pink carpet, its pale yellow petals incised with tiny teeth. Evening primrose contributes demi-tasse-sized saucers of porcelain white; other species of the same type bear long stalks loaded with cuplets of brilliant yellow. Ghost flowers have tiny blood-red specks decorating their ivory-tinted throats. Nama spreads out in burgundy blotches. Canterbury-bell phacelias are gentian blue. Desert mallows are miniature hollyhocks, the color of ripe apricots.

In a good year, desert wildflowers thrive under the kindly glow of the mild spring sun and abundant soil moisture. The desert is transformed as if by magic. One cannot step anywhere without crushing a wildflower. They grow taller and lusher with each passing day until the photographer no longer kneels low by his subject but merely stoops to point his lens at the particular flower in which he is interested. Pollen brushes off on thighs, not ankles — the desert has become a blazing garden in full bloom.

It is hard to believe, then, that in a few short weeks

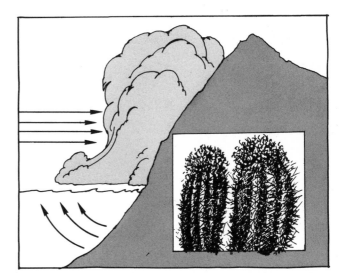

Cold ocean currents often parallel desert coasts.
As the moisture in onshore winds sweeps inland, it
becomes fog. Many plants living on such coasts
are surprisingly encrusted with lichen more
reminiscent of damp, green forests than of desert.

Even low mountains, like these peaks of the Mazatzal Range in Arizona, can snatch rain to nourish plant life.

these lovely patches of pink, yellow, creamy white, blue, and red will turn to straw and become a brown fuzz on the surface of the desert soil. But that is their inevitable end — the Western Sonoran Desert retreats to endure the long, hot, and for the most part rainless months of summer and fall. The flowering trees and shrubs such as palo verde, ocotillo, smoke tree, desert willow, and ironwood tend to keep their flowers a little longer. In time they, too, lose both blossoms and leaves, and settle down for the long wait.

The Eastern Sonoran Desert and the Arizona Upland are something else again. They receive local but signifi-

38

In many ways this is a mixed blessing. Summer-season wildflowers like the coral-tinted Arizona "poppy" brighten the desert floor. Grass springs up out of nowhere for the use of ranch stock. Water holes fill; ocotillo stalks become green wands. But the air is heavy with humidity. Flash floods tear down canyon floors, grinding down anything in their paths, inundating highways, damaging buildings. These violent storms are usually local in nature, seldom covering large areas. A mile away the desert will not receive a single drop. During the course of summer, however, most of the eastern sections of the Sonoran Desert are thoroughly drenched, at least once or twice. Under favoring conditions, even the western subdivision is visited by local showers. One recent summer, Palm Springs, Indio, and, closer to the Colorado River, the hamlets of Rice and Vidal—all suffered severe flash floods.

To summarize, as one travels east, there is a gradual reduction of winter rain and a gradual increase of summer precipitation. Indio has one true rainy season: winter. Tucson has two rain peaks: winter and summer. Big Bend National Park in Texas receives most of its rain in summer.

The Mojave Desert differs somewhat from its southern neighbor, the Western Sonoran. For one thing, much of the Mojave is higher in elevation; the desert floor varies from two to three thousand feet, then slopes down toward the Colorado River and sinks to 279.8 feet below sea level in Death Valley. It also has colder winters; frost can be expected during the coldest months, and snow, though light, falls occasionally. Rainfall is usually higher, but the Mojave Desert's south edge, east of the Little San Bernardino and the Transverse Ranges, is influenced by the subtropical high, and its central and northern sections are in the rain shadow of the northern Transverse Ranges and the Sierra Nevada. Its western extension is the picturesque Antelope Valley, sharpened to a point where the San Andreas Fault cuts across the Ridge Route, main north-south traffic artery leading out of the Los Angeles Basin.

A wandering burst of moist air may creep into the Mojave during the warmer months. The northern section, particularly the Owens Valley, has some summer convectional precipitation. Pacific storms tilting south from their usual easterly path and the western edges of storm masses generated over the Rocky Mountains may

cant thundershowers throughout the hottest part of the year. Though they are in the same latitude as the Western Sonoran Desert, one feature modifies their climates. They receive the benefits of being on the edge of the summer monsoon influx of moist air from the Gulf of Mexico.

bring additional summer rainfall. Nevertheless, the Mojave by and large is a winter-rain desert.

During a well-watered year, it displays the same wild-flower generosity as the Western Sonoran Desert to the south, but the peak is usually a month or so later. One may find sand verbena and desert marigold around Indio in March, lupine, desert candle, poppies and owl's clover on the hills near Lancaster in April and early May.

The Great Basin is farther north and even higher for the most part than the Mojave Desert. Snow falls each winter from storms crossing the Sierran crest or extending west from the Rockies. In general, precipitation remains low because of intervening mountains to the east and west and the distance from both oceans. Because of this freedom from maritime influence, the climate of the Great Basin is what is termed "continental." Seasonal change is pronounced—winters are cold and summers, particularly at lower elevations, are hot. Rain during this season is largely convectional, except for the same storm-edge conditions described for the Mojave. If moist air is aloft, local squalls race across the sagebrush plains, which soak in the downpour and saturate the air with their spicy odor.

The Navajoan Desert also has a continental type of climate. Winters are cold; summer temperatures vary from warm to hot. It is influenced by rain shadows cast by mountains to both the east and west, but convection-borne thunderstorms are not uncommon.

The Chihuahuan Desert has local spots of more severe aridity in the lee of some of its ranges, but this is mainly a subtropical desert—the result of horse latitude warm, dry air. Blizzards and cold fronts visit the Trans-Pecos and southern New Mexico from time to time, but most precipitation arrives in summer, in part because this desert catches the corner of the North American continent's summer monsoon as well as receiving the benefits of rain-bearing trade winds at their northernmost extension.

The Mexican sections of the Sonoran Desert complex usually have dry winters, but humidity begins to build up in late spring, heralding the approach of the wet season. As one progresses south, rainfall averages rise, with local variations due to relief and other factors. Vegetation thickens and increases in size, sure evidence of more moisture.

The uneven character of rainfall in the Mexican-American deserts may be traced in part to their differing origins — rain shadow, subtropical high-pressure system units, midcontinental location away from maritime moisture sources, or some combination of those factors. Add to these all the other climatic and topographical variables—innumerable mountain ranges and plateaus accumulating snow and rain on their high slopes; deep, almost waterless basins in between; coastal fog; erratic winter storms; altitudinal temperature changes—and one has a climatic recipe as unpredictable as the rising of a tricky soufflé.

The downslope drainage of cold air from higher altitudes plays a part, too. The higher deserts north of the Sonoran are uniformly cold during the winter nights; chilled and therefore heavier air slips off the higher slopes and settles in basins and troughs. There are areas in both the Mojave Desert and the southern Great Basin where frost is practically unknown; yet a thousand feet below, cold air accumulates and freezing temperatures occur regularly.

There appears to be strong evidence that a major trend is taking place in the climate of the Sonoran complex. It is getting drier, as demonstrated by a change in the vegetation south of Tucson. Proof of this hypothesis is supplied by a most interesting book, Hastings and Turner's *The Changing Mile* (University of Arizona, 1965). The authors have accumulated a series of matching photographs of certain places, one taken many years ago, the other recently. There is no doubt that many once-dominant plants have retreated in the face of species better adapted to drier and, of more significance, disturbed conditions. Much of this change is due to human interference, but the authors also conclude that a drying trend may account for some of this shift. Nothing is stable forever; change is the only constant. This applies to the apparently timeless desert landscapes as well.

*Joshua trees, silhouetted here against a flamboyant sunset,
are bizarre giants of the lily family, hallmarks of
the Mojave Desert.*

*Summer thundershowers are common in many places
in the desert. The new leaves of the ocotillo indicate
that substantial rain has already fallen here.*

Turret Arch, framed here by another arch, looks indestructible beneath its stalwart battlement. But its very presence proves that all rock exposed to weathering and erosion will finally be worn away.

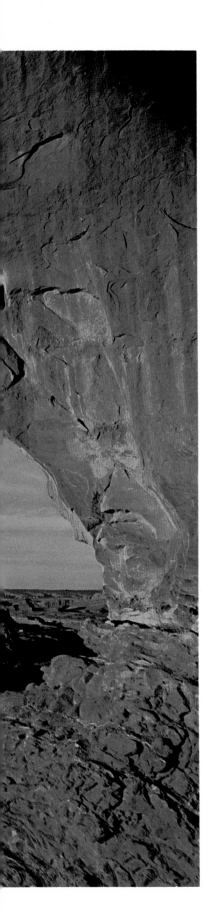

Wind-rippled dunes, such as these in Death Valley, form exotic sandscapes that change from moment to moment.

Many species of yucca mingle with ocotillo and other shrubs on slopes of alluvium washed from ranges in southern Arizona.

43

When dinosaurs trundled through
the mud of marshes and other wet places,
they unknowingly left priceless
records of their size and living habits.

Barren badlands and ancient craters,
snow-shawled mountains and alkali sinks—
Death Valley offers a natural showcase
of geological formations.

From the entrance pit of Carlsbad Caverns, countless tunnels
lead back into huge rooms adorned with mounds fringed with stony ribbons,
and spires and icicles of water-borne limy rock.

Red Rock Canyon, in the western Mojave Desert, is remarkable for its sharply tilted strata of orange-red and ochre.

47

CHAPTER 4

SKIN-AND-BONES COUNTRY

*The Basin and Range Province—where scenic mountains,
born of faults and volcanoes, punctuate the desert floor*

To appreciate the full drama of the Basin and Range Province, it is almost imperative that, at least once, it should be experienced at its worst. This applies to residents and visitors alike. Its problems and its uniqueness are all the more apparent if the encounter takes the form of a trip from some neighboring but very different environment, such as driving down into the desert from the crest of a bordering mountain range or high plateau.

There are several routes by which the traveler can experience the dramatic change from the cool green of mountain meadow and forest to the hot burden of the desert floor in summer — for example, Cedar Breaks National Monument (Utah) to the Escalante Desert; Tioga Pass to Death Valley; Idyllwild to Palm Springs (California). All of the real routes into the area, however, and more particularly into its hottest, driest sections, cross into the region from lower levels or over long routes where the change is so gradual that some of the contrast is lost.

To heighten the contrast and increase the desert's impact, take an imaginary trip. Begin on the foggy coast, near San Diego, perhaps; climb an eleven-thousand-foot pass of a mountain range whose highest peak is 14,569 feet; and descend into the Western Sonoran Desert. The shift from alpine landscapes to sea-level desert plains will be quick and startling.

Once the fog of the coastline is left behind, the hypothetical highway winds upward through chaparral-covered foothills. Along a stream swollen with the high water of late spring, alders and cottonwoods hold cool shadows in their newly foliaged branches. Climbing

higher, the road encounters lodgepole pine and a subalpine meadow. Granite crags loom over the roadway and limber pines huddle at their bases.

At ten thousand feet snowbanks reach the edge of the highway. The sky above is Prussian blue. A few scant alpine shrubs lie in the lee of protecting rocks. A highway turnout advertises itself as "Desert View." Far to the east is a gray-brown horizon, heat-hazed and sprinkled with tan-tinted hillocks. A large patch of white, the mineral residue of a dry lake bed, glints in the sun.

Now the big toboggan ride. In roughly twenty minutes the great sweeps of switchback take the traveler back down to sea level. The air grows noticeably warmer. Suddenly there are no more pines or firs — chaparral has taken command. At 3,500 feet the brush has thinned out, replaced by scruffy-looking bushes, clumps of cactus, and the slanting stems of last year's century plants and nolina. Slender wands of ocotillo burst up from the broken slopes.

The switchbacks straighten out, and foothill vegetation, sparse though it has been, yields to even more scattered patches of creosote bush, which dominates much of the lower desert throughout the continent. Now the highway plunges straight east across a basin of saltbush. Streaks of white alkali, looking deceptively like the snowbanks left behind, wind through the fine-grained soil.

The road ahead rises slightly. Silt gives way to sand; creosote bush returns, and with it the first long slopes of sand dunes that typify this area.

Out of the dunes and onto a gravel desert floor—the altitude has dropped to 500 feet. Shallow washes wind

Arizona's Salt River provides water for many uses. During the long years of its flow, it has dug a canyon of commanding size.

49

out of the surrounding ranges. Gaunt tree trunks follow the sandy pathways. Now the heat cannot be ignored if one's vehicle is not air-conditioned. It grabs throats, pounds heads, and seems almost too much to bear.

Across the river to the east are the Dome Rock Mountains—a cluster of blue fangs that look ready to bite the sky. Thunderheads hover over them. The highway continues northeast and drops around a promontory. There are the first alfalfa fields, wildly green in contrast to the sear plain just crossed. And trees are ahead, real trees with shade! But now there is a new torment — humidity. Evaporation from the nearby river, irrigated fields, the puddles of last night's rain shower, and the moisture piling up those clouds, along with the merciless 115-degree temperature, leaves sweat on foreheads and steam on sunglasses. Heat still lurks in the shade and waits relentlessly out in the summer sun.

IT'S BIG COUNTRY, this particular physiographic province—from southeast Oregon to the state of Hidalgo in Mexico, from southwestern Idaho to the Gulf of California. The entire East Coast, from Maine to Key West, extending inland for 150 miles, could be dropped into it with space left over. With the exception of the Great Plains, it is the most homogeneous geographic area in the United States or Mexico. The casual visitor would have a difficult time deciding, if dropped by helicopter while blindfolded, whether he was in western Texas, southeastern California, or central Arizona.

All of the creosote-bush country is in the Basin and Range Province — the Mojave Desert, the Sonoran Desert with its several subdivisions, and the Chihuahuan. The Great Basin is also a part of this vast region, though its vegetation is for the most part different from that of the lower deserts.

What is the unifying land-form structure of the region? It is deceptively simple. The earth's crust in the area is broken by numerous parallel, roughly north-south-trending faults—great cracks in the earth's surface along which movement, vertical or horizontal, has taken place. The Sierra Nevada, one of the western boundary ranges of the province, is probably the most impressive in size and grandeur of the North American mountain ranges made by fault action. Throughout the province are all sizes and shapes of similar ranges, from hillocks two to three hundred feet in height to great

A Primer of Rock Types

Rocks belong to three main groups, all of which can be readily observed in the bare landscapes of the southwestern deserts:

Sedimentary rock is composed of small rock particles cemented together—grains of older rock scrubbed off by erosion, accumulated masses of organic material, or volcanic detritus. Thus, sandstone is formed from sand, limestone from fragments of shells and other limy remains of sea creatures, tuff from volcanic ash. Ancient mud and silt deposits form shale or, when less well-compacted, mud- or siltstone. Conglomerates are collections of rounded gravel and pebbles held together by a matrix "glue." All of these sedimentary rocks were originally deposited in horizontal layers, but through millions of years forces in the earth's crust have warped, bent, tilted, folded, and sliced many of them.

Igneous rock has been formed from molten magma deep in the earth. If magma flows to the surface to cool quickly, as in a volcanic eruption, it becomes lava. If it remains underground to cool more slowly, as have the cores of some mountain ranges, it may become a batholith of granite.

Metamorphic rock is either sedimentary or igneous rock that has been changed by some combination of heat, pressure, or chemicals so that the new rock appears quite different from its parent material. Marble is metamorphosed limestone, slate metamorphosed shale. Large bodies of magma provide the heat, lateral pressure, and chemicals to alter nearby rock.

crustal uplifts reaching timberline or higher. Each of these ranges, because of their fault trends, is oriented along a north-south axis, although the unity of direction may not be apparent if the range in question is so small it is little better than a rock heap.

Piles of boulders, pebbles, and gravel fan out from entrances of gullies and canyons carved into the flanks of the ranges. Torn by erosion from the mother rock, these cone-shaped heaps often form encircling aprons around the desert hills.

Between the fan system of one range and that of an opposing range is a basin in which silt and minerals collect, washed down from surrounding slopes. These so-called alkali beds and dry lakes occupy the lowest level between surrounding ranges. During the wet season, runoff concentrates in the "dry" lake bed, to

Eroded "fossil" sand dunes can be recognized by strata that are thin and often tilted in relation to nearby beds. Sometimes they wear away to mounds of concentric rings.

Sedimentation: Sand and silt are carried downstream by a river, only to be dropped when it enters flood plains or shallow seas.

Grabens: Also called "rift valleys," these troughs in the earth's crust dropped when motion occurred along two parallel faults.

evaporate when drought returns. The Great Basin is a huge complex of such enclosed sinks. The Mojave, too, has many basins isolated from any contact with a river system. Such areas occur in the Western Sonoran Desert as well. Its largest basin is the Salton Trough, now landlocked, though many years ago it had access to the Gulf of California.

Almost all of the Eastern Sonoran Desert and the Arizona Upland are drained by the Gila-Salt River system. The Mexican Highlands and the Sacramento section have a number of drainless basins, but the Rio Grande pulls runoff from numerous canyons, washes, and valleys. The same is true for the Pecos River, a tributary of the Rio Grande, in western Texas.

Basin-and-range topography typifies much of northern Sonora and dominates the vast area between the Sierra Madre Occidental and Sierra Madre Oriental until it backs up against the Central Mexican Plateau. Internal drainage with no access to the sea is the rule rather than the exception here.

To summarize: three land shapes are almost universal throughout the province — bedrock mountains; encircling masses of alluvium collected in fans, which may or may not merge; and basin floors whose lowest levels hold dry lake beds and mineral deposits.

Monotonous? In places, yes, but with more variety than one would suppose. In some areas, volcanic activity has varied the typical fault-block patterns, and many of the ranges have colorful outcrops or series of rock layers varying in hue or texture. Some have eroded into striking shapes and forms—promontories, buttes, narrow gorges, grotesquely carved pinnacles, badlands, and other oddments of topography.

As soon as any body of rock thrusts its head above the surrounding terrain, it is battered by forces determined to demolish it. Volcano, fault block, upwarp, ridge fold—the gods of climate and weather rub their hands with pleasure, pull up their shirt sleeves, and get to work on the newcomer.

A process known as *weathering* first prepares the rock for the more serious onslaught of *erosion*. Both are accomplished by several means, some of which are shown in the figure on page 53.

Exposed to these and other types of weathering, the rocky structure is weakened and becomes prey for the inevitable forces of erosion. The so-called everlasting hills are not really immortal. Throughout the billions of years of the earth's history, mountain ranges have struggled upward only to be flattened by the nibbles of weathering and the gulps of erosion.

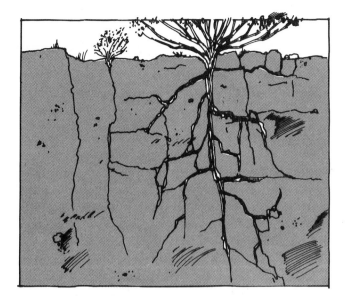

Weathering: When rocks are exposed to rain or chemical action, when they are split apart by roots or freezing water, they crumble away.

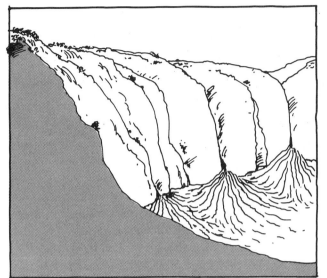

Alluvial fans: Characteristic of desert ranges are the fans of rock debris at their bases, a product of the weathering of the mother rock.

Most erosion is accomplished by running water and the grinding materials it carries along. Soft or weakened rock is particularly susceptible, and this is where erosion usually begins. Cracks become gullies, and gullies are widened to valleys; or, to use the terminology of the Southwest, cracks become arroyos, and arroyos widen to canyons.

Given time, the streams working on a particular range will lower its elevation and widen its valleys. The terrain softens; crags and sharp edges are ground down to hills and rounded contours. They, too, will eventually disappear. The streams of old age become more and more sluggish. They are part of a larger system whose origins may be many miles away. The closer the plain is to sea level, the more complex the system becomes, with oxbows—crescent-shaped lakes left behind by the changing stream bed—great loops or meanders where the current can hardly be detected, marshes, and the multiple waterways of a well-developed delta at the river's mouth.

That most famous of all desert rivers, the Nile, gave us the name for this type of topographical feature. The triangular shape of its system of branching outlets reminded geographers of the Greek symbol for the letter *D*. The Colorado River has a well-defined delta where it enters the Gulf of California. Small deltas can be seen in many places throughout the deserts. Watch for them where streams enter lakes, either natural or man-made. Alluvial fans are really nothing more than deltas "standing up" rather than "lying down."

Sheet erosion is caused by the general pounding away of surface soils by heavy rainfall. The sudden downpours of desert convectional storms push tons of silt, gravel, and sand to lower places.

THE ARID LANDS of the North American continent are showcases of geologic history and features, for deserts tend to develop certain typical land forms such as gorges and buttes. The unifying factor is the absence of restraining vegetation. The lack of protective cover helps compensate for the scarcity of permanent water flow, for the scant shrubs of most desert hillsides do little to lessen the impact of weathering and erosion.

Short-lived, storm-born streams, when they do flow, are "gully busters." Every guidebook to the desert has warnings about camping in washes and stream beds during the rainy season. People have been swept away by the rampaging current and cars buried in its debris. Nothing holds it back; it pours down the bare cliffs and bedrock hillsides to collect detritus and roar on,

flooding roads, stripping away bridges, and turning the desert floor into a muddy wasteland.

Violence is no stranger to the desert. There were placid times, however, when these bare expanses were floors of warm, shallow seas teeming with primitive forms of life. Then there were intervals when the region was covered with humid swamps. Giant horsetails, ferns, and cycads sheltered small dinosaurs and mammal-like forms during the Age of Reptiles.

About midway between the Dinosaur Age and the Ice Age, two major forces that have shaped the earth's crust were in full action—vulcanism and fault activity. Rocks from earlier eras indicate that similar events had occurred before in the region destined to become desert in a far-distant future. Volcanic action in southern Arizona and New Mexico during this period was quite different from the crater-building processes that were to change much of northern Arizona 19 million years later. There were no fluid slicks of lava running downhill like water here. The magma stored in underground reservoirs was stiff and pasty. When faulting and other crustal motion opened vents leading to the surface, the sluggish mass was unable to cope with the sudden expansion of gases so long kept under pressure. It was like opening a bottle of warm champagne—it blew and spewed all over the place in tiny bloblets, which cooled almost instantly to ash and dust. Blowing its top—or rather, its tops, for many craters were formed —was stage one in what must have been an awesome scene of destruction.

Stage two was even more savage. Thousands of tons of ash fell on the surrounding terrain, roaring down the slopes of the now-spent calderas in deadly clouds of hot gases and pumice particles. Nothing could possibly remain alive after this onslaught; all was buried under a choking blanket hundreds of feet thick.

There is evidence that a number of calderas popped their corks during this time. They occupied a stretch of territory from the Colorado River to western New Mexico. Chunks of ancient calderas can be seen near

Spool-like pinnacles in Chiricahua National Monument are eroded debris from an ancient caldera.

55

*Gentle winds ripple a dune's surface; stronger gusts carry loose grains of sand
to the crest and drop them down the smooth leeward face.*

Oatman, on the Apache Trail toward Canyon Lake, and in the Mogollon country west of the Rio Grande.

The accumulations of ash and pumice did not lie undisturbed. Faults were active, and mountain masses were being slowly thrust up along these breaks in the earth's crust. Many of southern Arizona's best-known ranges—the Superstition, the Chiricahua, and the Kofa, to mention but a few—are eroded blocks of consolidated debris from blown-out calderas. Even Camelback, in the heart of one of the more affluent suburbs of Phoenix, is a ragged little remnant of ash-flow rock.

Aside from the impressive scenery created by the erosion of such mountain blocks, underground activity was adding another dimension of wealth for future Arizonans. The great explosions shattered the crust surrounding the caldera and subterranean water loaded with dissolved valuable minerals bubbled up into the innumerable cracks and pockets within the area of destruction. As the water cooled, gold, silver, and copper deposits formed, each at its own temperature. These ore bodies and veins are the foundation for much of Arizona's mineral wealth.

More conventional volcanic activity has produced lava flows, cones, obsidian (volcanic glass) cliffs, and pumice beds in the Great Basin and the Mojave Desert. Hot springs and geyserlike jets such as those in the Mono Basin east of Sierra Nevada testify to the continued presence of magma at no great depth. Many geologists—and for that matter, thousands of tourists —would give their eyeteeth to see the Mono volcanic field come to life again.

Though the great canyons of the American West are concentrated in the plateaus to the north, and in Mexico's Sierra Madre Occidental east of Ciudad Obregon, central Arizona has some impressive canyon country east of Phoenix. The Salt River has dug itself a praiseworthy slot, which one crosses while driving northeast from Globe to the Mogollon Rim. Smaller gorges, many rich with pastel tints, are scenic features of the Indio Hills east of the Salton Sea. Carved out of loosely consolidated siltstones and conglomerates, the hills are labyrinthed with shoulder-wide crevices whose walls are thirty to forty feet high and as tortuous as rattlesnake tracks.

Northwest of Indio is a series of sand dunes with one formidable mound several hundred feet tall. An elongated sea of dunes runs northwest from the Colorado River, paralleling the Southern Pacific rail lines. Its crests and troughs are rippled by the desert wind, tiny wavelets caught in a moment of time. Only a few species of plants are able to live on dunes, and resident animals have made some remarkable adaptations in order to survive in their unusual environment.

Other smaller dunes are scattered throughout the Sonoran Desert wherever wind and landscape features combine for their creation. By far the most remarkable are those featured in the White Sands National Monument in the Tularosa Valley. Unlike most dunes, this shimmering, blindingly white expanse is derived from ancient beds of gypsum from nearby mountains.

Dunes are born when three factors get together: prevailing winds of sufficient strength to carry small particles; a supply of sand grains; and some obstruction that will force the wind to slow down and drop its load. The latter may be as large as a rocky outcrop or as small as a boulder or bush. As the dune builds, it provides its own restraining influence. For this reason, dunes tend to have long slopes on the windward side, and steep slopes on the lee. When the wind mounts to the crest, it is slowed enough to release part of its burden, but on the descent, back eddies stop its progress. It loses vigor as well as the rest of its load, which is dumped on the lee slope. The piled-up sand steepens to a certain angle, obeying a law of physics that controls the distribution of loose particles. After that slope has been reached, additional particles will not cling to the slope face but roll down to collect at the base. Where the wind is generally from one direction, there is a constant removal of sand from the long slope, only to be dumped on the lee side. Unless the dune is stabilized by vegetation, it will travel—slowly but surely—with the wind, drowning in sand whatever it can cover in its path. We find evidence of "fossil" sand dunes in certain types of crosshatched sandstone.

One noteworthy feature of the Chihuahuan Desert should be mentioned: the Carlsbad Caverns deep under the Guadalupe Mountains of southern New Mexico. One of the largest cave systems ever explored, it is a fantastic complex of rooms as large as Radio City Music Hall, grottos dripping with stalactites dozens of feet long, interconnecting passageways decorated with the tracery and fretwork of cave architecture. Its bat colony is one of the wonders of the desert world.

And so the drive across the Basin and Range Province continues—not so monotonous, after all. The blazing sun has disappeared, and a rain squall mists the ranges ahead. Soon the gray broom of the storm sweeps across the road. Lightning bounces onto the scarp of the small ridge beneath it, and tiny waterfalls spill off the broken cliffsides. Suddenly the car is filled with an unmistakable odor: the sharp, resinous, almost aromatic smell of wet creosote bush and dampened desert soil. Unassumingly, a small wash carries a thin stream of water and loosened gravel—a quiet but graphic reminder of how the desert was shaped.

CHAPTER 5

THE GRAND LANDSCAPES

*The Colorado Plateau—where wind and water have conspired
to create some of the most exotic landforms on the planet*

THE THIN, irregular tinkling of the lead sheep's bell drifted up the coral-hued walls of the narrow canyon. At times it was caught and scattered by the gusty winds of the great tableland. Now one could hear the high-pitched bleats of the lambs and the gruff rumbles of the older males.

Soon they came into sight. The aged ewe with the bell picked her sure-footed way up the last steep slope, treacherous with loose chunks of vermilion rock. The flock followed, nibbling here and there on the few, stunted, unmercifully cropped shrubs. Their matted coats, once white, had been tinted by the richly colored sand and soil of their grazing grounds.

Just then their herder appeared—a young Navajo girl not more than ten years old. She was shy and would not respond to a friendly wave or smile. With short commands, half Navajo, half spurts of sound used wherever animals are driven by people, she maneuvered the flock into a simple corral of juniper branches thrust into the rust-colored sand.

Behind her family's encampment blood-red, straight-sided mesas and canyon walls were picking up burgundy shadows. Juniper smoke from the hogan sweetened and spiced the wind, now slowly dropping with the sun. Soon clean-cut shadows disappeared. The blue haze of dusk softened the huge, angular distances, gradually dimming mesa and butte, arch and cliff, those almost unbelievable remnants of an ancient past. Monument Valley was slowly falling asleep.

Some miles away the Mittens, like giant upthrust hands, stood stark against the strengthening starlight. A murmur of Navajo, consonant clipped and vowel expanded, slowed and stopped. No gleam or glow shone in any direction until the horizon met the stars. Thus came the silence, the vast and heavy silence of a land without light.

MONUMENT VALLEY is but one of the many impressive landscapes of the Colorado Plateau, home of the Navajos and the Navajoan Desert. Though peripheral to the warmer and lower arid lands of the North American continent, the plateau's awesome scenery has become symbolic of the desert West. Its counterparts are few—the Sinai Peninsula, similar shreds of eroded rock in the central Sahara, Ayres and a few sister rocks in the Australian Desert—and none really matches this fantastic combination of mile-deep, terraced, and dissected canyons of apricot, sherry gold, and red; soaring leaps of naturally eroded stone arches; mesas and peaks dusted with snow; and slender shafts of Chinese red sandstone pricking the sky.

The western boundary is a high wall of fault block plateaus, breached in places by the Colorado, Virgin, and Sevier rivers. Just north of where the Colorado slows its cataract-infested dash to Lake Mead is the southernmost tableland, the Shivwitz Plateau. The Virgin River, creator of that wonderful jumble of gorge and butte, Zion Canyon, separates it and its next-door neighbor, the Uinkaret Plateau, from the Markagunt Plateau. The western cliffs of this high tableland cradle a natural "glory hole," Cedar Breaks. Over thirty tints and hues of red have been noted in its spires and gullies. These and several other plateaus complete the great rampart.

*Navajos believe that these skyscraper rocks in Canyon de Chelly are
the home of the sacred Spider Woman, who taught them to weave.*

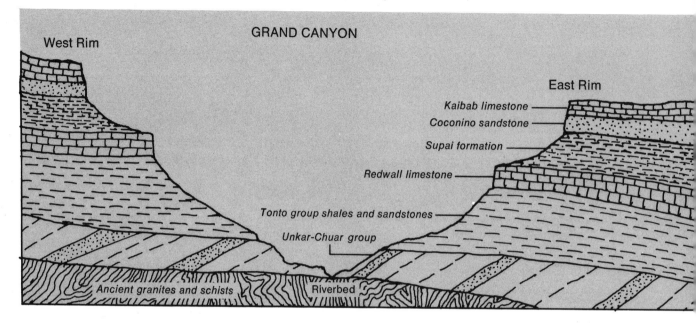

GRAND CANYON

West Rim

East Rim

Kaibab limestone
Coconino sandstone
Supai formation
Redwall limestone
Tonto group shales and sandstones
Unkar-Chuar group
Ancient granites and schists   Riverbed

GRAND CANYON offers a rare opportunity to actually see, layer upon layer, how the earth's crust is formed. Two topographical features make this possible: the Kaibab Upwarp, which brings deep-lying rock strata nearer to the surface, and the Colorado River, whose silt-filled waters slice through the upwarp and reveal its successive levels.

The tower at Desert View offers perhaps the best long-range vantage point to observe the geology, not only of the canyon itself, but also of the overlying formations to the north and east. This diagram simulates the scene from Desert View, looking northeast toward the Echo Cliffs. (Compare with the map on page 62.) Because the river bends just below this point, the North Rim becomes here the West Rim;

the South Rim, the East Rim.

Starting up from the bottom of Grand Canyon, one encounters the following strata: *Ancient granite and schist*—a mixture of metamorphic rock with granite intrusions that makes up the inner gorge. *Unkar-Chuar group*—beds of sandstone, shale, and limestone, the lowest (hence oldest) level to show evidence of living things. *Tonto Platform*—a broad bench of sandstone deposited on beaches of ancient seas and topped by a set of steps in the Tonto formation shale. *Redwall limestone*—spectacular buttes standing above the canyon floor and projecting from its walls, stained red by silt washed from the Supai strata just above. *Supai strata*—sandstone and shale with large amounts of iron oxide that give

Near Provo, Utah, the edge of the Colorado Plateau curves to the east, following the foothills of the Uinta Mountains, one of the few east-west trending ranges in the country. Dinosaur National Monument, near Vernal, has a fossil quarry where visitors may watch scientists painstakingly remove bones of the giant reptiles from their stony matrix.

The great uplift continues into Colorado. Its eastern boundary encloses Grand Mesa, the Uncompahgre Plateau, and Mesa Verde. Between the last two tablelands, the San Juan Mountains thrust a wedge of maroon and umber peaks. South of U.S. Highway 66, it curves southwest, bordering a huge lava flow that covers the colorful strata beneath.

Returning to Arizona, the southern boundary of the

plateau is demarcated by the famed Mogollon Rim, in places a forest-covered series of steps, hundreds of feet high. Farther west, the edge coincides with the Verde River, following its riparian greenery and canyon walls covered with vegetation typical of the Sonoran Desert. North of Clarkdale and Jerome, the Verde Valley is broken by the dramatic pink and cream bluffs of Oak Creek and Sycamore canyons. The southwest corner of the great plateau gradually decreases in elevation. A combination of rolling and rimrock country carries it to the Colorado River and the series of tablelands forming its western edge.

WITHIN THIS VAST, roughly oval uplift is a remarkable introduction to the story of the evolution of

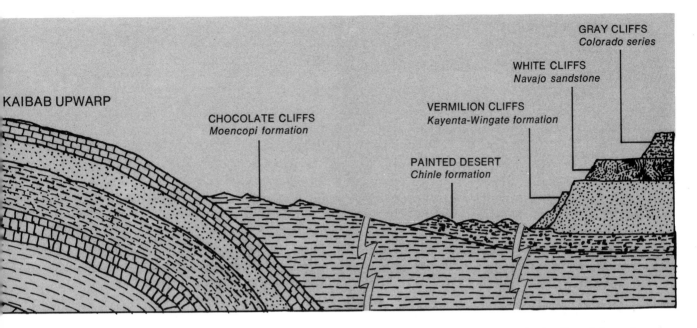

KAIBAB UPWARP

CHOCOLATE CLIFFS
Moencopi formation

PAINTED DESERT
Chinle formation

VERMILION CLIFFS
Kayenta-Wingate formation

WHITE CLIFFS
Navajo sandstone

GRAY CLIFFS
Colorado series

this series of steps a vermilion hue. *Coconino sandstone* and *Kaibab limestone*—perpendicular gray-buff cliffs that form the canyon's rimrock.

Extending north and northeast from the Kaibab Upwarp are a series of step-like, receding scarps topped by terraces of rock, each younger and higher than those preceding: *Moencopi formation*—a deep red stratum of shaly sandstone, which overlies the Kaibab limestone beyond the upwarp and is capped by other strata forming the Chocolate Cliffs. *Chinle formation*—easily eroded pink and lavender shale and sandstone that make up the delicately tinted hillocks of the Painted Desert. *Wingate and Kayenta formations*—two rosy-red sedimentaries, that give the name to the Vermilion

Cliffs. *Navajo sandstone*—massive fossil sand dunes from another age, the basic rock of the White Cliffs, eroded in Capitol Reef National Monument and elsewhere to form gleaming white domes sitting atop a flame-colored base of Kayenta-Wingate. *Entrada* and *Carmel formations*—sandstone layers underlying the Gray Cliffs, not colorful but sculptured into interesting shapes by erosion and laced with dinosaur bones and rich beds of coal.

With time, these successive strata have been scrambled in many places by warping and faulting, but the visitor can still find the marvelous story of geological history written again and again on exposed cliff faces and canyon walls throughout the Southwest.

life and its various habitats. Nowhere is it more dramatically revealed than in the Grand Canyon, where one foot can rest on sand left by yesterday's high water, the other on rocks of the era before the beginning of life. One of the famed features of the Grand Canyon is the record of the earth's history it exposes to view. The Colorado River and its tributaries are like knives cutting deep slices from a wondrous geologic layercake. The base upon which the strata were deposited is deep in the canyon's Granite Gorge, through which the river runs today. Hiking or riding up any of the several trails that begin at river level, one can follow in imagination the change from lowly, one-celled forms of life such as bacteria to man with his unique capabilities.

Leaving the ancient base rocks, the trail winds slowly

upward. Where it passes an outcrop of the Unkar series, the visitor makes the "great leap," as these marine sediments contain evidence of plant life, coral-like creatures, and worm tubes and tracks. Another important feature of the lower canyon is the Tonto platform. During the period when its various strata were being deposited, life was becoming more complex—trilobites, pillbug-like little animals, and other marine fauna dominated this portion of geologic time.

Where the trail wanders up onto the highest layer in the Tonto group, the canyon reveals an enormous gap in its story of life on earth. There are no rocks from the millions of years during which a most important biological "invention" took place: the development of the backbone. The first air-breathing animals—so-called

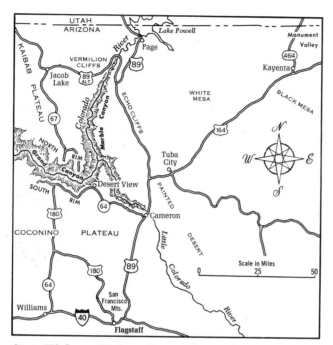

State Highway 64, from Desert View to Cameron, offers the traveler a rare chance to "read the ages."

sea scorpions—evolved in these missing periods, too.

Once on the Redwall, one sees evidence that plants had invaded the land, fishes were plentiful, and amphibians—a significant group of "transition" animals—were coming on the scene. A second big time gap occurs between the Redwall and the Supai strata—the development of land-dwelling animals such as insects, primitive amphibians, and reptiles. From the top of the Supai formation to the rim of the canyon the rocks all belong to one period, the reign of amphibians and the rise of more and more specialized reptiles.

Topping out of the Grand Canyon on the South Rim, the traveler must close his introductory "textbook" for a while. To begin the next chapter, he must head east to Desert View, a visitor center located on Navajo Point. Accustomed by now to regarding upper rock layers as younger than those below, he may find it very disconcerting to learn that, as he faces northeast, he looks *down* on rock formations much younger than those upon which he is standing.

As he drives down the slope of the great Kaibab Upwarp to the trading-post village of Cameron, in places roughly paralleling the gorge of the Little Colorado River, he is approaching the first outcrops of the

chocolate-red Moencopi formation, deposited on top of the Kaibab limestone, the creamy-white rock that is highest, and therefore youngest, of the Grand Canyon strata. Driving past cliffs and road cuts revealing the rosy-brown layers, he descends to the western edge of the Painted Desert, whose strata are even younger than the Moencopi beds he has just passed.

From Cameron (4,201 feet elevation) on the Little Colorado River, he can either turn north to the high plateaus and canyon lands of northern Arizona and Utah or climb the slow grade south to Flagstaff (6,905 feet), a charming little town set among yellow pines. If he chooses the latter route, he follows U.S. Highway 89 as it crosses layers of Moencopi formation until they are lost beneath cinders and other detritus from recent volcanic activity.

Should he head north from Cameron, within a few miles the traveler is confronted by another decision—he can opt for the North Rim of the Grand Canyon via Jacob Lake or discover the fascination of the Navajo country by going northeast on U.S. Highway 164. In either case, the textbook is well into another chapter, the Age of the Dinosaur. The Moencopi rocks are its introduction.

The Echo and Vermilion cliffs are colorful Chinle-Kayenta-Wingate formations overlooking U.S. Highway 89 on the east en route to the Marble Canyon bridge and following U.S. 89A on the north from the bridge to Jacob Lake. The same richly hued rocks, deposited later than those of the Painted Desert, appear in parts of Zion Canyon, along the road to Monument Valley, and throughout much of Capitol Reef National Monument. A number of natural bridges and arches, elegant examples of erosional artistry, are typical of these rock beds as well as of younger rose-to-orange strata.

U.S. Highway 164, heading east into Navajo land, winds between the mauve, lavender, and gray hillocks of the Painted Desert, then in a wide, uphill curve mounts the sunset-colored scarp of the Echo Cliffs. The sand by the side of the road continues to be salmon-colored, but to the left is White Mesa. Though mostly true to its name, it has random tinges of color and a natural arch one can see from the road if he knows where to look for it.

The highway continues to rise steadily until it crests Marsh Pass. Black Mesa looms to the right, named not

The gorge of the Little Colorado meets the main stream far from its origin in the White Mountains. Beyond, outcrops of rock break the surface of the plain.

for black rock beds—these formations are typically tan or gray—but for thickets of juniper and piñon pine. From a distance, these short-trunked cone-bearers appear to be black rather than green or brown. Like White Mesa, Black Mesa is an enormous platform. All but one of the Hopi villages sit atop fingerlike extensions of the great tableland or at their bases. The rock of Black Mesa dates from the time when primitive mammals were eluding the fangs of the huge reptiles that had dominated the world for so long but were soon to become extinct. Within minutes, the traveler has gone from midway in the Dinosaur Age to its close.

During the era of these impressive animals, another biological milestone was passed. The dinosaurs gradually separated into birdlike and mammal-like forms, but the periods that witnessed the development of to-

day's birds and mammals are not too well represented on the Colorado Plateau. Rocks and fossils from these later epochs can be found elsewhere in the North American deserts, however. Rich fossil beds are common in places in the Mojave Desert. Bones of early horses, camels, and other mammals that had long since disappeared by the time early man entered the New World are scattered on the barren hills and plains near Calico and in the hills behind Barstow.

Most visitors to Utah include the famed Bryce Canyon in their itinerary. Its rocks are young in comparison to those of the Grand Canyon; called Pink Cliff formations, they are like icing on rich geologic pastry beneath. Ranging from golden yellow to deep crimson (depending on season and time of day), the spires appear to have been whittled out by man rather than by forces

63

of weathering and erosion. Rocks of this same period appear in Cedar Breaks and in rosy-hued bands on the sides of the Aquarius and other plateaus west of the Canyonlands of southeastern Utah.

T HE HIGHEST ELEVATION and most recent rocky masses of the Colorado Plateau are volcanic in origin. Looming over the Grand Canyon are the San Francisco Peaks, surrounded by cinder cones and craters, the clustered offspring of fiery parents. Volcanic plugs—thick, viscid lava hardened in the throats of volcanoes long since eroded away—are scattered about the Four Corners region. Notable examples are Shiprock and Aglatha Peak, east portal of the entry to Monument Valley. (The west portal, directly opposite, is Owl Butte, carved from an imposing cliff of red sandstone.)

Other mountain masses, particularly in the Canyonlands country of eastern Utah, were formed when intrusions of viscous magma heaved up the sedimentary overburden. Navajo Mountain and the Henry, Abajo, and La Sal mountains were formed in this manner. The last-named range is a photographer's dream when it is snow topped and framed within the red curves of Delicate Arch, deep in Arches National Monument.

To the great good fortune of the buyers (and sellers) of photographic film, this is a fabulous world of color, chopped up into masses and shapes that readily compose into stunning pictures. You can't go wrong. Though late afternoon enriches color and intensifies shadows, whenever you shoot, whatever you focus on, you are likely to get a winner.

The credit for this vast collection of perfectly posed landscapes belongs to four fortuitous circumstances: the geologic accident of upwarps and plateaus; layers of colorful rock, some soft and easily eroded, others hard and resistant to erosional wear and tear; a great river system, which in spate from winter snow melt or summer flash flood carries huge loads of grinding material from nearby mountains and mesas; and time.

It was once thought that wind, especially when loaded with abrasive material during sandstorms, was responsible for natural arches and fins—those clusters of thin, upright, planklike rocks, characteristic of many areas on the great plateau. Water, however, is really the operating agent. Arches are caused by water's seeping into cracks of fractured rock, freezing there, and thus expanding to break away a slab—and in time another slab. Eventually, there is a gaping hole. Natural bridges, on the other hand, are the direct result of running water, which, even if intermittent, hammers away at a fin that obstructs its flow.

A collection of pinnacles, each sporting a "hat" of different color or shape, is another erosional feature. One such group is found in Goblin Valley, east of Capitol Reef National Monument. The cap rock is more resistant to erosion and protects the softer material beneath. The staircase bases of buttes such as those found in Monument Valley are also the result of the alternation of hard and soft layers—shales and mudstone between a hard sandstone, for instance.

The great canyons are truly children of rivers. The Colorado created Grand, Marble, Glen, and Cataract canyons. One of its tributaries, the Green River, is responsible for Labyrinth, Gray, Desolation, and Red canyons, as well as Flaming Gorge on the north slope of the Uinta Mountains. Two other tributaries, the Dirty Devil and Escalante rivers, have had a hand in shaping some handsome gorges east of the Aquarius Plateau. These are remarkable achievements considering that the great uplift began only several—some authorities say a dozen or so—million years ago.

As the Colorado Plateau slowly arched higher and higher, the Colorado River and its tributaries steadily ground deeper and deeper. Great drainage systems, like the Mississippi, gradually reduce their landscapes to more mature surfaces, eventually producing a level plain. By rising while the rivers were cutting, the plateau has managed to remain young in the sense that it has not been tamed into gentle hills and valleys.

Years and water, uplift and rock types have created the Colorado Plateau—that marvelous highland of the North American deserts where immensity is commonplace, dramatic beauty is taken for granted, and man, if he chooses, may be very much alone.

This colorful canyon upstream and northeast of Moab seems tame compared to the gorges the same Colorado River has carved downstream at Canyonlands and Grand Canyon.

*Colorful and impressive as it is, Grand Canyon has more to offer than being a
photographer's delight. Much of our planet's history is told by the rocks of the great gorge.
Their fossils, sequence, and composition are marvelous clues to the past.*

Desert View is an excellent place to get acquainted with the seemingly contradictory time sequence introduced by the Kaibab Upwarp. Facing north or east, one looks down on rocks younger than those on which he is standing.

*Many mountain ranges
of the desert have
golden aspen thriving
in isolated groves.*

*These petrified rainbows
were once trees whose
plant tissue was gradually
replaced by minerals.*

*Snow is no stranger
to high desert plains and ranges.
Here wind-driven snow clings
to storm-bent trees.*

*The relentless Colorado River,
reinforced with silt from its tributary
the Green, grinds a tortuous path
through Canyonlands National Park.*

*All of the rich color
of Bryce Canyon is enhanced
by the long rays of a rising
or setting sun.*

71

PART TWO

NATURAL
COMMUNITIES
OF LIFE

*Golden poppies and desert dandelions,
cascading down a slope below Mount San Jacinto,
explode the myth of the "lifeless" desert.*

73

Gulf fritillary.

Burrowing owls.

Bighorn sheep.

Kangaroo rat.

Desert tortoise.

Rhinocerous beetle.

Leopard lizard.

Raccoon.

Cactus wren.

Kit fox.

Badger.

Ridge-nosed rattlesnake.

*The adaptable mule deer, found throughout much of western America,
ranges into the Southwest, too, particularly in wooded areas.*

Yellow trumpet flower.

Desert lily.

Arizona "poppy."

Desert willow.

Sacred datura.

Sego lily.

Beavertail cactus.

Spanish bayonet.

Indian paintbrush.

Claret cup hedgehog cactus.

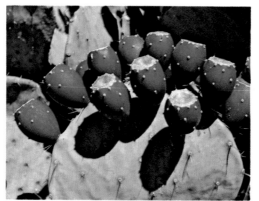

Cactus and fruit.

Desert mariposa.

After the spring rains, the desert floor becomes a garden. Here California poppies mingle with lupine in the shadow of Mount Turnbull, southern Arizona.

Most of the year the ironwood tree looks like a woody skeleton, bereft of foliage and flowers, but in spring it suddenly breaks out in masses of pink blossoms.

Baja California has some unusual desert plants: the "sprouting asparagus" or boojum tree (right), century plants (center), and giant cardon cactus (left).

79

Bigtooth maples seek moist places along streams, as here in Oak Creek Canyon, Arizona. In fall their foliage turns pink or scarlet.

CHAPTER 6

PLANTS OF THE CROSSROADS REGION

*Immigrants from many places and natives that through
millions of years have adapted to an arid life*

Adaptation, the amazing ability to meet the stresses of changing environments, to survive in a coyote-eat-rabbit world or a habitat burdened with severe drought, is the proud outcome of the miracle play of evolution. As naturalist-photographer David Cavagnaro says: "Things live where they do because they can."

During the millennia in which plant and animal species evolved, wandered in from other biotic regions, or stopped to reconnoiter the multiplicity of possible homes in the Mexican-American deserts, they grouped into associations termed natural communities. Natural communities are collections of plants and animals, living together in a specific environment, which have adapted or are adapting to that environment and to contact with each other. Species unable to live there have disappeared or are leaving. Nature does not play favorites; it's a matter of adapt or leave or perish.

Organisms, and ultimately species, have two things going for them: heredity, which passes characteristics from parent to offspring through the genes; and mutation, a sudden change in appearance, behavior, life processes, or body parts. Most mutations—and there is still some doubt as to their cause, though cosmic rays have been suggested—are usually unimportant to the organism or actually harmful to it. A mutation leading to deafness would be of great disservice both to the original mutant and, more important, to its children. Mutations are more than just one-time phenomena. They are recorded in the genes and transmitted to offspring, unless the mutation is so harmful that the organism dies before maturity.

On the other hand, if the mutation could help the organism adjust to a certain environment or escape its predators, it would have hit the jackpot in the game of survival. For example, the first desert plant with the ability to grow succulent leaves in which water could be stored, and to transfer this ability to its descendants, had advanced profoundly its species' efficiency in coping with long rainless months.

Natural communities, therefore, are laboratories of evolution. Though they may have undergone periods of environmental change, such as fire, cyclical rhythms of climate, or some type of catastrophe, by and large the members of biotic communities have made the great adjustment in one way or another. They have adapted to most of the limiting factors operating in a particular environment.

In terms of the continent's bi-national deserts, the structuring of plant and animal types in accordance with elevation was first brought out in an early study of the American Southwest. The system was based on the zones of vegetation found as one progressed from the bottom of the Grand Canyon to the top of the San Francisco Peaks.

Some books still continue to refer to these zones, but it appears more realistic to use a new system based on the collection of typical organisms into natural communities. For the most part these areas are named for their most numerous and characteristic plants; hence, the oak woodland community, the creosote brush scrub community, and so forth. A few have names from more exotic sources: chaparral, tundra, and taiga — words taken directly from other languages.

Flowering Joshua trees make an attractive frame for the snow-sprinkled Tehachapi range, northern boundary of Antelope Valley. Lancaster, Palmdale, Barstow...

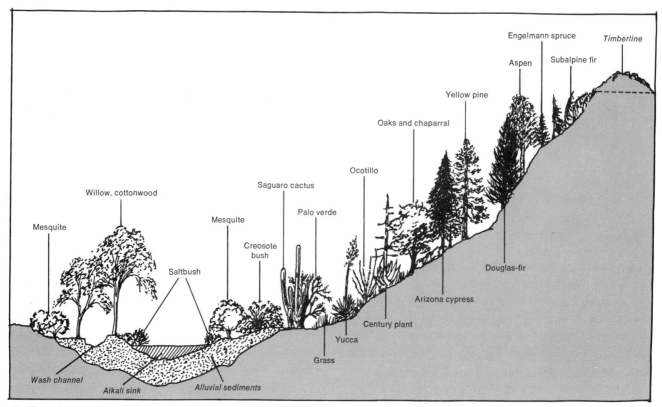

In desert mountains, rain and cold increase with elevation, so the zones of plant life change:
scrub, savannah, chaparral, and woodland. Conifers common to cooler times survive at upper levels.

The diversity of the North American deserts cannot be overemphasized. Some forty-five natural communities are found here. Contrast this with an area of comparable size in the northeastern United States and adjacent Canada, which, though its annual rainfall totals up to fifty inches, supports only some twenty communities. Clearly the differences between the two regions contradict the long-held belief that the desert is a relatively featureless stretch of undifferentiated scrub.

A PLANT IS MORE than a collection of leaves, stems, roots, and such reproductive parts as flowers and seeds. It is a unique factory designed not only for its own survival but also for the animals that feed upon it. One of the major steps forward in evolutionary history was the development of organisms able to produce food from the energy of sunlight, chemicals in air and water, and a substance within the organism that stimulates the chemical reaction. These organisms, of course, are plants, and the process is photosynthesis. Plants use the food they make to produce leaves, woody tissue, flowers, and seeds. Unfortunately for plants that live in dry regions, all of these processes require the passage of gases in and out of openings in leaves, where most food-making takes place. Water vapor also escapes through these leaf pores, or *stomates*. Desert plants cannot afford to lose much moisture, so water-conserving mutations that took place in certain species of plants were very helpful (see figures on pages 83, 84, and 85).

Most desert shrubs have small leaves with a hairy, waxy, or leathery skin, enabling them to retain cell moisture. Some, like the ocotillo, or coachwhip plant, lose all their leaves at the end of the wet season. No leaves, no openings through which precious water can leave the plant. Similar mutations have occurred in other desert species such as the palo verde. Unlike ocotillo, palo verde has green bark on its trunk and larger branches. Food-making bodies are located in these parts of the tree and continue to carry on limited photosynthesis despite the absence of leaves. As most of the desert's cacti have substituted spines for leaves, the food-manufacturing function has been transferred to stalks and pads.

Desert plants that stick it out during rainless months have a number of other adaptations. Root systems are usually wider, longer, or both. Many visitors comment upon the spacing of desert shrubs, as if gardeners had arranged them just so many feet apart. Nature, not man, is responsible for this seeming aloofness on the part of many perennial plants of the desert plains. There is just so much water available, and competition for soil moisture is severe. Thus the spreading root network of one bush seldom has much contact with that of a neighboring plant. There is also evidence that some desert species discourage competition by releasing substances into the soil that tend to inhibit the growth of too close neighbors.

A large group of desert plants, including the most spectacular wildflowers, use another tactic. They simply refuse to maintain leafy tissue and juicy stems during the dry months. Instead, they spend the most taxing periods as seed or buried bulbs, holding onto a tiny spark of life that will burst into bloom when the soil has sufficient moisture. Because of this behavior, some authorities believe these "ephemerals," should not be classed as true desert plants. When conditions are favorable, they germinate, grow, and bloom, as improvident with water as wildflowers in a mountain meadow.

The alkali sinks of the Basin and Range section of Mexican-American deserts pose a special problem. They are heavy with various salts to the point that most have no plants at all where minerals are most concentrated. Specialized vegetation does grow around the rims of sinks, but only a few species are capable of tolerating such salty soil.

Plant life has evolved to make use of the physical principle that water will enter—actually pass through—the membranes of root tissue *if* the solutes in the cell sap are more concentrated than the solutes in soil water. In other words, soil water "wants" to dilute the cell sap until both liquids have the same amount of dissolved substances such as salt. Since cell sap usually has more solutes, roots can do their job of absorbing soil moisture.

Now reverse the situation. Suppose there are more solutes in soil water than in a plant's cell sap. The plant will lose water rather than absorb it, and thus wilt. This is the situation in an alkali sink. One would expect that such soils could support no plant life at all, but sinks are rimmed with flourishing shrubs and grassy "meadows." The secret? Again, adaptation. Some species excrete excess salt from their leaves; others exert effort to concentrate their cell sap. Many salt-tolerant plants such as pickleweed and desert greasewood are succulent, storing the water they have worked so hard to get in thick leaves or stems.

IT IS APPARENT that the vegetation of the American Southwest (and Mexico's Northwest) has many environmental conditions with which to cope. Add altitude and temperature to soil types and water availability, and one can begin to understand the reasons for the multiplicity of desert communities.

Altitude, even if no more than a shift of several hundred feet, has a major influence on vegetation. It accounts for patches of mesquite-dotted grassland disappearing into oak thickets, which in turn open out to forests of cypress and juniper. Nowhere in the West can the land escape the consequences of distance above sea level.

Altitude is close kin to latitude, another geographic factor of extreme importance. The deserts of North America continue to the forty-fifth parallel and as far south as roughly the twenty-second. The area is rela-

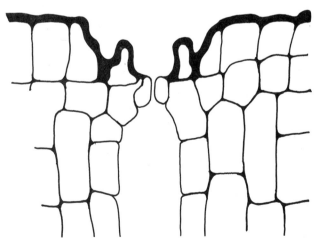

Stomates—pores in leaves that allow gases to pass in and out—are often recessed in desert plants to avoid drying by direct solar rays.

tively small in comparison to the Sahara and other major deserts, but because of altitude diversity, latitudinal width, and greater wetness of neighboring regions, which send an occasional wandering storm or moisture mass over their dry frontiers, it enjoys a richness of community types that is remarkable for a generally hostile environment.

Why does Wyoming share species with Chihuahua? What do the forests of Canada and San Luis Potosí have in common? An "archipelago" of highland islands is distributed through the western deserts. The high plateaus and Mexico's two great sierras are such insular heights, crowned with aspen and yellow pine. Between them are numerous valleys, many too low and thus too dry for more than arid scrub.

Plant traffic has not been in only one direction. For a very different set of reasons, a number of tropical species have ventured north of the Mexican border, among them a form of Cordia that in season bears masses of white flowers; types of manioc; members of the pineapple family; a tropical hop bush; coralbean, shrub sister of the beautiful coral trees of the tropics;

and several mimosas. The remarkable fact is that these types, most of them originally from the humid tropics, have found the desert compatible.

Without doubt, the island ranges of the desert are intriguing meeting grounds for representatives of such diverse regions as the subarctic and the tropics. Yellow trumpet flower (*Tecoma stans*), found all through lowland and mid-elevation Mexico and Central America to northern South America, flourishes on rocky hillsides in southern Arizona, for instance, at the base of Kitt Peak, while five thousand feet above, Douglas fir and other trees common to British Columbia live in an environment equally suited to them.

A similar thread in the pattern of regional interaction is the convergence of eastern and western floral elements within the desert Southwest. Because of topographical modification and climatic events that occurred many millions of years ago, early in the Age of Mammals, the plant species of western North America differ significantly from those of the eastern half of the continent.

The dry Great Plains, heart of the grim Dust Bowl in

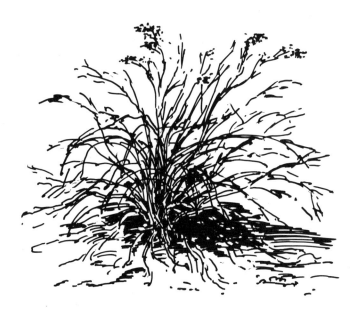

During prolonged periods of drought, desert shrubs such as the creosote bush reduce their need for water by maintaining life in just a few branches.

The barrel cactus and most of its succulent relatives can store water in their pulpy flesh and thus survive many weeks of desiccating heat and zero rainfall.

the 1930s, continue to be a barrier between the plant communities of the eastern part of the continent and those of the West. No eastern oaks grow west of the short-grass country; no western pines occur east of the Great Plains. There are several major exceptions to this rule, however: subarctic coniferous trees extending in a broad band from Alaska to Newfoundland; weeds that enjoy—and exploit—continental distribution; eastern riparian trees and shrubs that escort the Mississippi system deep into western territory until plains cottonwood nods to narrowleaf cottonwood, its Rocky Mountain counterpart in western Montana; outliers of red cedar (really a juniper) and bur oak on ridges in northwestern Texas and Oklahoma; and several riparian species almost ubiquitous throughout the country, such as box elder.

Low and irregular rainfall is not the only environmental feature that prevents thirsty eastern species from invading the West. The Rocky Mountains are an effective barricade, too. Where they descend into the broken country of the Mexican Highlands, however, numerous passes and valleys no higher than three or four thousand feet break up the continental crest. A number of typically eastern plant types have pioneered westward through these gaps, notably sugarberry, black cherry, soapberry, pokeberry, American spikenard, poison ivy, and shinnery oak. The Big Bend country of southern Texas is a real convention ground for visiting plant species—persimmons from the South, a cypress from Arizona, an orchid from British Columbia, and desert olive from Mexico.

The largest convocations of seemingly incompatible plants are in northern Mexico, where desert and mountain plants typical of mid-latitude arid regions, and sky-island vanguards from more northerly strongholds, meet such tropical representatives as strangler figs, wild palms, and kapok trees.

Interior and coastal California is relatively isolated from the rest of the continent, sealed off by deserts, mountains, and climatic differences. Hence, much of the state's flora has developed independently. Nevertheless, a type of *Clarkia*, a tall, graceful pink wildflower, represents a group of plants that struck east from coastal California. These journeys probably took place when the climate in the intervening regions was not so harsh as it is today.

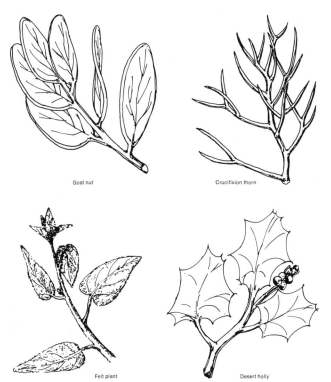

Goat nut

Crucifixion thorn

Felt plant

Desert holly

Leaves are one place where desert plants are likely to lose precious water, because their pores, or stomates, allow the escape of vapor into the atmosphere. Plants have evolved many adaptations to meet this threat to survival: some, often thorny species, have few leaves or none at all; some lose their leaves in the dry season; others have upright leaves that expose a minimum of surface to the sun; still others have pale or hairy leaves, which reflect heat.

Regardless of all this cross traffic, the great majority of plants and animals of the desert belongs to it alone. Endemic species, those restricted to one location, vary in their distribution. Some desert plants, like the Joshua tree, range over portions of several states. Others—a certain locoweed on Mount Charleston in Nevada, for instance—are confined to one canyon or ridgetop.

Even so, full-fledged plant species do not spring from the ground like soldiers from buried dragon's teeth. They all descended from ancestral types, which in many cases no longer exist. For a number of desert species, their place in the botanical scheme of things is most obscure; and the search for their background and history can be an engrossing study. Little by little, the

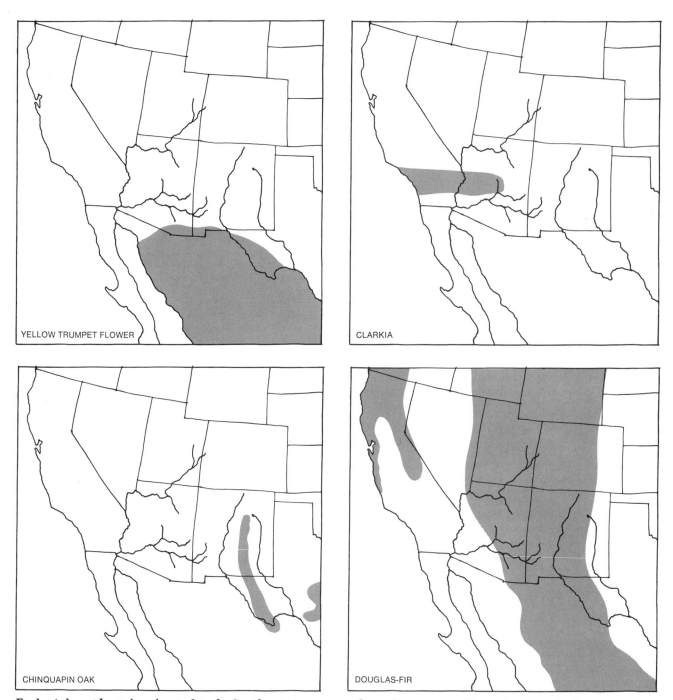

Each of these plants immigrated to the Southwest from somewhere else: trumpet flower from tropical America;
clarkia from California; chinquapin oak from the East; Douglas-fir from the Northwest.

plant scientist gains insight in regard to their distribution and position in certain natural communities.

The clues are fossils, remains or imprints of organisms preserved in rock. Since only certain rock types preserve organic remains, the record of past life is not complete. Geologists have enough fossil material, however, to get an idea of what life and its environments were like.

The climate, at least in what was to become the North American deserts, was warm and moist following the time of the dinosaurs. There is evidence of large, shallow, inland seas. Vegetation reflected a climate much like the humid tropics of today. It extended as far north as southern Canada and included wild figs, trees of the avocado group, and cinnamon trees.

About midway between the last of the dinosaurs and the beginning of the Ice Age, another type of plant life evolved. Western North America was becoming increasingly cooler and drier. Vegetation had to adjust to decreasing rainfall and new seasonal rhythms. In California this meant dry summers. In other parts of the continent, colder winters and warmer summers settled into their own climatic patterns.

The drying-out process, resulting finally in typical desert plants, began thousands of years before the advent of drought. Small localities (microsites) in certain soil types and on south-facing exposures, were habitable only by plants able to withstand dry environments. Spreading northward from their outposts, probably in the Sierra Madre range of western Mexico, they very closely resembled the present-day chaparral species of California, Arizona, and the highlands of western Mexico. Types of madrone and other typical brush and woodland plants are clearly recognizable from fossil remains, uncannily resembling their modern counterparts though they lived millions of years ago.

Several millennia before the Ice Age, drought-adapted plants had spread throughout a large part of California and the southern half of the Great Basin, with smaller patches scattered from Oregon into Mexico. During the same period, several mountain ranges had buckled up along the coastal slope and in the interior, casting rain shadows that encouraged the distribution and adaptation of dry-climate plants.

Though the Ice Age induced periods of increased rainfall in many parts of the Northern Hemisphere, local areas remained relatively dry. The little patches of drought-tolerant plant associations began to produce species even more adapted to extremes of aridity and heat. Chaparral and woodland retreated to desert uplands or toward the Pacific Coast. Plants that had adjusted to drought widened out more and more as con-

ditions became drier at the close of the Glacial Age. Present-day desert vegetation was born.

IT CANNOT BE STATED too strongly that climate, soil, and topography perform as a trio. Each is an instrument in the final production: a natural community. The soils of the desert, in keeping with its other peculiarities, are unlike those of other regions. They do not accumulate in *horizons*—specific zones in the subsoil where various types of activity take place. They are often heavy with minerals deadly to plant life. They are not rich in humus but can be very fertile when treated with care. They are deep on valley floors, nonexistent on bedrock slopes. They produce sand dunes and lunar expanses of so-called desert "pavement"—flat plains of pebbles, each rock settled neatly, side-by-side into place, by the wind removal of separating sand.

Most mid-latitude deserts reach a sea coast somewhere. Quite frequently the meeting place has striking scenery, and Baja California is certainly no exception. The contrast between land and water is sharpest where desert ranges dive directly into the sea. The stark profiles of a waterless land suddenly drown.

Along most desert shores there are several transition communities. Mangroves are encountered south of 27° latitude at Mulege on the gulf side of Baja California and from Guaymas south in Sonora. Other types of desert shores include tidepools (where the rocky substrate is suitable), sand dunes, beach strands, lagoons separated from the open surf by sand spits, and salt marshes.

Salt marshes are strung along the coastlines of the North American deserts wherever the terrain allows. Coastal salt flats in a desert are paradoxical: they have probably the richest plant life of the entire desert, with the exception of oases. Careful observation reveals that most salt-flat vegetation is composed of a few select species—pickleweed, cord grass, a coastal form of salt grass, and several very special members of the daisy family. And they thrive! A mud flat thick with cord grass has been estimated to be more productive of nutrient material than an equal acreage of corn!

Once away from the immediate shoreline, the matrix plant association for that particular area becomes dominant. In places on the Pacific side of Baja, a savage tangle of needle-sharp century plant leaves prevents

Smoke trees, common to desert washes, look like soft, gray puffs in the distance, but at close range they are armed with sharp thorns.

much human reconnaissance. Lichen-crowned cacti, dependent on the fog generated by a cold offshore current, fill the empty spaces. And if this vegetation is grotesque, it is surpassed by the boojum trees and elephant trees of the interior.

The matrix plant for most of the Sonoran and Chihuahuan deserts is the creosote bush. One soon learns to see it as the background for a number of variations. Washes in the Western Sonoran Desert support smoke trees, desert willow (not a true willow but a member of a largely tropical family whose best-known member is the jacaranda tree), mesquite clusters, and palo verde trees. These arboreal forms depend on the moisture concentrated in wash floors.

Where permanent surface water occurs, either along streams or in springs, the character of the desert changes completely. This is the home of plant types not really typical of desert environments. Such trees and shrubs are water wasters because they can afford to be. Contrast a towering cottonwood tree with thousands of large, bright green leaves, all with hundreds of stomates through which water vapor can pass, to a wizened burrobush, typical shrub of arid plains. Its tiny, light-gray leaves are thrifty with the precious fluid. The wild

palms of western desert oases are as extravagant with water as their cottonwood neighbors, so they, too, must live near permanent surface or subsurface moisture.

Alkali flats occur in basins of both the creosote bush and the sagebrush deserts. As the soils become increasingly saline or heavy with minerals, shadscale scrub takes over from the prevailing matrix community. The plants of this scrub are dried-out-looking little shrubs, most of them scalebushes in the goosefoot family. Their seeds are enclosed in capsules that look like cornflakes glued along the fruiting stem.

The heart of the sink usually is plantless. Made up of fine silt and located as a collecting basin for drain-off water, it is either bone dry or a waterlogged mass of salty mud—in either case a most unfriendly environment for vegetation.

Sand dunes have their own little clique of vegetation types adapted to live in this particular habitat.

Summer rains in the eastern sections of the Sonoran Desert and the adjacent Chihuahuan Desert modify the arid terrain. As one goes east from the Colorado River, the density of large columnar cacti—saguaro and, in the southern Sonoran Desert subregions, organ-pipe and cardon—increases, to a point. Then, east of Tucson,

88

saguaros disappear. The Chihuahuan Desert of Texas, southern Arizona, and New Mexico is singularly devoid of giant cacti.

Throughout the summer-rainfall deserts, arboreal (tree-size) plants occur in arroyos, along canyon sides, and even on open slopes. Kidneywood, desert rosewood, Mexican mulberry, and littleleaf sumac join palo verde, mesquite, and other more ubiquitous desert trees. Typical plant mixtures in washes and drainage ways include Apache plume, desert willow, white thorn—also an open-plain species—and desert broom, which in seed time has huge white, feathery masses atop the dark green stems. In contrast to the spartan expanses of California deserts, hillsides of these more-watered areas support not only thick mixtures of typical desert trees and shrubs, but also infiltration of species from neighboring biotic provinces.

One of the most notable features of the summer-rain deserts is a carpet of grass. The Navajoan Desert shares many grass types with the short-grass plains to the east. The Eastern Sonoran Desert, Arizona Upland, Mexican Highlands, and the Trans-Pecos become almost miraculously green in the hot season, particularly to the eyes of one used to the rainlessness of the Mojave and Western Sonoran deserts. He is apt to have assumed that the same climatic stranglehold had clamped down on the entire West.

Semidesert grassland, or savanna, is another piece in the plant mosaic of the southwestern deserts. It usually occurs at three to four thousand feet elevation, above the desert plains proper. Though this community enjoys somewhat high rainfall, soil type has a good deal to do with distribution of grasses. They often occur in soils derived from limestone (which tend to be dry in nature) and in deep soils of fine texture. The latter pro_____ine condition. Water cannot _____e lower soil depths, particu-larly _____ are impervious caliche layers. It is trapped _____ under the surface, going no deeper than a ____ or so. When moisture is present, it often creates heavy, waterlogged clays. But since the water is so close ___ the surface, it dries up quickly, leaving the fine-textured soil powder-dry. Grass, which grows rapidly, is ___ perfect plant type to make use of this now-you-have-

it, now-you-don't water supply. After the first good rain, in almost a matter of hours, the grass seeds have germinated, or as in the case of perennial types such as bunch grass, the plant becomes active. New shoots appear, and if weather is benevolent, additional rains quickly bring the plant to seed-production stage. The rains cease, the soil dries out, and stems and leaves shrivel and die. Seeds wait in the now thoroughly desiccated soil for the next rainy season; perennial grasses retain life in their root masses, which will respond to the same stimulus.

The Chihuahuan Desert is typified by several shrubs absent from western deserts—tarbush, sandpaper plant (its tiny leaves are as rough to the touch as its name suggests), and mariola. Creosote bush and ocotillo continue to be the most common matrix plants.

Once above the desert floor of central Arizona and New Mexico and in many places in western Texas and northern Mexico, chaparral takes command. It is closely related to a well-known coast and foothill scrub in California, and most plant scientists assume that the two communities, though separated by hundreds of miles, share common ancestral stock.

One dominant community above the mid-altitude scrub is *encinal,* or oak woodland, a tranquil and pleasing landscape of oak species (silverleaf, gray, wavyleaf) peculiar to the American Southwest and Mexico, but not to California. The under layer of vegetation is usually grassy, with patches of chaparral or plants typical of arid savannas—yucca, century plant, and such.

The other important woodland type is the piñon pine–juniper dwarf forest scattered throughout the Colorado Plateau, here and there in the Great Basin, and as far west as California. Tracts of the grotesque tree lily, Joshua tree, form another type of woodland. It often occurs with piñon pine–juniper associates.

At appropriate altitudes, the desert removes its influence. The high islands of cool temperatures and plentiful rainfall escape the general impoverishment of desert latitudes. The cone-bearing trees of the north, seemingly so out of place in plant-community maps of the North American deserts, maintain their lofty homesteads. They have not had to make the big adjustment of their desert compadres to live in a land where water is scarce.

CHAPTER 7

CREATURES OF THE DESERT

*Specially-evolved animals that sleep through the long,
hot summer or hide from the noon-day sun*

THE CASUAL TRAVELER speeding along Interstate 10, barricaded behind the closed windows of an air-conditioned car, is not likely to see much wildlife—probably nothing livelier than a calf at a water trough. His natural conclusion: few animals live in the desert.

How surprised that traveler would be to learn that some deserts are rich in diversity and number of native fauna. Of the ten or so biotic regions in Texas, the Chihuahuan Desert of the Trans-Pecos has the largest number of mammal species; there are more types of reptiles in the American deserts than in the rest of the country; there is a large number of birds that reside in the desert and are seldom found elsewhere.

Animal life in the deserts includes an amazingly wide range of types, from sea anemones in tide pools on rocky desert shores to mountain lions, aloof but watchful for passing prey. There are desert fish, desert toads, and a huge horde of desert insects creeping, crawling, flying, pupating, hatching, laying eggs, and biting unwilling victims. There is even a desert whale. Some species such as crossbills—pomegranate-red birds whose bills are specially adapted for coaxing nuts out of cones—remain in coniferous forests characteristic of higher elevations. Others wander in from neighboring biomes, such as ocelots and jaguars from tropical forests and woodland thickets.

Like plants, animals have had to adapt to extreme heat and shortage of water to survive in the desert. Some have acquired through evolution special characteristics that help them to deal with these problems. Several species of rodents, for example, can acquire all the mois-

ture they need from diets of green vegetation. Wood rats survive on the juicy pads of opuntia cactus. Most carnivorous lizards rely on the water present in the insects they consume. One rodent, the kangaroo rat, needs no water at all from sources outside itself; it depends upon its unique metabolic system actually to "make" water from the dry seeds it eats.

So many creatures living together have adjusted to make the most of what food and water there is. How do large colonies of wild mice, rats, and ground squirrels make do with such small resources? One would suppose a fierce competition for the poorly stocked larder. Here the story of survival has another remarkable chapter: each species has developed a set of living habits that differs, if only slightly, from those of its relatives. One ground squirrel feeds during the day, its cousin at night. Some mice rely on seeds of one type of plant, others on another type. Leaves and juicy stems are the main menu for one species of rat; roots are the staple for another. Feeding systems based on the food preferences of their residents are masterpieces of evolutionary engineering. Their efficiency, their ability to s... species even in harsh envi... out of available resourc... biological triumph.

Communities bordering... tered at oases, where life ca... something else. The richest... many warblers, orioles, bunt... tanagers, and chats—work thro... for insects and other tidbits.... are more common in desert ma...

The handsome pronghorn antelope sheds its horns every year but retains the bony core from which a new set will grow.

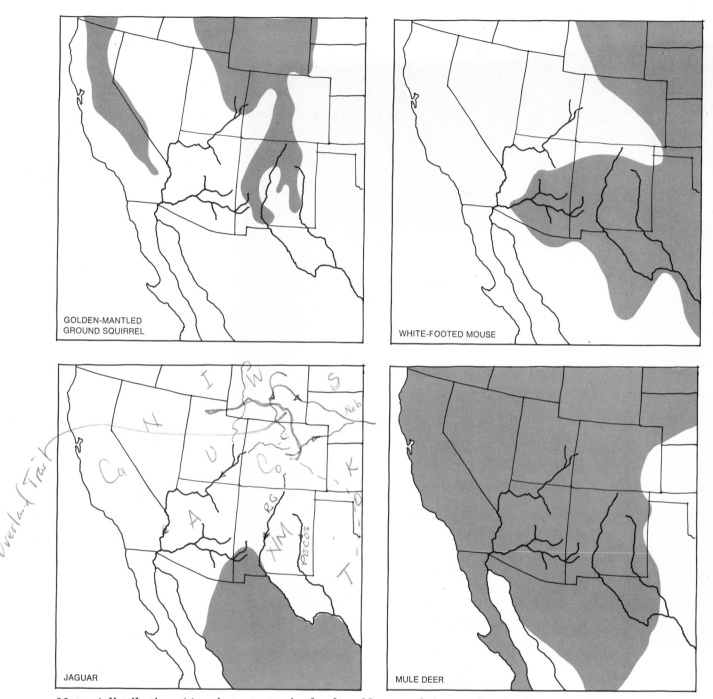

Maps of distribution of four important animals—the golden-mantled ground squirrel, eastern white-footed mouse, jaguar, and mule deer—demonstrate how species from the four points of the compass have extended their range into the biotic crossroads of the Mexican-American deserts. The desert kangaroo rat, on the other hand, evolved here.

frequent the larger pools of permanent streams.

Birds possess one very important advantage in the battle to survive—mobility. They can fly to where the water is. And fly they must, for they have to drink at regular intervals. One of the ways birds cool themselves is by opening their bills, exposing tongues and moist mouth parts to evaporation as a dog does. This is effective but water-wasting. In compensation, birds often remain in the shade, resting during the hottest hours. They are mostly day creatures, nevertheless, and may frequently be seen around springs and seeps. Sleeking their plumage is another way birds protect themselves from heat and dehydration; their feathers serve as insulation.

Plants, by the very nature of the vegetable kingdom, are stationary, unable to evade the furnace-like fury of the desert sun. They cannot pull up their roots and walk away. If they are to adapt at all, they must do it by biological change. Animals are more fortunate. Many of them have managed very successful adaptations simply by changing their life style. Two of the most common patterns are *nocturnalism* and *estivation,* a state of dormancy akin to hiberation except that the animal becomes torpid during summer, not winter. Both are ways of escaping the twin perils of desert life, heat and desiccation.

A number of animals, particularly rodents, drowse away the daylight hours resting in burrows they have excavated in soft sand and gravel. Other species seek shelter in rocky clefts or beneath overhanging shelves. Still others retire into brushy thickets or under trees of streamside or oasis. Wood rats build large nests of twigs and debris in which they rest during the day.

Not only is the air temperature in these nesting places much lower than in the open sun, but the humidity—particularly in the burrows—is higher. Each denned-up animal is surrounded by a tiny cloud of air vapor produced by its own breath. Its habit of sleeping through the hotter hours is further adjustment. The more a warm-blooded animal works in hot weather, the more water must be evaporated to maintain normal body temperature. People keep cool by perspiring from sweat glands located in the skin; dogs and other creatures pant. In either case, precious water is lost to the atmosphere. To maintain proper water balance, animals that keep cool by some means of evaporation must drink sufficient amounts of water to make up for the loss. Its scarcity in the desert, where high temperatures demand a great deal of evaporation, is one of the circumstances that make arid regions ruthless environments.

Thus, the night-active pocket mouse, holed up in his cool den by day, has three ways to conserve his body water: inactivity during the hot hours, remaining in a cool environment, and cushioning himself from drying air by the use of his own breath.

There is an extra bonus in this life style—protection from day-active predators such as hawks and an occasional coyote. Desert animals, like those of other habitats, have evolved many useful ways to elude their enemies. To guard against invasion by hungry snakes, which also use rodent burrows as daytime dens, the pocket mouse piles sand in strategic places within the burrow complex.

So many animals, predators and prey alike, are nocturnal that the unaware visitor is likely to interpret their absence from the daytime scene as absence altogether. Most snakes, owls, and such carnivorous mammals as skunks, kit foxes, and gray foxes are nocturnal. So are a large number of herbivorous mammals—wood rats, various types of wild mice, and some desert ground squirrels. They may begin activity in late afternoon and continue on to sunup, but as soon as the sun recovers from the apathy of dawn, they vanish into their retreats.

Nonetheless, even a summer day is not totally devoid of observable animals. They may be inconspicuous, but alert eyes should not have too much difficulty spotting some of them. Lizards, for instance, are there in profusion.

Reptiles seem to have that combination of evolved biological features and living habits that gives them an advantage in the game of desert survival. Their scaly skin and waste-voiding efficiency both help them to conserve water. Their cold-blooded nature makes them sensitive to temperature change, and spurs them to develop living patterns that are harmonious with environmental temperature.

One frequently sees snakes and lizards sunning themselves during the early part of the day, warming up for the business of food-gathering. While still cold from the night, they are unable to pursue insects and other small creatures that make up reptilian diets. (Two exceptions are the ferocious-appearing but gentle crested iguana and the chuckawalla, largest of California's lizards—both vegetarians.) By noon, however, most desert lizards scamper into crannies or under bushes to escape the sun's heat. They will spend the hottest hours in the shade, though they can often be seen scurrying from one bush to another, tails held up away from the heated ground. Reptiles are also sensitive to cold, and in the colder deserts many of them hibernate during the winter months.

Jackrabbits and cottontails move about in daytime as well as during evening hours. Like other diurnally active creatures, they are inclined to rest during the warmest time, usually seeking shade of some sort. The charming little antelope ground squirrel, or flicker-tail, is another mammal undaunted by high air temperatures. He can be seen skittering across the road and darting into the scrub. Many resident birds such as phainopeplas—the male's black plumage, crested head, and red eyes are unmistakable—are most active in the

During the warm hours of the day, many rodents are tucked away in burrows or other micro-habitats. Plants also use small variations in the desert mosaic, growing larger in shady places or where local conditions increase the amount of soil water available.

morning, but one can expect to catch glimpses of them at any part of the day.

NOCTURNAL CREATURES have based their adaptation on the day-night rhythm of nature. Other species have taken advantage, instead, of its seasonal rhythms, with instinctive responses of migration, hibernation, or estivation.

Most of the Mexican-American deserts have a "dead season" (in some areas there are two), when animals are scarce. Some, like their human counterparts, leave for friendlier climates when the weather is harshest. Others retreat to long intervals of dormancy deep in subsurface dens, often having evolved a life cycle in which their least vulnerable stages occur during this recess. Eggs and seeds are examples of this process. The season of greatest rainfall in a given area and the particular peril an animal is seeking to escape—heat, cold, dryness, or famine—determine whether this animal is dormant in winter (hibernation) or summer (estivation). In both processes, metabolic rates fall to a minimal, torpid level.

In the Great Basin and the Navajoan Desert, the quiet times tend to occur from late fall through midspring. Temperatures often drop to freezing, and blizzards careen across the high plateaus. Many animals, including ground squirrels and reptiles, enter hibernation, dropping into a deep sleep that places little drain on their body resources. Activity resumes just before the summer rains arrive in June, to continue to September. During the summer, many birds arrive as visitors.

The Mojave and Western Sonoran deserts share some of the longest periods of inactivity in the entire North American desert complex. From early summer to early winter, except when given temporary relief by an occasional storm, plant life is dormant and animal energy at low ebb. A few species, one a desert toad, estivate.

The Mojave Desert, higher in elevation than its neighbor to the south, has longer, colder winters. Many of its mammals and most of its reptiles hibernate from late November until midspring. The Western Sonoran has fewer winter-dormant animals. By February, its floor is already turning green, birds are beginning their journey from the tropics, and lizards venture out into the warming sun.

When the wet season coincides with the cooler part of the year, as it does in the Mojave and Western So-

The Road May Be Blocked

A grand tumble

2.13.75

GRAND CANYON

giant wall of sandstone has fallen into the
rado River near Lees Ferry, creating a
rapids which one scientist says may block
el by large motorized watercraft.

r. Steven Carothers of the Museum of
thern Arizona came across the new rapids
miles downstream from Lees Ferry. The
e wall fell leaving a nine-foot-wide channel
boats when the water is flowing below 10,000
ic feet per second.

That river is blocked to motorized traffic
t now," he said.

he National Park Service said it has no
is to clear the channel, but river experts
make a detailed study. No river-running
it has requested that the rocks be moved
cials said.

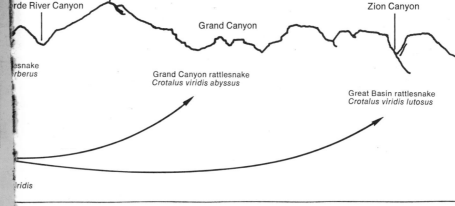

cies, partly because of natural barriers. For example, the prairie
hanges in climate and landforms have isolated some of its descendants.
from their relatives in color and markings.

rly spring burgeon
of hibernation, and
ywhere. Awakening
ecome generous with
mammals, reptiles,
Larvae creep out of
from cocoons, slowly
erge. Now the desert
rings with an avian dawn chorus. Territorial marking
songs pour out from domineering mockingbirds and
Scotts orioles. Natives are already mating and beginning to raise broods; and a host of migrants wing in
from the south, the first of the "tropicals," many in
bright breeding plumage.

The desert night is more alive than ever. Owls spread
wide gray sails and drift off for mice and other rodents.
Their prey forage among the new seeds and tender
leaves and stems. Litters of these small wildlings are
being born in the burrow systems, soon to emerge on
their own, seeking their share of the goodies of springtime. Bats ghost out of caves and crannies. Poorwills
and night hawks tear across the sky, their outsized
mouths scooping up flying insects, which are in plentiful supply. Beetles hurtle through the air, knocking into
lighted windows and collecting around lamp posts in
populated places. Snakes, lean from their months of
sleep, linger on paved roads soaking up warmth from a

sun that hours earlier disappeared behind the mountains to the west.

In deserts farther east, particularly those regions that
enjoy two wet seasons each year, the times of waiting
are relatively short: one in the fall before winter storms
bring rain or snow (depending on latitude and elevation); the other in the late spring before the start of the
summer rains. Low temperatures in uplands and scattered highland islands enforce a period of inactivity
from late fall to midspring.

Springtime activity in the two-wet-season deserts may
continue without much interruption into summer. Re-
juvenated by the first thundershowers, insect life seems
richer than ever; cicadas shrill from every tamarisk
tree. Birds hustle about, bathing in the rain pools left
by the short-lived storms. New wildflowers replace those
of spring, and fields of so-called Arizona "poppy" lie
like cloth-of-gold covering the dead stalks of April's
evening primrose.

Seasonality displays some peculiar quirks. One tiny
creature, the tadpole shrimp, "learned" long ago not to
depend on chance rainfall to fill its water hole. It drops
into total dormancy and stays that way sometimes for
years, buried in dry silt, until released by a flood that
fills its pool sufficiently for renewed activity. The rain
stops and the pool dries up; the tadpole shrimp burrows
into the muddy floor, which soon dries out, too. There

The horned lizard looks archaic and menacing to strangers in the Southwest —reminiscent of reptiles of the Dinosaur Age—but it is a gentle creature.

the little crustacean, now unconscious, waits on and on. Once more the reviving rain comes, and again the tadpole shrimp emerges—much to the surprise of the chance visitor who wonders where on earth it dropped from, here in the middle of the desert!

In Death Valley, a small fish known as the desert pupfish faces a crisis much like the one the tadpole shrimp once faced: water is gradually being pumped from its pools. Other species live in streams that are slowly drying up. Will they too be able to adapt to the new conditions? Where the threat is of man's making, will it be too fast to allow the slow changes of natural adaptation? It is too early to be certain, but some of these endangered species already show a remarkable tolerance for the increased salinity of their watery homes.

The first pocket mouse to have a pale coat in the white gypsum dunes of southern New Mexico was luckier than he knew. He was much less noticeable than his darker fellows. Hawks, owls, and other predators soon lost him as he scampered over the sand. His offspring

shared this trait and became even paler in color. Thus, a strain of white pocket mice lives in the dazzling sand piles, perfectly matching its background and successfully eluding its enemies. These mice are another example of adaptation of a species—that marvelous determination to "hang in there," aided by what favorable chance comes its way through inheritance or the good fortune of a useful mutation of its own.

IN PRACTICE, the plant and animal kingdoms, which have been discussed separately here, form a single community. Plants feed animals; conversely, without the billions of tiny chompers and chewers that help reduce plant and animal remains into soil, the green earth would be barren. Any number of close and traditional relationships exist between certain species of plants and animals. Yucca moths pollinate yuccas, which in turn protect and feed the growing moth larvae. Scrub jays bury acorns, often in places best suited for the young oaks that later sprout from them. On the other hand,

Ornithologists had long assumed that birds did not hibernate—until a poorwill was discovered resting dormant in a rocky cleft in the desert.

some plant-animal relations are definitely harmful to one of the participants. Pine-engraving beetles damage the bark of pine trees; aphids suck the juices from leaves of preferred plants.

Complicated as these interdependencies and interrelations appear, there is another strand in the web: animals relate to other animals in a variety of ways. They may be mutually helpful, such as two horses standing side by side and head to tail, each swishing flies from its companion's face. Or they may be dire, like the pounce of a bobcat upon a hapless cottontail.

Thus, each natural community has animals adapted to the same environmental features that control the plants—climate, topography, and soil. In addition, the animals must get along with one another and with the plants, using them in many ways for food, shelter, lookout posts, and so forth.

These communities of living things can be identified most practically by their dominant plant species. After all, animals can migrate from one plant community to

another if conditions are not favorable, but individual plants are tied forever by their nature to the spot where they first found life.

Mesquite and tamarisk thickets harbor a number of animals dependent on their typical plants for several reasons. Tiny yellow-headed verdins build grapefruit-sized nests in the foliage. Phainopeplas and other birds relish the tasty fruits of a form of mistletoe to which mesquite trees are hosts. Seed-eating rodents harvest the contents of the pods so conspicuous at certain seasons. Bees and other insects use the pollen from the fuzzy flowers, while lizards clamber up and down the rough bark watching for such prey. Even to man, mesquite shade is welcome in summer, and its wood has long supplied ranchers with fence posts and firewood.

The Joshua tree, a giant lily typical of the Mojave Desert, is another such apartment house. It is landlord to an oriole that seldom nests anywhere but in its dagger-sharp leaves; a tiny lizard lives on the termites active in the dead wood; wood rats use its debris for nest build-

Another desert dweller that is frightening to many people is the hairy spider, or tarantula, but this insect-eater is quite harmless if not molested.

ing; a moth visits its flowers to lay her eggs, and without her help, the tree's seedlings could never begin life.

Unstable though they may be, dunes are also home for several animals adapted to their shifting surfaces. The sidewinder, a form of rattlesnake, uses a peculiar looplike motion for better traction. Horned lizards, the "horny toads" so loved by most children, wriggle down into the sand when danger threatens, leaving only a few telltale wavelets to mark their hiding place. Another lizard has long, fringe-edged toes that help it navigate through loose sand, in much the way foot fins are used by snorklers.

In saguaro land, several birds are so unmistakable as to be symbolic of the giant cacti. The elf owl, one of the smallest of his group, lives in abandoned nest holes dug in the succulent cactus flesh by gila woodpeckers and Mearns flickers. Down in the draws thick with palo verde, desert willow, and catclaw, cardinals and pyrrhuloxias whistle and call.

The desert grasslands and the oak woodlands just above them support a somewhat different set of animal residents. The mice of the sand patches are replaced by harvest and grasshopper mice, confined to grassy slopes and valleys. Acorn woodpeckers work at their trade of hammering acorns into crevices in living bark or dead wood of old snags.

Up in the coniferous forests crowning the sky islands, elk and deer browse through brush or graze in open meadows. After the start of summer rains, these wide glades are Paisley shawls of color: harebells, gilias, penstemons, cone flowers, and paintbrush brighten roadsides and grassy verges. Bears are not uncommon, and several predators, from mountain lions to skunks, help balance the plant-eating animals.

Desert tide pools are communities of another kind. They support great colonies of seaweeds and masses of marine animals adapted to the rhythms of seashore life —tidal rise and fall, and breakers boiling in endless parade, particularly on continental edges. Here live sea stars, sea urchins, barnacles, sea snails, and a host of other crab-type, slug-type, worm-type creatures of great variety and number.

Lagoon and sand-stand communities are typified by burrowing creatures. Crabs, clams, tube worms, and numerous other shore dwellers take shelter in the easily penetrated substrate. They make contact, nevertheless, with the surf upon which they are dependent for food, oxygen, and moisture when high tides flood their lairs.

The North American deserts are as much meeting grounds for animals as for plants. In earlier times wapiti (the American elk) and even bison were reported in the northern sections of Chihuahua and Sonora. Mule deer, pronghorns, and black bears share the dry thickets of Sinaloa and Chihuahua with coatimundi, peccaries, armadillos, and an occasional ocelot. All of these latter species wander north across the border into the Big Bend country, southern New Mexico, and Arizona.

A number of typically Mexican birds regularly nest in the American Southwest—vermilion flycatchers, with caps and chests of brilliant red; rose-throated becards; Rivoli's and violet-crowned hummingbirds; and painted redstarts. Several of these colorful species even make their way west to the California deserts. Nesting vermilion flycatchers visit an oasis near Palm Springs each year, and pairs of coppery-tailed trogons breed each summer in Madera Canyon just south of Tucson.

Traffic from the East has been consistently increasing —whether because more species of typically eastern birds are reconnoitering new territory or because there are more bird watchers to note what has always been a pattern is as yet undetermined. Perhaps it is both. At any rate, the count of Baltimore orioles, American redstarts, and scarlet tanagers grows larger each year, with indigo buntings, lark buntings, and several strictly eastern warblers, such as ovenbirds, becoming almost commonplace. At the same time, birds characteristic of the California coast are also being gleefully entered into the life lists of Arizona bird watchers.

Insect life has found desirable homesites in many areas of the desert. Insect collectors discuss with excitement their latest trip into southern Arizona and their discovery of strikingly handsome tropical beetles, moths, butterflies, and wasps.

Such boreal representatives as lesser fritillaries and butterflies known as "alpines" stretch from the arctic to South America via the stepping stones provided by the Rockies and other ranges. One eastern giant silk moth reaches the Southwest by a most intriguing route: up the Appalachians, across Canada, and down the Cascades and the Sierra Nevada to arrive at last in Arizona and Mexico.

The great variety of species found in the deserts is probably nowhere more apparent than among reptiles. Every year new species are reported in the vicinity of the various research stations in the mountains of the Southwest. The reasons are several. As discussed earlier, reptiles are biologically well adapted to desert survival. Also the crossroads location of the Mexican-American deserts allows an inflow of many types of reptiles from the plains, the Pacific states, and particularly from the tropics. But perhaps the most important factor is the terrain of these particular deserts, which encourages speciation. There is a veritable mosaic of different habitats, many of them mountain islands or isolated washes with no avenues for biological communication with similar environments elsewhere in the same desert. Consequently, immigrant creatures from other areas who take up residence in each of these places must do their own adapting in their own ways. This, of course, results in branching of the family tree, as shown in the diagram on page 95.

Desert reptiles are clear evidence that that master of biological invention—evolution—is still at work. New species continue to develop and old species develop new ways to live in new places, all adding to the wonder and richness of animal life in the Southwest.

PART THREE

THE MARK
OF
MANKIND

This early pueblo village excavated on Black Mesa
and the nearby coal slurry pipeline (from which modern
Hopis will profit) symbolize changing patterns
in the marks man has left on the desert.

CHAPTER 8

HUNTERS OF THE HAIRY ELEPHANT

*Ice Age wanderers who first followed the game from Siberia
over the Bering Land Bridge and into the great Southwest*

WHO WERE THEY, those ancient people who came to the Southwest in the shadowy times of prehistory? Where did they come from? And when did they arrive in the New World? Scientists have clues to all three answers.

Though archaeologists are not unanimous in their opinions, most authorities in this field tend to regard Asia as the ancestral home of the American Indian. Many present-day American Indians have characteristics that indicate origins in common with oriental people: skin, eye, and hair color; eye folds, more or less pronounced, observable in several tribal groups; and the so-called "blue spot" at the base of a newborn baby's spine. Differences between the two racial groups can be attributed to the fact that one remained in Asia to follow its ethnic destiny, and the other left the homelands to populate a whole new hemisphere—no mean feat for a primitive people in completely unfamiliar territory.

Archaeologists agree on certain essentials—the early travelers were hunters in search of large game, which they attacked with carefully crafted projectile points; and they crossed from Siberia via the Bering Strait. There is some disparity regarding the last assumption, however. One school favoring the notion that the crossings were on dry land, since the strait is shallow and the ocean level dropped considerably during the glacial periods, and another holding that the ice of the winter-frozen strait could have supported the weight of men and their equipment. Until a few years ago, a third point of agreement was the route: down the east side of the Rocky Mountains and from there branch-

ing into California via the Southwest, into the Southeast, and into Mexico and Central America. Further migrations distributed the American Indian from Newfoundland to the Straits of Magellan, from Point Barrow to the Yucatan Peninsula.

One of the most cherished points of argument among students of American archaeology has been *when* this vast migration started. Theory has swung back and forth as wildly as a pendulum in an earthquake. Geologists calculated that a land passageway was open across Bering Strait during the last interglacial period, that is, just prior to the final advance of the continental ice sheets about seventy thousand years ago. Ancient man might have entered the New World at that time. The same route was again available after the retreat of the great glaciers, roughly ten to twenty thousand years ago. Here the battle lines were drawn. Did early man arrive in the New World before the last ice advance or after?

Both sides gathered data and mustered arguments in defense of their positions. Those favoring the earlier entrance cited a fact of major significance—the great diversity of languages and cultural patterns. If presumably the first intruders into the virgin New World came from a single ancestral stock, how could they have broken up into a veritable Tower of Babel in just a few thousand years? California is a prime example of this linguistic separation. When de Anza's party plodded up Coyote Canyon east of what is now San Diego, there were roughly one hundred thirty-five language types spoken by California Indians. Some of the dialects were related to those used by tribes in

The earliest tribes in the Southwest depended on the meat and hides of game for their survival. (Diorama in Mesa Verde National Park.)

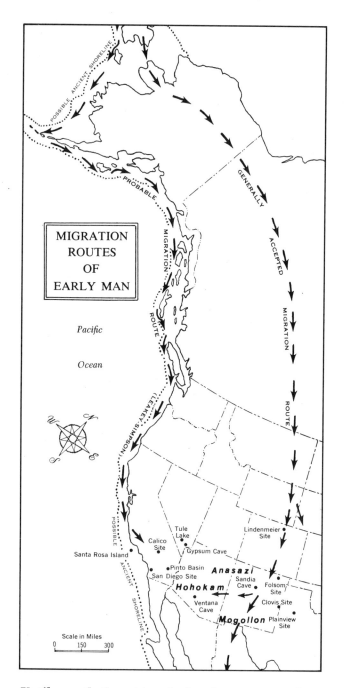

MIGRATION
ROUTES
OF
EARLY MAN

Pacific

Ocean

Tule
Lake
Calico
Site
Gypsum Cave
Santa Rosa Island
Pinto Basin
San Diego Site
Anasazi
Sandia
Cave
Hohokam
Ventana
Cave
Mogollon
Plainview
Site
Lindenmeier
Site
Folsom
Site
Clovis Site

Scale in Miles
0   150   300

Until recently the supposed migration route of early man was east of the Rockies. Now some archaeologists believe he traveled south along the Pacific Coast.

northern Canada; others resembled the speech of Indian groups in the eastern part of the continent; still others were unrelated to any language whatsoever.

Cultural diversity was just as pronounced. There was (and still is) no "Indian way of life." Life styles varied from simple seed-gathering (the Miwoks of California) to the construction of complicated irrigations systems (the Papago of southern Arizona). Craftsmanship ranged from the crude baskets and pottery vessels of the seminomadic Navajos to the magnificent gold jewelry and elaborately decorated buildings of the Aztecs and their predecessors. The life of the Plains Indians centered around buffalo; that of the Haida, around salmon.

The argument that it would have taken many thousands of years to produce such diverging cultures and habits is countered by pointing to the adaptability of the human race and the possibility that successive migrations from Asia brought new traits and introduced new techniques as man stepped slowly toward more sophisticated civilizations. There is also evidence that peoples other than those of mongoloid stock visited the New World before the official "discovery" date of 1492. Their presence could also help account for physical and cultural differences in what, by and large, is a homogeneous racial type.

WHAT SCIENTISTS DO KNOW about these early peoples is based upon a number of significant archaeological "finds," many of them at sites in the desert Southwest. At first, the age of the artifacts was estimated from study of associated bones, the layers of rock or rubble in which they were found, and nearby topographical features of known age with which they could be correlated. New techniques of dating developed in the atomic age are proving more reliable, but for the most part they have substantiated the "educated guesses" of traditional archaeology.

Several of these sites are landmarks in the history of archaeological discovery in the West. Not only can they be dated with reasonable accuracy because of the nature of the site, but each is distinguished as the place where a certain characteristic type of projectile point was first found. In nearly all instances, the points were found with bones of extinct forms of animals—horses, camels, bison, mammoths, and mastodons. Evidently these "kill sites" were the packinghouses of ancient times. They were often located by streams or lakes, where the larger animals tended to

Though both hunter and prey disappeared long ago, there is plenty of evidence that the "hairy elephant," or mammoth, was an important resource for early nomads.

congregate in search of water, or in caves, which provided shelter for the early hunters. When the caves were used or occupied by successive groups of prehistoric Indians, invaluable dating material was left for the archaeologist. Each group left its garbage heap on top of the debris discarded by earlier occupants. Digging down through these accumulations is like turning the pages of a book backward into time.

Sandia Cave is one of the most important kill sites in the Southwest. Radiocarbon-dating places its earliest use at roughly 10,000 B.C. The lowest level with signs of human occupation has a large number of bones and projectile points of a distinctive type—one side has a "shoulder," where a chip has been flaked off, breaking the otherwise symmetrical leaf shape. All such points, regardless of place of origin, are called "Sandia points" in honor of the discovery site.

Also in New Mexico, the Clovis site, where several types of stone artifacts were found with mammoth remains, lies on the western edge of the Great Plains —quite a different habitat from Sandia Cave, which is in mountainous country east of the Rio Grande. There is evidence that Clovis points were contemporaneous with Sandia points in that they have been found together in several kill sites. The Clovis excavation also revealed the presence of tools made of bone, another material easily worked by those early people.

By 1960, most archaeologists specializing in the New World were happy to accept what appeared to be a stabilized southwestern prehistory. Radiocarbon–dating was confirming their original assumptions that early man and his tools were active in the area at the end of, or just following, the last great ice advance. Universities and foundations were sponsoring digs in

At a dig near Barstow, California, archaeologists have unearthed stones that may be a fire hearth made by primitive men 50,000 years ago.

a number of places. Throughout the summer, parts of the Southwest were overrun by earnest-looking youngsters armed with camel-hair brushes and digging trowels. The camaraderie of their unabashed enthusiasm became clouded only occasionally when ambitions locked horns or summer heat invited siestas instead of painstaking labor in trenches that were like slots of hell.

Digs flourished in the pine woods and in caves whose floors were beds of every kind of rubbish from bat guano to potshards. Gypsum Cave, in southern Nevada, yielded evidence of a series of tenancies: modern-day Indian occupation; use during the great Pueblo Culture days; even earlier residence by the predecessors of those apparently tireless builders of ancient apartment dwellings, the Anasazi; layers of giant sloth dung; and under it all a surprise—two fireplaces that provide unmistakable proof of human occupancy.

Pinto Basin in Joshua Tree National Monument, Ventana Cave in southern Arizona, Lindenmeier site in northern Colorado—the list of places important in New World prehistory grew longer with each passing year. The cultures responsible for the finds became more real, more imaginable as their tools, crafts, and ways of life emerged from the overburden of successive peoples and life styles.

What were these early hunters like? They were skilled at making stone knives, scrapers, and projectiles with stone or bone points. Those who lived in the desert wandered about in small bands, resorting to caves when shelter from the elements was required. They killed their game with spears or darts, usually employing the atlatl, or spear thrower—a kind of artificial extension of the hunter's arm that increased propelling force and precision of aim. The women gathered seeds, roots, fruits, and other edible plant material. Gradually they developed such grinding implements as milling stones to ease their rough menu. They either brought the use of fire with them or discovered its usefulness on their own; such fire-making tools as drills are found in Hunter Stage sites.

The early hunters knew the value of furs for warmth, perhaps from their ancestral homelands far to the north. Their most sophisticated knowledge included the use of manipulated natural fibers. They made nets and baskets, and even wove articles, such as

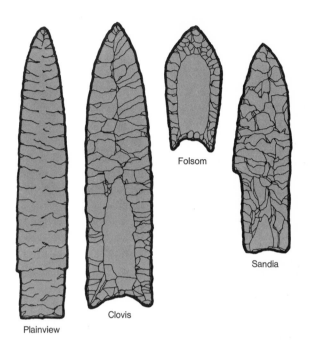

Folsom

Clovis

Sandia

Plainview

By the time early man arrived in the New World, he was skilled in making projectile points in a variety of sizes, shapes, and flaking patterns.

head straps, to facilitate transport of heavy objects.

And what of their prey—the dire wolves, saber-toothed cats, tapirs, giant sloths, horses, camels, extinct forms of bison and pronghorns, mastodons, and the hairy elephant (or woolly mammoth) whose demise remains a mystery to this day. The disappearance of these Ice Age mammals is cause for much discussion and conjecture. What caused their total extinction? Were these hunters, so poorly equipped in terms of today's sophisticated technological devices for killing other living things, capable of totally wiping out widely distributed and wonderfully adapted species? Some think so. Others stress the increasing dryness of the Southwest, which imposed intolerable conditions of environment on these particular creatures. However, these same or related species also vanished from regions in the Western Hemisphere where rainfall continued to be abundant. One type of pronghorn remains in the West, and the American bison flour-

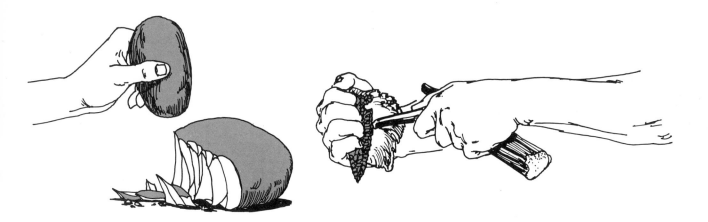

After the hunter found the rock he needed for a projectile point, he chipped flakes from the core.
Then, using leather as a cushion, he shaped the point with a tool made from an antler.

ished on the Great Plains until white men and their rifles all but exterminated them.

It seems that nobody really knows why these magnificent assemblages vanished. The scientists who eventually find the answers to this fascinating problem will be candidates for a very particular Hall of Fame—the solvers of evolutionary riddles. They will tell us why the dinosaurs died out and why penguins continue to thrive in their bleak environment.

Meanwhile, activity at the digs continued. Folsom points turned up with consistent regularity. Bones of extinct mammals were right where theory said they ought to be. Scholarly papers and monographs flowed from university and museum presses. Student archaeologists argued, flirted, took pictures, cleaned bones, got tans, and secretly longed to make the fabulous discovery that would set their pit-bound little world on its ear.

But not all was as serene as the orderly life on a dig would suggest. Some experts were thinking, why should we accept, willy-nilly, the dictum that man first entered the New World no earlier than ten to thirteen thousand years ago? What about that site in southern Nevada, Tule Lake? Radiocarbon-dating suggested that man had been present there thirty thousand years ago. The Old Guard shook their heads and "carefully reevaluated" the data. The site was occupied only about thirteen

thousand years ago, they pronounced, and that was that.

Other archaeologists, however, were puzzled about a site in San Diego where, at the time of a street excavation, charcoal from a possibly man-made hearth was discovered, along with what could be crude tools. They were radiocarbon-dated at 20,000 B.C. And there was the Santa Rosa Island find—a chipped implement and burned bones dating back more than thirty thousand years. Early hearths turned up in Texas. Roughly executed scrapers and chopping stones, totally lacking the elegance of the earliest projectile points yet discovered, littered the ground in some areas and tumbled out of exposed strata in others. The debate began again.

Upon further investigation, there was no really clear-cut, undeniable evidence of human presence as early as the carbon dates for these sites suggested. The fires could have been natural in origin, the "artifacts" shaped by weathering or erosion. Things seemed to be settling down again. Anxious archaeologists, with confidence in their original estimate of the time of man's arrival now restored, relaxed and went back to their Clovis points.

But not for long. A visiting English archaeologist, Dr. Louis Leakey, wandered into California. Since Dr. Leakey was famed for his discoveries in East Africa, few American scientists were aware that he was also very interested in ancient man's entrance into and progress in the New World. Dr. Leakey would visit

Early Basket Makers still lived in caves and hunted with atlatls, though they had developed some simple agriculture. (Diorama at Mesa Verde.)

America from time to time, give some lectures at various universities, drive around the countryside for a bit, and then leave.

All the while there had been some stubborn diehards in California who just could not forget that fire hearth under San Diego's Texas Street and the chipped pebbles of Santa Rosa Island. When Dr. Leakey and this little group got together, the outcome was equivalent to the capture of an Abominable Snowman. Not only was early man's entrance period pushed back by thousands of years, the southbound migration route was drastically changed as well.

Dr. Leakey agreed that the Bering Strait was a land bridge at the time the first men crossed it. Capable of fashioning the rough but effective slaughtering devices of the early Stone Age, they had swarmed across the tenuous fingers of land that linked the Old World to the New, in pursuit of the game that abounded on the unmanned continent.

He did not agree, however, with accepted theories of the path of these migrations. Instead of the inland route, he proposed the likelihood of one along the coast, on the now-submerged continental shelf that was then exposed by the same water-locking glaciers that created the Bering Land Bridge. He pointed out the advantages of a leisurely journey southward along the shore, making use of freshwater streams flowing into the ocean and of fish, shellfish, and game available along the coast. He expects that undersea exploration will one day provide evidence of this proposed route.

As for the timing of the migration, Dr. Leakey joined the cause of those who believe that the interval of time between 10,000 B.C. and the present is much too short to account for the enormous diversity of language and cultural patterns that characterizes the American Indian. But more evidence was needed to prove it.

SHORTLY AFTER DR. LEAKEY's reconnaissance of the Southwest, the waiting crew of the San Bernardino County Museum got the word: dig at Calico, whose only claim to fame at that time was as a kind of Disneyland resurrection of a ghost town. Dr. Leakey had chosen the area because of its location on an alluvial fan and the evidence of a nearby Ice Age lake—both of which could be geologically dated.

The archaeological team dug up, peered at, collected, evaluated, and studied a huge trove of bits and pieces, most of them found *in situ* around the dig's headquarters. A few items were significant — stone tools such as hand axes, whose chipped edges indicate crude attempts to increase their efficiency, and a fire hearth whose construction could not possibly have been a "natural accident."

If all we have learned about American prehistory is reliable, if all the techniques so carefully developed in the archaeological field are still valid, then the Calico dig places ancient man, crude scrapers and all, in the New World at least fifty thousand years ago. *Homo sapiens* is no newcomer! He has shared this vast hemisphere with its other residents for a long, long time.

By A.D. 450 to 750, late Basket Makers were also making pottery, hunting with bows and arrows, and growing much of their food supply. (Diorama at Mesa Verde.)

CHAPTER 9

PEOPLE OF THE DITCH

*The Southwest's earliest farmers, who made pottery and pithouses
and the first irrigation canals—centuries before Christ*

WHATEVER THE EXACT TIME of his arrival on this continent, man has lived in the southwestern deserts for thousands of years. Hundreds of little bands wandered from cave to lake to spring, searching for food, anxious for water. Unlike their descendants, whose ruined structures and empty dwelling places are important features of the desert landscape, the early hunters and gatherers made little impact on the land. This period in the history of man in the New World has been designated as the Hunter Stage and extends roughly from 10,000 to 5,000 B.C.

It appears that the chippers of Folsom points (see page 107) never ventured very far west of the Rocky Mountains. Similar points have been unearthed in the eastern half of the continent, but by and large, Folsom people were southwestern. Sites with other types of early stone projectile points have been found in many places in California, in southern Nevada, and east to central Texas (Plainview points were named for a find near Lubbock, Texas).

Presumably every Indian in the Western Hemisphere had an ancestor who crossed Bering Strait. Following the herds of game southward, these ancient immigrants separated into tribal bands. In time, distinct cultures developed that had certain features distinguishing one life style from another. But they were not totally isolated; a traffic in ideas and trade items crossed mountains and deserts—and followed rivers and passes, cross-fertilizing the cultures. Thus the prehistoric tribes of the American Southwest learned much from their neighbors to the south, just as the Pilgrims learned from Indians to get along in the new land.

The early hunters of the desert left no pottery shards and no arrow shafts, just widely scattered heaps of bones, bits of twined fiber, stone implements, and charcoal. They must have been as skilled in hunting as the Bushmen of Southwest Africa and as tough as Arctic explorers. They had something in common with all people confined to harsh environments—the ability to survive.

Their contemporaries on the Great Plains and prairies to the east remained hunters right up to the time of conquest by the now-romanticized cavalry of the 1870s. The Sioux and the Crow so perfected the art of living off an animal, the American bison, that they have become classic examples of a sophisticated hunting culture. On the other hand, their neighbors in coastal and interior California developed a peerless seed-gathering economy (though fish and other animals were also part of their diet). Neither group ever seriously became involved with agriculture until the white invasion. Nor did they construct permanent dwellings. Hunters must be mobile, ready to follow the game wherever it leads them. Even gatherers of seeds need a measure of independence.

The peoples of the Southwest, however, did not have access to the great herds of bison that roamed the plains east of the Rocky Mountains or to the abundance of acorns and shellfish along the Pacific Coast. So, unlike their neighbors, these tribes were forced to change—adapt or perish.

As early as 7,000 B.C., an offshoot of the hunting tradition, termed the Desert Culture, sensing the potential in a region so abundant with diverse habitats,

*With only Stone Age tools and their own muscle-power, early farmers
called the Hohokam dug a complex series of irrigation ditches.*

Pithouses, believed to have evolved from cave dwellings, were used by both the Mogollon and the Hohokam. Postholes were sometimes in the pit floor, as here, sometimes in the ground surrounding the pit, as in the Black Mesa ruins (page 118).

began to concern itself more with gathering and collecting of food than with hunting as such. Projectile points are found in camp- and cave-sites of this period, but they had developed some new refinements. Some had notches just above the base to make it easier to bind the head onto a shaft. Some were serrated, or "toothed," along the edges. *Manos* and *metates* became standard equipment of the desert household, as did mortars and pestles. Clearly, these people were no longer content to wear down their teeth by a diet of unprocessed, hard-shelled seeds.

Sometime between 5,000 B.C. and A.D. 1, the same urges that pushed the ancient dwellers along the Nile River into planting barley and making mud huts began to stir among the desert Indians. Major changes occurred in their way of life, though not simultaneously throughout the desert region—some tribes evolved a given technique earlier than others.

There is little doubt that many of these skills, such as pottery-making and agriculture, crept in from culture centers in Mexico and Central America. Others were home grown, the outcome of experimentation by someone with an idea. Genius is not confined to a laboratory or a desk. The person who had the notion that attaching feathers to the base of an arrow would increase its stability and flight distance was in every sense a genius. Many minds were at work in those long years of developing distinct, viable, and rich patterns of living.

All the early desert settlers (as distinguished from the nomadic hunters before them) constructed their simple homes in much the same way, evidence of an already established tradition that has lingered to the present day. They were round pits, up to thirty-five feet in diameter, with steps leading down from the ground surface outside. Storage areas were excavated into the sides of the room, and a fire hearth was located in the center. Several pithouses constituted a village. The largest appears to have been used for ceremonial purposes, ancestor of the kiva chambers still found in every Pueblo village.

Cruder structures of the same general nature have been discovered in the San Pedro Valley of southeastern Arizona. Although smaller and less complex, they were presumably built in the same period. One, east of Tucson, may turn out to be the oldest recognizable man-made housing structure in the Southwest.

A PERMANENT DWELLING PLACE provides more than shelter from the elements. During the early stages of the Desert Culture, caves often served variously as living quarters, storage places, and killing grounds. However, since caves were not very numerous, particularly in the southern deserts, temporary shelters for equipment and food were probably erected during the years of wandering in this harsh land.

There is the key word — *wandering*. Hunters and gatherers cannot settle into permanent quarters. They must follow the caribou, walk about for witchetty grubs, track down the elephant. Life is a round of water holes and campsites, a judging of season and time. When are the wild gourds ripe? Have the wintering geese returned to the tule swamp? Always move on, move around, move back—but move.

People who live in houses—structures that have immovable walls, solid floors, "built-in" storage areas, and more or less permanent roofs—are tied to that piece of real estate, especially if they lack transportation other than their own feet. There is no folding the tent and leaving for better hunting grounds. Food sources must be close to home, whether the neighborhood supermarket or a patch of beans and corn. Settlements, in the sense that most of the inhabitants live there year around, are the direct result of one of mankind's most significant discoveries: if one plants certain seeds in the

A small arena at Wupatki ruins appears to be a ball court, suggesting cultural exchange with ancient peoples who built similar courts hundreds of miles to the south.

soil and somehow they get water, they will grow and yield food.

Even today, many desert tribes supplement their diet by harvesting such native food resources as cactus fruits and the nuts of piñon pines. Hunting wild game, in some areas, is still a traditional and inexpensive means of obtaining protein. But the tending of crops and its related industry, livestock-raising, are landmark developments anywhere. In deserts, they are monumental.

Though agriculture frees time for one to do more than merely survive, there are new responsibilities attendant on growing crops. Weather is more important than ever; rain must come, and at the right time. Baskets have their uses, but other vessels are needed for storage and transport. Tools must be invented to break up the stubborn soil and harvest the crops. Rules must be made and obeyed, lest a covetous neighbor steal a family's corn or, worse, their land. And to whom does the land belong? Shall a person own it outright, or shall the village fathers decide which parcel he may work? Do children have the right to continue using the land upon which their parents grew crops?

Agriculture and animal husbandry brought an orderliness into living. If things went well—and they usually did—food-getting was no longer an endless, time-consuming trek. Now there was leisure, time to make personal adornments, time to enjoy the company of tribal brothers, time to discover ways of coping with

Extensive adobe-walled ruins are comparatively rare in southern and central Arizona. One, La Ciudad, has been excavated right in busy Phoenix and has yielded some ancient treasures.

all the new problems crop-tending introduced.

Though a number of authorities agree that the first crops to be domesticated were among the wild species in the region, the arrival of corn, or maize, was a vital turning point. It is highly doubtful that corn ever grew wild as far north as the American Southwest. In all probability, it was first domesticated in the central highlands of Middle America. Its origins are still somewhat obscure, but its ancestral species most probably resembled a living relative called *teosinte*. Another primitive species in the group is pod corn. There is evidence that both types are responsible for the development of modern corn.

The earliest known collections of corn cobs in the American Southwest are from caves in western New Mexico. The cobs are tiny, hardly larger than a man's little finger. Corn appears to have arrived not alone but as part of a domestication complex that included gourds, squash, and beans. By the year A.D. 1, corn and its companions were flourishing in garden patches in the Mogollon culture area of southwestern New Mexico, southeastern Arizona, northern Sonora, and Chihuahua.

Ruins of pithouses and debris dumps in occupied caves reveal the growing affluence and sophistication of the new farmers. Pottery shards are plentiful, some

attractively decorated; bows and arrows were replacing the more cumbersome darts and spears; and digging sticks and other farm implements had been invented. It was believed that somebody or a group of somebodies controlled the wind and rain, sun and frost. Could they be appealed to in some way, to assure the crop's success and the community's well-being?

Concrete evidence of a growing interest in the supernatural and its influence on the affairs of men is sometimes difficult to find. The discovery of several burial sites in which certain rituals had been followed indicates that a rich ceremonial life existed. The religious facet of simple cultures is often very complicated, abounding in myth, elaborate public displays, and ceremonies deep in sacred chambers.

BY 300 TO 200 B.C., two important cultures were differentiating out of the generalized Desert Culture base — the *Mogollon* in the mountain-mottled wilderness of the upper Salt and Gila river systems, and the *Hohokam* of the desert plains to the west. While the Mogollon people were grinding hammerstones almost to a polish, smoking reed cigarets, learning to roll dice, and practicing on flutes, the Hohokam were making pottery, irrigating their fields, and slowly evolving

Many types of pottery have been found in prehistoric sites. These simple jars were made with coils of clay; one was left corrugated (left), the other smoothed out (right).

a culture of their own under the saguaro cacti and mesquite trees of wash and hillside.

Because many traits were shared by the Mogollon and Hohokam cultures, there is good reason to assume that Mexico was mother to both. The sites of the Hohokam villages are scattered in the valleys and uplands of the Salt-Gila river drainage complex. Several of the better-known digs boast names with local color such as Snaketown, on the Gila River near Chandler, and Sweetwater. The Hohokam were potters par excellence, achieving striking designs of grays, reds, and browns, with glitter added to some. One wonders what impulse nudged the first potter to toss a handful of mica flakes into the wet clay she was shaping. Perhaps it was to strengthen the finished jar or bowl. Whatever her purpose, it sparkled and was pleasing. The wanderers of old, the bone gnawers in dank and smelly caves, had come a long way, indeed.

Mexico seems to be the source of another artistic achievement—the molding of little human torsos, which bear a marked resemblance to figurines from central Mexico. The pronounced female anatomical features of some of the little statues suggest concern about fertility. Crops must grow, children must be born, or the tribe will cease to exist. Survival is tantamount.

Even in the early stages of Hohokam culture, houses were changing from the classic pithouse shape (see diagram on page 114). Not only were the buildings square rather than round, but some were more "house" than "pit."

About the time that Christians and lions were confronting each other in Roman amphitheaters, two basic cultures of the American Southwest and northern Mexico were settling into patterns that eventually became two quite distinct ways of life. Almost from the beginning, Mogollon and Hohokam pottery makers used different methods. The former shaped their vessels by placing coils of clay on top of each other and smoothing them out by scraping the surface with a pebble or other polishing tool. The Hohokam used coils, but they also employed the paddle-and-anvil technique. They placed a "pancake" of clay over a mold and used a wooden paddle to pat the clay into shape.

Eventually both groups were to refine their techniques and become masters of the craft. Designs became more colorful, elaborate, and rich in esthetic appeal. Each pueblo or major settlement developed its own characteristic shape, color, and style of ornamentation.

While the Mogollon influence was spreading north and somewhat to the east and west of its center of

origin, the Hohokam culture was tightening its hold on the river system it had colonized so long before. While crusaders were marching off to the Holy Land, Hohokam were excavating huge ball courts for a difficult and complicated game. The idea must have been imported from what was to become Latin America, where similar courts have been found. The point of the game was to strike a solid rubber ball through rings attached to the sides of the court. The use of hands and feet was forbidden—not even a little finger, although shoulders, hips, and heads could be used to score. One of the most interesting items in the prehistory of the Western Hemisphere is that, although the game extended into South American, the *only* rubber ball ever found came from a site in desert Arizona.

Not only were the people of the Hohokam culture interested in competitive sport; they were given to what the stern-browed Puritans would have referred to as "ostentation and vanity." They carved exquisite little bracelets and other ornaments from shells. Stone beads and pendants inlaid with pieces of turquoise have been found in a number of sites.

WHILE SOME WERE MAKING JEWELRY and carving stone effigies and bowls with a high degree of craftsmanship, others were involved in a more ambitious project. The Hohokam were an enterprising, highly organized group of people, quick to recognize useful ideas that traveled north from Mexico; they appreciated the time and leisure afforded by a reliable food source; they knew the temper of the desert, its capricious rains, its sullen heat; and they lived alongside rivers, permanent streams that gave them water the year around. It was inevitable: why not divert some of that water for their crops instead of relying on undependable clouds?

With very simple wood and stone tools, they dug an intricate system of irrigation canals. The sheer physical effort and social organization required for such an undertaking staggers the mind when one stops to think how it must have been accomplished. To take but one problem, how were the tons of earth that were removed from the ditches transported elsewhere? There is only one answer. People had to stoop down, scoop up the dirt, place it in baskets or pots, and carry it to the dump site. Back and forth, back and forth. Tiresome, repetitious work, but it meant water—dependable, life-sustaining water.

Roughly one hundred years before Columbus set sail, the Hohokam broke with a tradition they had kept for thousands of years—the pithouse. For some time the people of the irrigation ditch, so knowledgeable in many ways, had known about their cliff-dwelling neighbors to the north, the Pueblo people to be discussed in the next chapter. But desert plains lacked the topographical features that invite cliff-type "apartment houses," so the Hohokam did not abandon their pithouses until history was just around the corner. Their first surface houses were simple—huts of wattle and mud with posts to support a brush-and-stick roof. Summer shelters, open-sided and brush-roofed, apparently came into use at about this period, as well.

We probably will never know what possessed these diggers of ditches and planters of corn when they suddenly began to erect huge, multistoried compounds of adobe with walls four-and-a-half feet thick. No doubt they were influenced by their northern neighbors, but there is an intriguing feature peculiar to these structures: many of them were divided into rooms much too small to live in. There is speculation among archaeologists that the people continued to live in more traditional houses around the compound.

Only one great ruin of this period is left, Casa Grande in central Arizona. Now a national monument, it has been roofed by the National Park Service to protect its adobe walls from what little rain occurs during the desert year. And what of the Hohokam? They remain, growing cotton, making baskets, tending irrigation ditches—only now they are called the Pima Indians.

This square pithouse was unearthed on Black Mesa. Small holes around the perimeter once held poles to support a wood and brush superstructure. The entrance was on the far side.

CHAPTER 10

THE ANCIENT ONES

Basket makers and cliff dwellers who vanished mysteriously but left their trace in a gallery of remarkable architecture

AGH, IT WAS COLD! Namlo stepped out onto the persimmon-red sand, scuffled and littered in front of his cave. On three-fire nights, the ground was always covered with glittering hoarfrost that hurt the soles of even his toughened feet. He pulled the robe of entwined fur strips more closely about him. He must send Atama for more firewood.

Hunkering down in the slowly warming sun, he thought. His family needed meat. Ground maize was all very well, but cold bodies need hot meat. He knew that a hunting party had set out yesterday for the canyon, but they had returned without the cheerful hubbub that meant success. He supposed they had taken no more than a rabbit or two for their own families—a deer would have meant meat for the whole band.

They were a small group, not a large village such as those to the east, near what would one day be Durango, Colorado. Namlo, Atama, and their family lived in a rocky shelter, deep under a protecting overhang. The fireplace and sleeping area were close to the entrance, the storage pits farther back. Other bands built crude dwellings for themselves, part cave and part pithouse. Like the houses of the Hohokam, their contemporaries to the south, the roofs were covered with clay. Unlike the Hohokam, however, these people often decorated the roof tops with designs representing animal tracks and claw marks.

Who were they, Namlo and his sometimes hungry family? Archaeologists have given them the name of Basket Maker II. Their predecessors, belonging to an earlier culture known as Basket Maker I, are obscure. Scattered over the Colorado Plateau and adjacent up-

lands are sites indicating the presence of an early Desert Culture–type people who lived there from perhaps several thousand to two or three hundreds years B.C. Their way of life was hunting and gathering, not much different from the ancestors of the Hohokam and Mogollon farther south, but these northern nomads were destined to evolve from huddlers in cold caves to builders of the most impressive structures in the prehistoric desert West.

As the name implies, the Basket Makers did not know how to make pottery until later stages of their cultural development. They practiced simple agriculture but also continued to hunt with atlatls, some of which have been found in Basket Maker sites. The area of greatest concentration for these early people was on the Colorado Plateau in the drainage of the San Juan River, a tributary of the Colorado, in what is called the Four Corners country today.

Though it is somewhat difficult to date the beginnings of this intriguing culture complex, most archaeologists are willing to compromise on about year A.D. 1. From these relatively humble beginnings were to come Spruce Tree House, Wupatki, and the great D-shaped pueblo of Chaco Canyon.

There appears to be no question that these relatively isolated people were influenced by revolutionary developments occurring to the south. It was inevitable that pottery would enter their life style, just as after a certain period all the cultures in the American deserts would share the ability to make baskets. One wonders how the intricate art of basket making developed. Though each group gathered its own materials and

Deep under a protecting cliff of sandstone, Inscription House, one of three well-known ruins in Navajo National Monument, has remained almost intact.

121

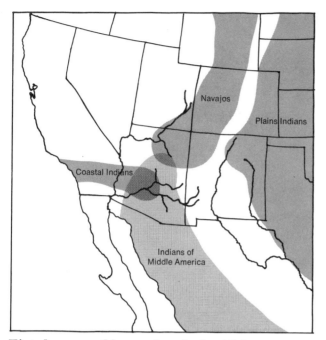

Tinted areas on this map show the "traffic" in cultural traits among Southwestern peoples: shells from California; ball courts and parrot feathers from Mexico; bison horns and hides from Plains to the east. From the north Navajos and Apaches moved in with their entire cultures.

devised its own methods, shapes, and designs—as they still do today—the basic techniques were the same: the coil and the twill.

In the coil method, the container is built up by a continuous spiral coil of pliant twigs and grass. Bark strips or other plant material is used to wrap the coils tightly and to "sew" them together. Most coiled baskets are either bowl or urn shaped and may be deep or shallow, depending on the purpose for which they are intended. Some are almost traylike, though twill work is more commonly used for this shape. A variation of the coil method is twining, a much simpler and often coarser technique by which radiating rods are fastened together in the center and intertwining rods are "woven" between them. Twilling is actually a form of weaving. The fibers are cut into lengths of even width, often flattened between the teeth or some other instrument, and then woven together. The pattern is seldom the simple in-and-out stitch with which we are most familiar; warp fibers often skip several woof strands

before picking up the weave, and vice versa.

Baskets have many uses in a primitive society. They can be so tightly woven that they are waterproof or, if coarse, they can be sealed with pitch, as the Navajos do today. They can be converted into cooking vessels by dropping hot rocks into a basketful of raw ingredients. They are storage jars, berry-picking buckets, baby cradles—and collector's items of increasing value today.

Atama made coiled baskets. She also made a simple sandal of pounded yucca leaves, a fiber useful for many purposes. The Basket Maker II sandal typically had a square toe and occasionally was decorated with a buckskin fringe. And Atama knew the art of true, though primitive, weaving. Bark and yucca-leaf mats woven in a simple over-and-under pattern have been found in a number of Basket Maker II sites. These people also knew how to make "cloth" bags, weaving them by a twisted-twine method that does not use warp and woof threads strung on a loom. Fur and feather robes, warm and long-wearing, were made in much the same way.

Like most hunters, the early Basket Makers utilized the skins of their prey, softening the leather by chewing, rubbing it with fat, or other methods. Bags and other containers and cradle liners were among the uses of this versatile material.

Bows and arrows were yet to come; these people were still atlatl users, probably as skillful as any in the world. The actual weapon, though often described as a dart, was really a small spear. An ancestor to the true arrow, it had feathers at the end of the shaft. The head was fitted with elegantly crafted little points, some notched at the base, others showing secondary pressure flaking, a refinement designed to give a sharper cutting edge.

As Namlo crouched by the entrance to their cave, Atama assessed their remaining food resources. Behind their sleeping quarters was a pit in the floor of the cave, called by archaeologists a "cist." It was a circular hole several feet in diameter and a foot and a half deep, carefully lined with slabs of the rich orange rock that was characteristic of their canyon-tangled homegrounds. In it was stored the harvest of the previous season.

Each summer, Atama and her older children took their digging sticks down to the soft, sandy soil of the canyon bottom, not far from a spring, where they dug into the soft earth, planting the seeds of maize, beans, and squash. The heat within the canyon walls was

This prehistoric jar has small "handles" that were probably used to attach a carrying cord.

almost unbearable, even to these hardened people. It bounced back and forth between the sandstone slabs like a caged animal. But there were sweeter times when the rains came, like kindly fathers determined to help this little band. Then the long green fingers of the squash plant would creep out to the rubble that, broken from the towering walls overhead, gathered at their bases. The corn, dwarf cousin to Iowa's giant plants of today, finally produced little swellings here and there, the tiny cobs whose few kernels would be stored in the pit of the family's cave.

Atama sighed. At best, there were enough corn and dried beans to last until the moon was full two more times. By then, the sun, at rising time, would strike the rock just above the sleeping skins. The days would be warmer. The deer would come into the canyon looking for the newly sprouting shoots of the shrubs and small trees growing in the floor of the canyon; the ground squirrels would come out of their winter holes. Namlo would put out nets to catch this badly needed meat, if they could but last the rest of the winter.

THE BASKET MAKER II PERIOD, to which Namlo and Atama belonged, was evidently at its height around A.D. 200 to 300. By about A.D. 450, Basket Maker III, a more developed culture that led to the beginning of the Pueblo complex, was in full flower. It, too, seems to have been concentrated in the San Juan River drainage

One of the largest prehistoric pueblos is the great D-shaped Pueblo Bonito in Chaco Canyon.
In this painting, builders are at work on some of the finest masonry in the Southwest.

with a peripheral spread throughout much of the southern Colorado Plateau.

The great distinction between the two later stages of Basket Maker culture is the introduction of pottery. The Hohokam and Mogollon people were already making fired and decorated pottery. There is no doubt that, for the Basket Makers, acquiring this skill was a step toward the rich culture that was to follow. At first, their pieces were unfired; the clay was simply formed in some way and dried in the sun. This method produced a very fragile vessel, unwatertight unless coated by some waterproof material. It appears that the earliest clay containers these people made were fashioned by lining a

basket with clay to which crushed plant material had been added, so as to prevent the clay from cracking while drying. After the lining dried, it shrank and could be removed from the basket.

Firing the clay container was the next logical step. Some authorities believe that the discovery of the durability and watertightness produced by subjecting the formed vessel to great heat was accidental. Perhaps some pieces of unfired pottery broke and fell into a cooking fire; the owner noticed the difference, and the process was perfected. Others think that the idea traveled north from cultures already familiar with the procedure and was quickly adopted. By this time, pottery was a trade

this type have been found near Grand Falls on the Little Colorado River in northern Arizona. Either walls and roof were one structural unit, with poles bent and fastened together in the middle, or the pithouse had a post-and-beam roof. Both types of house were covered with brush and plastered.

Tiny, highly simplified human figurines of clay have been found in Basket Maker III sites, indicating another possible cultural contact with people to the south. The figurines are always female and, curiously, poked full of holes.

It is during this period, around A.D. 650, that the atlatl and dart gave way to the bow and arrow. Rather gruesome evidence of the weapon change was turned up by an archaeologist in Canyon del Muerto (which, ironically, means Canyon of Death) when he found a mummy of a woman with an arrow still in her body. Evidently she had been killed around A.D. 600.

The Basket Makers II and III were not only concerned with the absolute necessities, however. We have evidence that they were also very interested in beauty and personal adornment. Toward the end of the period, they excelled in certain types of twining and weaving, apparently proud of fine craftsmanship. Ornaments of bone, shell, and particularly feathers have been found in many Basket Maker sites, and pottery was becoming attractive for its own sake. The stage was being set for the next act, and the same actors would remain—there was no great break in cultural tradition. Though both people and ideas may have infiltrated from other cultures and regions, by and large the Pueblo peoples had Basket Maker ancestors. They simply elaborated on their heritage.

D EFINITE EVIDENCE of Pueblo I culture characteristics dates from around A.D. 700. Though the main center for its development was still in the San Juan–Little Colorado river region, its influence widened out to include the Rio Grande from what is now Santa Fe to slightly south of Albuquerque, and west almost to the present Arizona-Nevada border. Archaeologists often refer to prehistoric Pueblo people as the Anasazi, borrowing the term from the Navajos, who called them the "Ancient Ones."

One indicator of the change in culture was a change in pottery. Up to this point, Basket Maker pottery had

item, and the pottery techniques of one tribe could be quickly assimilated by another.

Among the Basket Makers, the notion of decorating pottery soon followed that of firing. In time, this area would be producing literally tons of handsomely decorated pottery.

About the same time, the Basket Makers came out of their rock shelters. Perhaps the tradition of pit-type houses trickled in from other cultures, but there is good reason to believe that, if so, it was influenced by some of the ways of their own past. It has been suggested that some pithouses seem like little more than an enlargement of the grain cists in the ancient caves. A few of

The size of Pueblo Bonito is even more impressive when one considers that it was built with the most primitive tools. Circular foundations were for kivas.

been confined to two colors—Lino gray and Lino black-on-gray. Forms tended to be bowl-like, perhaps in imitation of basketry. The late Basket Makers were the only potters in the prehistoric Southwest to make true spouts. Some of the ladles, which may very well have been inspired by gourds and other natural materials, had hollow handles with tips through which liquids could be poured.

The designs were, admittedly, crude affairs, but they were a beginning toward making everyday living more enjoyable with things pleasing to the eye. Pottery continued to become more decorative, more varied, more innovative as the Pueblo period advanced—luckily for archaeologists, who depend upon pottery sequences to help correlate datings.

In some places, a major change occurred in the process of pottery manufacture as well. It is believed

that the firing of clay vessels had been carried on for hundreds of years, mother teaching daughter the art. However, among the late Basket Makers and early Pueblos, a new tradition began—probably by sheer accident—when the *reduction* method of firing came into use.

With this technique, the dried and decorated pots are placed in a firing chamber that excludes oxygen, so that the minerals in the paint cannot oxidize. White or gray backgrounds are the result. By contrast, a kiln in which air is allowed to circulate freely produces rich colors of red, brown, and ochre. It has been strongly suggested that this new approach to pottery color and decoration was a result of Mogollon innovation—another example of the push and invasionary force of their ideas. At any rate, the Pueblo people probably traded for the colorful containers at first and then learned the process for themselves.

Sometime during the transition from Basket Maker III to Pueblo I, another new idea appeared, probably meeting disapproval, at first, among more conservative tribesmen. One can imagine a group of old cronies sitting in front of a pithouse and worrying about this new idea. Think of it—building houses right on the ground, with rooms put together and not even a suggestion of a pit for the foundation!

In one famous site near La Plata in southwestern Colorado, apparently both factions won. There are a number of adjoining surface rooms, used partly for storage and partly for living, but there are pithouses *inside* some of these rooms as well as scattered about outside. There is speculation that this village may be the earliest collection of connected surface rooms in the American Southwest. Considering that this was the beginning of stone masonry among these Indians, what remains today shows surprising refinement.

The transition period appears to have been a time of experimentation with both old and new: square pithouses, round ones strung together in a complex of rooms, groups of above-ground circular rooms. It was as if anything was acceptable, as long as there was some type of storage and shelter for living. Wattle—the time-honored stick-and-plaster construction—was still being used, but rock mortared by clay was also becoming common.

During Pueblo I and II eras, the business of living continued without too much change from late Basket Maker days. Crops were planted; babies were born and tended; old men of the village grumbled. It is almost certain that the weaving of cotton had entered the Pueblo world by this time. Though a species of wild cotton does grow in the area, it seems logical that a domesticated variety was introduced by those ready exporters of ideas, the Hohokam.

Around A.D. 900, the Pueblo culture entered a period of pronounced expansion. Though the center of development remained in the general area of the San Juan–Little Colorado river complex, Pueblo III concepts of architecture and ways of life radiated outward. Shards of trade pottery have been found as far west as California, as far south as Tombstone, north into the Uinta Basin of Utah, and east of the Rio Grande in northern New Mexico. Small villages seem to have

popped up behind every piñon pine and in every rocky cranny. Meanwhile, the pithouse was by no means abandoned; its use continuing in some regions while large, impressive surface structures were being built in others. That it eventually led to the *kiva*—an underground room for ritual and clan activities—appears unquestionable.

The ruins of the classic Pueblo period (III) are those that are most familiar to people visiting the Southwest. Well constructed, often protected from the worst of the elements by their placement in cliffs and under rocky overhangs, and many times set in unintentionally dramatic settings, they have a singular appeal. Some of the pueblos were in rocky shelters, such as salmon-pink Betatakin, crouching under a graceful arch in Navajo National Monument. A few were actually excavated in tuff—soft rock of the type exposed in Frijoles Canyon near Los Alamos. Others are built in the open, like Pueblo Bonito, the great D-shaped "apartment house" in Chaco Canyon (here extremely good masonry work has no doubt aided its preservation).

Living quarters were cramped, with fire pits in strategic places, and were often entered through small, keyhole doorways, whose shape is still unexplained. Many had lookout towers, such as at Square Tower House in Mesa Verde National Park. Those who lived in cliff or hillside villages had to climb either up or down to draw water and tend crops. They planted their fields with much better grades of corn than their ancestors used, either developed locally or imported from neighboring tribes.

While the Pueblo culture was expanding, the Mogollon was also pushing southward into northern Mexico. The high point of the Mogollon advance is Casas Grandes, a well-developed settlement in Chihuahua that appears to have flourished from A.D. 800 to 1400.

PRECISE DATING of ruins such as Casas Grandes is done by a variety of methods. Traditionally, archaeologists have relied on pottery shards, sequential layers in rubbish heaps, and other artifacts. More recently they have used radiocarbon-dating. However, another technique was developed by A. E. Douglass, a climatologist at the University of Arizona, which has proved very useful. Dr. Douglass, in seeking a way to compile accurate climatic records far into the past, hit upon the idea of examining the width of tree rings—the wider the ring, the better the growing season. From old, just felled trees he was able to determine the climate pattern in certain areas of Arizona for the past several hundred years. But he wanted to go back even farther. Why not examine beams from pueblo ruins? In this manner, he discovered matching tree-ring patterns when he compared certain beams. Thus, a time sequence could be established as a certain ring pattern in the older, inner heart of one beam matched the ring pattern in the younger, outer rings of an older beam. By enthusiastic sleuthing and help from archaeologists, he found the right beams and traced an unbroken record back to late Basket Maker times. The science of tree-ring study has since become an invaluable aid in understanding southwestern prehistory.

THIS WAS A TIME of cultural intermingling. The Indians of the desert were not isolated from the rest of Indian America. The Southwest was as much a crossroads for the Ancient Ones as it was, and is, for plants and animals.

An interesting "intersection" culture appears to have flourished in the Flagstaff area from the eighth to the fifteenth century—the Sinagua people, who, judging from their artifacts, had a rich and diversified way of life. Theirs was such an admixture of traits from north and south that it is difficult to know just which affiliation was stronger. Small ball courts similar to those in Yucatan have been found as far north as Wupatki, a little heap of jewel-red ruins, out on the grass-covered plains of the Moencopi formation. Even in this arid land, the Sinagua grew crops, particularly after the eruption of Sunset Crater, whose volcanic detritus left a layer of fertilizing, water-retaining ash.

Meanwhile, another small group, the Patayans, were making do with a heat-tortured climate in an area that was, however, rich in water. Their headquarters were along the Colorado River—just about where the innumerable resorts, along the string of dams that have tamed the river, are now busy with guests throughout the air-conditioned year. The Patayans designed their homes to provide shade and take advantage of what breeze might come their way. They appeared to be jealous of what must have been a strategic position, for a number of buildings that are presumably forts have been found. There is evidence that the Patayan influence was felt as far east as present-day Prescott.

A busy shell trade was carried on with the Indians of the California coast, who had access to much desired shells. There is also evidence that traits and trade goods from the Bison Culture to the east became part of Pueblo ritual. And from the north came not a mere culture trait, not even necessary or wanted trade goods, but a whole culture—the Navajo.

No one has as yet solved the mystery of the decline of the highly advanced Pueblo way of life. Bits and pieces remain in the existing pueblos of today, along the Rio Grande and on isolated mesas here and there, but no one now lives in Cliff House. The ancient kivas are empty of all but tourists. What caused the inhabitants to abandon such sophisticated domiciles? Disease? A severe and prolonged drought? Perhaps it was those raiders from the north, the Navajos and their cousins the Apaches, for raiders they were; it was their way of life, just as growing gourds was the Anasazi way. In time, the invaders changed, became peaceable, and learned more settled living from their Pueblo neighbors. Now Pueblo and Navajo have a mutual enemy—those who would destroy their beautiful desert home.

Spruce Tree House in Mesa Verde National Park is a fine example of prehistoric Pueblo architecture.

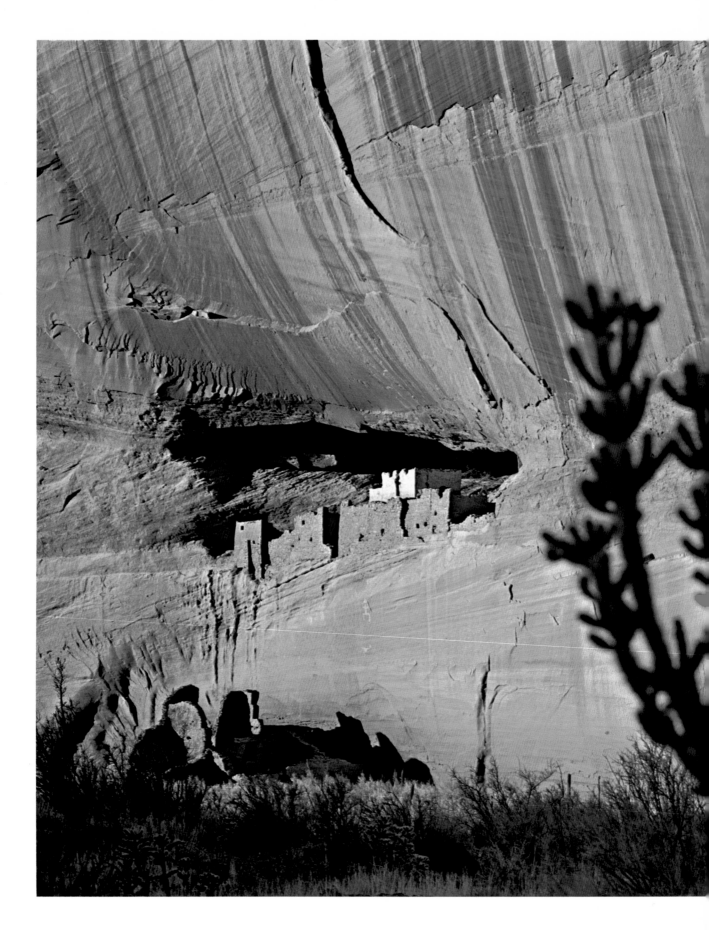

Canyon de Chelly, famed for
its spectacular gorges, also has many
Pueblo ruins such as White House.

In Monument Valley a Navajo weaver prepares yarn for a rug with a design of dancers and corn.

Age-old pastoral traditions that came with the Spanish survive in the Navajo nation.

A Hopi artisan sits with comely dignity amid her pottery, in a photograph taken in 1890 and hand colored for sales to tourists.

Anza and his second expedition readying to leave the Presidio of Tubac in October, 1775. Father Font and two other friars are on mules. Before painting this, artist Cal N. Peters did meticulous research into the details of life and travel in the period.

CHAPTER 11

IRON TIDE OF CONQUEST

*The coming of the padres and conquistadores, who found
more souls than gold in El Dorado*

THE FIRST DISCOVERIES by Columbus were some offshore islands and a continental rim. Then Cortés marched to high, watery Mexico City, captured it, and founded New Spain. Downslope to the north, spreading out like a cornucopia, lay a new world to explore and pillage. Within a decade Spaniards, on horseback or afoot, were kicking up dust in sunny desert valleys to the north. Men itched to penetrate into the interior of the enormous space that stretched on and on beyond the angular and ever-drier horizons.

And generations of discoverers and conquerors, regal, ecclesiastical, or brutally commercial, did tramp northward into the unknown to hunt for fabled cities or to exploit known ores and grasslands. Europeans with ideas for conversion, colonization, and profit, men impelled by the young energy of the Renaissance, made free with an ancient land. Within three centuries a thousand stabilized local civilizations would die crushed, and the environments they had slowly adapted to would linger devastated or in jeopardy. Life patterns long evolved by men and wild animals would expire. Instead, imported civilizations would flourish, worshipping divinities novel in the area, planting Old World seeds, and breeding vast herds of exotic creatures such as cattle, horses, and sheep.

But first, by accident, ahead of any panoplied procession, four ragged wanderers walked the breadth of what is now the southwestern United States and northwestern Mexico. In 1528, after a shipwreck on the Texas coast, Alvar Núñez Cabeza de Vaca, two other Spaniards, and a Moorish black named Estévanico

slowly worked westward, with long halts as captives, toward countrymen in Mexico. Núñez's skill as an amateur surgeon in cutting an arrow from deep in a native's head won hospitality from tribesmen, who shared their foods, including cactus fruits. The Spaniards gawked at bison—tawny or black, with small horns like those of Moroccan cows, and with long flocky hair, fine fat flesh, and useful skins. The Núñez party crossed the Big Bend country to the Rio Grande, where they found the Jumanos. These intelligent farming Indians got their salt and meat from the salt flats and buffalo plains to the north. They urged Núñez to tell the sky to drop rain for their melons, beans, gourds, and corn plants.

After eight years of wandering in a desert world as fresh and unspoiled as the Asia Marco Polo had crossed two hundred and fifty years before, the party reached western Sonora. They made their long way southward past a hospitable village near what is now Ures, where Indians gave them hundreds of open deer hearts, and into the region of today's Hermosillo. The men met Indians who already feared slave-hunting Christians from farther south, where Nuño de Guzmán had been assaulting and ravishing the pueblos on the Río Yaqui.

Núñez overtook four such Christians on horseback, "who were astonished at the sight of me, so strangely habited as I was. They stood staring at me a length of time, so confounded that they neither hailed me nor drew near to make an inquiry." Leaving the slavers, who continued to hunt down Yaquis and others (and helped engender hostilities that would last for more than three centuries), the wanderers proceeded on to

*This Taos man incarnates the courtesy, dignity, persistence, and intelligence of a people
who have preserved the inner essence of ancient ways amid modernization and tourism.*

Culiacán. They reported on the enormous wilderness to the north, including rumors of its rich cities. The pedestrians had been the first Europeans to describe bison and to traverse so wide a stretch of the continent from the rotund Gulf of Mexico to the linear Gulf of California.

The Franciscan missionary Fray Marcos de Niza responded to the tales of riches. Accompanied by Estévanico, Indian interpreters and servants, Marcos set off from Culiacán to find the seven rich cities, which Guzmán had been seeking. The Marcos party went north, following the Pacific slopes of the Sierra Madre Occidental until they came to the Gila River and worked eastward and northward to the Zuñi villages. There, perhaps because he carried medicine rattles thought to be magical, Indian leaders killed the black, ardent, confident Estévanico. They turned back the friar, who glimpsed but did not enter a Zuñi pueblo. He returned to report to the viceroy and the governor of New Galicia, Francisco Vásquez de Coronado, that he had seen one of the seven cities of Cíbola, whose inhabitants wore turquoise ornaments hanging from their noses and ears. New Spain buzzed with talk of treasures equaling those of Peru.

In 1540, under the command of Coronado, an army of about three hundred horsemen (including gentlemen of rank), four priests, and eight hundred Mexican Indians left Compostela. They celebrated Easter in Culiacán, the outpost of Spanish civilization, and headed north. Strings of mules carried elaborate equipment. There were droves of Iberian longhorns—rangy, speedy, tough, and with little edible beef on them—and droves of sheep, goats, horses, and pigs that were small, muscular, and tender as rubber balls. The long, straggling expedition was a livestock ranch in motion, with Old World trappings. The horsemen wore steel helmets or engraved *celadas,* with or without visors, plate armor or chain mail, and leather coats. They carried shields of metal or bullhide, decorated with paint, and swords, parrying daggers, spears, or lances. The party was equipped with the latest weapons from the royal arsenals of Spain—with several dozen each of crossbows and matchlocks and a half-dozen cannon.

Like Marcos, Coronado avoided the Chihuahua Desert on the east and the lower Sonoran Desert on the west by staying in the western hills of the Sierra Madre with its rivers, streams, and springs. He went up the Sonora River Valley, crossed to the San Pedro River Valley, and held northward until he reached the Gila River. He turned northeastward, crossed the Little Colorado, and drew near the Zuñi towns.

One day, when the advance party was encamped about two leagues from the first town, some well-hidden Indians suddenly gave a great yell. Although Coronado's men "were ready for anything, some were so excited that they put their saddles on hind-side before."

So wrote Casteñada, historian of the expedition, who went on to describe the arrival at Háwikuh, the city glorified by Marcos's report: "The next day . . . when they saw the first village which was Cíbola, such were the curses that some hurled at Friar Marcos that I pray God may protect him from them." Háwikuh was "a little, unattractive village, looking as if it had been crumpled all up together. There are mansions in New Spain which make a better appearance at a distance."

After a skirmish, Coronado moved in by force. Though the village of sticks and mud had no gold to grab, it had welcome food: pine nuts, corn meal, corn, and tame turkeys, and in cisterns, where snow and rain collected, lay pools of sweet water.

The party proceeded eastward past the amazing high mesa town of Acoma to the Rio Grande towns, where Coronado abruptly expulsed the inhabitants of Tiguex, near the present Bernalillo, and housed his men there. During two years of arrogant occupation, he sent expeditions in all directions. One squad went beyond the Hopi pueblos and discovered the Grand Canyon. Coronado himself was decoyed across the mountains and the Río Pecos, and far into the great buffalo plains beyond.

He returned to a cold reception in Mexico, for though he was a success as an explorer, Coronado was a failure as a conquistador. He had no gold. Casteñada wrote that the expedition "has made it easy to see the difference between the report which told of vast treasures, and the places where nothing like this was either found or known. . . . I do not know whether this will furnish ground for pondering and considering the uncertainty of this life."

ALTHOUGH CORONADO'S FAILURE in 1542 ended for half a century any spectacular northern caval-

Frederic Remington's version (in black and white) of Coronado's expedition tramping through sun-blanched desert in search of the Seven Cities of Cíbola.

cades, the workaday mining and ranching frontier pushed steadily forward on the east side of the Sierra Madre, so that by 1580 the edge of settlement was 850 miles out from Mexico City and near the present Hidalgo del Parral. Here were the mines of Santa Bárbara, together with a Franciscan mission founded in 1565, and the mines of San Bartolomé, with a mission founded in 1570. North and east of these outposts lay major barriers—two huge, relatively sterile interior drainage systems of intermittent salt lakes, alkali flats, sand dunes, and waterless land for hundreds of miles. One area covered much of northern Chihuahua. The other, south of Río Conchos, covered much of eastern Chihuahua and western Coahuila, including the Bolsón de Mapimí.

In 1581 Fray Augustín Rodríguez and two other Franciscans, Juan de Santa María and Francisco López,

together with Indian servants, Captain Francisco Sánchez Chamuscado, and nine soldiers, set out from San Bartolomé for New Mexico. The party embodied the conflict of state and church, for the men were "fortified," according to one of the soldiers, "with the hope of attaining temporal and eternal reward." They pioneered a new route via rivers to New Mexico. They went down the Río de Parral to the Río Florido and down it to the Río Conchos, then down it to the five Indian villages at the junction with the Rio Grande, where they introduced Christianity before following the big river north past the swamps below the present Juárez and on north to the Indian pueblos, where Indians killed Fray Juan. When the expedition left to return to Mexico, Rodríguez and López stayed behind to serve as missionaries, only in turn to be killed by natives. Chamuscado died on the way to San Barto-

El Morro headland in New Mexico, an autographed cliff bearing inscriptions by Oñate, Vargas, and others.

lomé. The written account of the trip first used the name New Mexico. Of the fifty states in the Union, only Florida has an older name.

Other parties followed the roundabout river route. One, that of Antonio de Espejo, returned down the Pecos to the Rio Grande, thus opening a new road.

Then came the establishment of a major new route, the royal road that would connect Mexico City directly with the upper Rio Grande Valley. Don Juan de

Oñate, a wealthy silver-mine owner of Zacatecas, financed his own colonial expedition and outfitted it mostly in Zacatecas before heading north via Fresnillo, Nombre de Dios, and Durango to the edge of his civilization, at Santa Bárbara. From there on his scouts, particularly the sergeant-major, Vicente Zaldívar, broke a trail that ran from the Río Parral northward to where Ciudad Chihuahua was later founded and then on almost due north over mountain saddles, past occasional hot or cold springs, brackish ponds, dry streams, and deep, formidable sand dunes (Los Médanos) to a ford in the Rio Grande near the later site of El Paso del Norte.

It was in early 1598 that the Oñate expedition left Santa Bárbara in a procession three miles long—eighty-three wagons, carriages, and carts and seven thousand head of livestock destined to be eaten on the way or used to establish farms in the distant north. There were 130 men—soldiers or colonists—together with their wives and children. The guardian soldiers wore defenses against either European hand weapons or native American arrows. They wore light half-suits of armor of Flemish or German make. On their heads they wore plain helmets, cabasets—simple, potlike iron helmets with chain mail hanging from the back and sides and under the jaw—or morions—cocky, hatlike helmets that held a feather. The horsemen put their feet in solid iron stirrups, sometimes cross-shaped, with silver engraving, and they carried broadswords, Italian *schiavona*, with hand guards and blades a yard long. Some blades bore engraved inscriptions such as

DO NOT DRAW ME WITHOUT REASON

DO NOT SHEATH ME WITHOUT HONOR.

Oñate's men had no crossbows, preferring such modern armaments as the wheellock carbine, however awkward, the flintlock musket, and the miquelet lock, which had a good shoulder fitting.

In the Chihuahua Desert on Holy Thursday, the feast of the Blessed Sacrament, the men knelt before a representation of the Holy Sepulchre and begged forgiveness for their sins. At night there was prayer and penance for all; women and children came barefoot to pray. "The soldiers," according to Villagrá, the historian on the journey, "with cruel scourges, beat their [own] backs unmercifully until the camp ran crimson with their blood."

In southern New Mexico, Oñate followed the waterless ninety-mile Jornada del Muerto, which took three difficult forced marches, mostly at night. The river to the west was in a precipitous channel too narrow to be followed.

Oñate's advance party arrived in northern New Mexico well in advance of the main wagon party, which took five months to make the tough seven-hundred-mile journey. Oñate not only established the direct route between the mission frontier of Nueva Vizcaya and the mission frontier of Nuevo Méjico. He also bloodily "pacified" the pueblos, successfully colonized New Mexico (the second permanent settlement in what is now the United States), founded the first capital of the province at San Juan, organized the first mission system among the New Mexico Indians (seven districts under eight Franciscan friars), and introduced the cult of the Penitentes, the Third Order of St. Francis, as evidenced on Holy Thursday.

Oñate explored as much as Coronado and Chambuscado did, and he began the custom of autographing the cliff now called Inscription Rock at El Morro. He used up his fortune and resigned under severe criticism in 1607, partly because of his pathologically brutal treatment—murder, torture, mayhem—of Ácoma citizens. Three years later he was the hero of Villagrá's prosy, frank epic poem in thirty-four cantos, *Historia del Nuevo Méjico,* published in Alcalá, Spain, the first poem about any section of the United States.

Oñate's second successor as governor, Don Pedro de Peralta, founded Santa Fe—"Holy Faith"—a walled city with a plaza and a fortress *palacio,* which became the new capitol. Spanish New Mexico now had both a mission system and a permanent capital city to match established settlements in southern Chihuahua, and it was the beginning of a century of religious expansion in the lands between. By 1617 there were eleven Franciscan missions in New Mexico and forty-three by 1626, from Pecos in the east to Ácoma and Zuñi and Hopi in the west, from Taos in the north to El Paso del Norte in the south. Inside Chihuahua, during the course of two centuries, the Jesuits and Franciscans each established a score or more missions and convents. Notable Jesuits—Juan Fonte, Joseph Neumann, Tomás de Guadalajara—worked in the mountainous Tarahumara region and among the tribes in the rough western area. The Franciscans labored along the Río Conchos in the lowland valleys and plains. Far to the east, where the Conchos joins the Rio Grande, Fray Alonso Oliva founded a church and settled converts. A penitential man, he was still wearing his habitual iron girdle with prongs embedded in his flesh when he was buried.

The missionaries sought to replace the time-tested planned communities of the pueblo Indians and the

Mission San José de Tumacácori, a relic in the 1860s.

functional, often camplike *rancherías* of the nomadic tribes with the age-old Roman-planned communities of Iberian culture. The missions set up not only the church but an entire system of farming and grazing, of industries such as weaving and tanning, of education and government. Indians learned about horses, cows, goats, and sheep, about apples, peaches, wheat, onions, and grapes. They received instruction in music, letters, and crafts. The fathers intended to combine conversion with training to produce citizens of New Spain.

Some missions were only minor *visitas,* or subchurches; others were centers of population and power. One such was the limestone Pueblo de las Humanas, now the ruins in Gran Quivira National Monument. Another was Cicuyé, east of Santa Fe, once a stalwart town of nearly five hundred warriors, where the Franciscans built a towering church "of peculiar construction and beauty, very spacious, with room for all the people of Pueblo." It had great pine beams, dragged from the Sangre de Cristo Mountains, and high clerestory windows to let light shine in on a religious stage. An inscription read: *Venite ad sanctuarium Domini Quod per Matrem suam sanctificavit in aeternum.* The Cicuyé church and pueblo eventually fell before the attacks of Comanches. The final citizens emigrated westward to the Rio Grande, and the ruins today are in Pecos National Monument.

In pueblos and settlements that survived along the Rio Grande, old mission buildings remain in regular use, such as at Santo Domingo or San Ildefonso, at Zuñi, and downriver from present Juárez and El Paso at Ysleta, Socorro, and San Elizario. Refugees fleeing

southward from the Indian rebellion of 1680 established a mission and convent at Nuestra Señora de Guadalupe del Paso del Norte (Juárez), which served local Manso and Suma Indians and also some transplanted Piro and Tewa Indians from the north.

In 1697 on the Río Chuvíscar, some two hundred and fifty miles to the south, Franciscans founded the mission of Nombre de Dios for the Conchos Indians. A town of silver miners and farmers grew up near the mission. In 1718 it acquired the name La Villa de San Felipe de Real de Chihuahua. The silver mines at the mining town of Santa Eulalia some miles away came to be known as the richest in the world.

The Franciscan Order was largely in charge of the wagon trains. Once every three years these trains brought supplies north from Mexico and took back produce from New Mexico. There would be two sections of sixteen heavy-service wagons pulled by eight-mule teams. Each section had a *mayordomo,* a captain, and a dozen soldiers. The lead wagons flew the royal banner. But in the late seventeenth century the Apache raids on supply trains put transportation more and more in the hands of military and civil authorities, and as Chihuahua grew in importance, its merchants took over the control and the profits of the royal road from Chihuahua to Santa Fe, the great trade route through Apachería.

While the Chihuahua–New Mexico frontier with its unifying great river grew stronger from Oñate's time on, Arizona—part of New Mexico—remained a wilderness, and the western Mexican frontier from Sinaloa northward crept slowly, with no particular distinction. Pimería Alta (northern Sonora and southern Arizona), like the Californias, remained blank on the charts.

THEN, BETWEEN 1687 AND 1711, came the activities of Father Eusebio Kino, S.J. This Austrian from the Tyrol, a Renaissance man, had been offered a professorship in mathematics at a Bavarian university before he went to Mexico as a missionary. He worked in Baja California until he transferred his energies to the desert mainland, with a headquarters at Mission Nuestra Señora de los Dolores on the Río San Miguel. During his twenty-four years there he made fifty journeys, some a thousand miles long, exploring from the Río Sonora to the Gila and from the San Pedro to the

Colorado. Sometimes he rode forty or more miles in a day, traveling with few soldiers and sometimes only with Papagos, Pimas, Sobaipuris, or the tall Yumas and Seris. He converted and baptized thousands of Indians in scores of tribes, founded missions, and built churches. To feed the missions, he became in effect a benign cattle king, founding a score of ranches from Santa Bárbara deep in Chihuahua to San Xavier del Bac near Tucson. He inspired Father Juan María Salvatierra, S.J., founder of the permanent missions in Baja California, and he was the careful historian, in *Celestial Favors,* of his own imperial labors in the arid borderlands.

Kino had even fewer Spanish colonists than the Franciscans had on the Chihuahua Trail, so even more than they he was carrying out the Spanish policy of colonizing the frontier by incorporating the natives into the system. He was working for both church and state as he brought European civilization, including fruits and vegetables, to the civilizations already there. He urged the king to the "reduction"of Apachería by means of missionary effort. He hoped to see trade ties develop eastward and westward, with the Indians and Spanish in Nuevo Méjico and the Indians in Alta California. In 1710 he was urging Philip V to push the conversion of California and to create Nueva Navarra in the region of Pimería Alta; his map of this area is famous.

A fellow Jesuit wrote that this busy, many-sided man, who would sit up all night reading, "neither smoked nor took snuff nor wine . . . nor had any other bed than the sweat blankets of his horse for a mattress, and two Indian blankets. He never had more than two coarse shirts, because he gave everything as alms to the Indians."

After Kino's death his missions were continued, but the Jesuits lost control in 1767 when Charles III of Spain suddenly expelled the Jesuits from his empire with sealed orders. It was a time in Europe of anti-clericalism, power struggle inside the Church and in the royal courts, controversies over the doctrine of grace, and the rise to influence of the pietistic, mystical Jansenists and the secular deists and enlightened despots. Foes charged that the Jesuits were too intellectual, cold, and syllogistic, also too involved in mercantile and political activities.

Franciscans from the College of the Holy Cross in Querétaro moved north to take over the missionary work. Among them were Fathers Juan Díaz and Francisco Garcés, who helped strengthen Spanish control. At the Indian village of Tumacácori, for instance, where Kino and the Jesuits had never been able to do more than to hold occasional services, the Franciscans set up a mission headquarters and began, around 1800, to build a big church. In turn, the Franciscans reached an impasse after Mexican independence in 1821. The new country could not defend the missions against hostile Indians and ended the custom of subsidizing missionary activity.

Already by 1645 a vast social change had begun in the imperial area on the east side of the present-day American Southwest and southward deep into Coahuila and Chihuahua, south of the bleak Bolsón de Mapimí and its dusty fringes, and on to cities such as Durango. The change was that hunting and gathering communities—Querechos and Tejas (Comanche and Texas Indians), Jumanos, Apaches, and others—were learning to ride horses and eat horses stolen from haciendas and outposts. Indians of mountain and plain were evolving into skillful riders and raiders, mounted warriors. The Spanish never learned to cope with them on the open plains and in the twisting canyons from Raton Pass to Torreón and westward to the Río Altar and the Gila.

After 1700 the Spanish began establishing a border line of presidios, forts manned by soldiers with families on nearby farms, as a means of keeping marauders out of important parts of the cattle and horse country. The Apaches, a varied and widely distributed group, became the principal antagonists clear across the region. Also, there were Navajos and Utes to the north, Mojaves to the west; on the east were the Comanches. At the time of the Comanche Moon, the first full moon each September, after summer rains had filled all the waterholes, Comanches from the high plains trotted south across Texas to Persimmon Gap (now an entrance to Big Bend National Park), forked around the Chisos Mountains, forded the Rio Grande, and pounced down for a warm, well-fed winter in the Chihuahua cattle country and the sunswept Bolsón de Mapimí.

These aggressive native nations were only part of

The presidio at Tubac, as sketched in the early 1860s.

the frontier problem that Spain faced. Far to the west Alta California, though nominally a Spanish possession, lay open and exposed to the acquisitive eyes of Russians and Englishmen. In response the government used the Pacific sea route to establish missions, presidios, and pueblos, beginning with San Diego in 1769. The next move was to join the skimpy north-south series of settlements in California with the parallel north-south chains of settlements in the interior, those scattered west of the Sierra Madre, where Kino had labored, and those stretching like a meridian from Santa Fe to San Bartolomé.

Exploration began again. In 1776 Fray Silvestre Vélez de Escalante investigated westward from Santa Fe toward San Gabriel in California. The great obstacle to a direct route was the maze of deep, tortuous Colorado River canyons. Escalante's route wandered far to the north, to the basin lakes of Utah. After he turned around in southern Utah, his homeward way through northern Arizona and on to Albuquerque was much more direct.

The modest Escalante expedition was important for exploration, and it left names on the land. It pioneered part of a trail to the Pacific. But it was far overshadowed in importance by the Anza expedition of 1774–1775, which first established a land route from mainland Mexico to the California coast.

Don Juan Baptista de Anza, a native Sonoran and a highly competent captain of cavalry in the royal presidio of Tubac, south of Tucson, undertook to open a line of communication between Tubac and Monterey, California, by way of the Gila and Colorado rivers. The expedition, commissioned by the viceroy, the gov-

ernor, and the captain-general of New Spain, was less lavish than the grand processions of Coronado and Oñate two centuries before. There were thirty-five loads of provisions—munitions of war, tobacco, equipage, "& other things necessary for an unknown country." In the party were thirty-four persons including two Franciscan fathers, twenty volunteer soldiers, and five muleteers, together with more than a hundred mounts and sixty-five beeves to walk along until eaten.

The route ran through northern Sonora, past the mines at Arizonac, past small mission settlements such as Oquitoa and Caborca, with fertile fields and quiet Pimas and Papagos, to Sonóitac with its old Jesuit mission, and then across a long, almost waterless stretch to the Gila River and down it to "the rivers," where the Gila joined the Colorado. There the Yumas —giant Indians, many of them over six feet tall— celebrated by throwing fistfuls of earth up into the air. The Yumas crowded around to study "our persons, our clothes, and other things used by us." Anza gave the Yumas an ox to eat, regaled them with glass beads and tobacco, and studied their appearance. Men and women alike painted their faces with black and red colors. The men had three to five perforations in their ears and wore earrings in all of them. They perforated their noses and thrust through a cluster of feathers or a sprig of palm frond. They did up their hair in diverse fashions with a fine river mud, and over it they scattered a powder that gave a silvery luster. To protect this coiffure, they slept sitting up.

These unwarlike people had fat horses and good riverbottom fields of wheat, maize, beans, melons, and calabashes. It was February, yet so mild and irrigation water so abundant that Anza foresaw vineyards and citrus orchards, for "the fruit would not be exposed to danger from frosts."

The Colorado was at its usual low winter stage. The Yumas guided the party across a ford where the river was only about four feet deep and something less than six hundred feet wide. The king's arms for the first time crossed the Río Colorado del Norte. To celebrate, the commander had men fire off some rockets. "This volley pleased the Yumas, although the roar frightened them so that on hearing it they threw themselves on the ground." The expedition made its difficult way across the hot, sandy, salty desert west of the river, into the Borrego Valley, and toward the promised water and verdure of the southern California coastal plain.

It was in the demanding desert that Fray Francisco Garcés, ever the eager missionary, gregarious with the Indians, cried out in his diary: "Oh, what a vast heathendom! Oh! what lands so suitable for missions! Oh! what a heathendom so docile! How fine it would be if the wise and pious Don Carlos III might see these lands!" It was this Garcés who later went off alone to explore the river above Yuma, commune with the Mojaves in their villages, and "discover" a route crossing the Mojave Desert westward to the Tehachapi Mountains and central California.

The second Anza expedition, in 1775–1776, was the first overland crossing with families. It started out in September from the presidio of San Miguel de Orcasitas, east of the present Hermosillo, with twenty families of soldiers and four of settlers, who with the soldiers and servants made a total of 177 persons. They went north past Magdalena and Nogales Wash to the church at Tumacácori and the presidio of Tubac, where the party grew to 240 persons, including three Franciscans. With 355 beeves and 695 horses and mules, they moved north through Papaguería, to the *visita* of mission San Xavier del Bac, to Tuquisón, pioneering a new route for mass migration. At the prosperous, admirable Pima villages on the Gila, they turned west, downstream. After days of freezing weather, lack of firewood, and delays caused by sickness, a childbirth, and a woman's death, Anza reached the Yuma villages again.

Father Pedro Font, diarist extraordinary of the expedition, noted that the Colorado, like the Río Yaqui he knew, was low in winter but given to sudden rises from March to July, when it spread over land and deposited fertile silt.

In May, on the return trip from San Francisco, the Anza party, now only forty in number, found the river at a high stage with whirlpools, and crossed on rafts. Yuma women swam over pushing loads in their *coritas*. The remainder of the return trip reversed the route of 1774—Sonóitac, Quitobác, Caborca. Always the way was crooked because of the need to seek out water and pasturage, to camp at *tinajas* (pools) in rocks, *pozos* (springs), and *zacatels* (patches of coarse grass). And always, too, there was Indian danger. Since the party had passed north through Tumacácori, the Apaches had destroyed it. Anza returned safely to Orcasitas on June 1, 1776, after a trip of three thousand miles.

WHILE THE SPANISH colonial government faced problems of defense and the missions had their ups and downs, the caravans between Chihuahua and Santa Fe, annual affairs since around 1750, gained solidly in importance. Chihuahua itself grew to be a city of twelve to fifteen thousand persons, with paved streets and walks at right angles to each other, and with a fountain amid a main plaza. On the south side was an ornate cathedral with twin towers, on the west the mint and treasury, on the north the legislative hall and the granary, and on the east the governor's palace. Nearby stood the church of San Francisco, a chapel, an academy, and barracks. In 1807 miners were at work in fifteen mines in the environs, thirteen of silver and one each of gold and copper. Smelters smoked in the suburbs, and slag and cinders encircled the town. Then as now, polluting meant prosperity and wealth for the mine owners and poor health for miners and smeltermen.

The merchants of Chihuahua dominated the New Mexicans' economic life with a variety of devices for monopolizing and shortchanging and entangling in debts. The summer caravan, camping northward for forty days, carried boots, shoes, cloth, chocolate, sugar, tobacco, liquors, paper, ink, books, and ironware, especially tools, arms, keys, plow points, daggers, and needles. In the late fall the return caravan brought the standard provincial goods—wool and hides, buffalo robes, Indian blankets, pine seeds, salt, El Paso brandy distilled from El Paso wine, and slaves—captive Ute and Apache women and girls.

Men tunneled for ore in many places—in the silver mines near Arizonac, where nuggets weighing 2,250 pounds had been reported in 1736; in busy gold or silver mines from Galisteo near Santa Fe to Cusihuiriáchi in the Sierra de Metates southwest of Chihuahua. But the one sure commercial enclave, the one firm axis in the great deserts of Apachería, was El Camino Real, the regal trade route that Oñate had opened up in the year Philip II died, when there was yet no permanent non-Indian settlement in Virginia or Massachusetts.

CHAPTER 12

RED MAN'S TROUBLED PASSAGE

*Indians of the "vast heathendom"—their culture before the Spanish
entrada and their plight as vassals in its wake*

IN THE CENTRAL ELEMENTS of civilization, the Europeans, like their Mexican and Anglo descendants, had nothing basic to give the New World natives, who already had systems of farming and hunting, government, religion, education, ethics, family relationships, crafts, and arts. In its way each tribe was a going concern. While there were great variations and contrasts in everything from physique to language, the evidence from the earliest records is that at first the Indians, from Apaches to Zuñis, kept their word. Until they sensed or experienced aggression, they were hospitable. They gave or sold food to exploring parties, provided guides, pointed out water holes, and sometimes provided expert and advanced medicinal assistance. Many tribes, notably those that irrigated, were inclined to peace rather than to use of arms. Fighting was more often a ritual than a calculated act, but any tribe, when attacked, fought with skill and ferocity. The most warlike were the nomadic mountain and plains tribes, who had been raiding the pueblos since the thirteenth century.

The Spanish often accused the Indians of laziness and petty thievery, of stealing with their toes as with their fingers, but the Spanish at the same time were eyeing local soil, ores, and women with a view to possession. What the Spanish brought in were new systems of organization, physical novelties, and social disasters. Even as Cabeza de Vaca was winning admiration from aboriginal Texans for his surgical skill, his countrymen at Culiacán had introduced chattel slavery and struck terror into the agricultural communes of the Yaquis.

Coronado evicted whole towns, moved his men into the rooms, and ate up the stored food. He demanded cloth or clothing for his men. Once, as the Indians complied and took off their own cloaks, some soldiers stripped Indians of cloaks that they wanted "without ado, not stopping to find out the rank of the men they were stripping, which caused not a little hard feeling" since headmen were thus maltreated. In return, the Indians killed a guard and ran off many horses and mules. Coronado sent his army to catch and punish the guilty, to bring back no captives, but "to make an example of them so that the other natives would fear the Spanish."

This led to a battle in the pueblo. The Spanish gained the roofs and used their muskets and crossbows to make good shots. They dropped fire into kivas, the sacred subterranean chambers where some Indians were hiding. When Indians made the sign of the cross, meaning peace, several aldermen from Seville made the same sign. The Indians put down their arms and received pardon. Many entered the captain's tent. But then the captain, not knowing of the peace arrangement, ordered two hundred stakes prepared to burn as many men alive. When the Indians saw that they would be tied and roasted to death, there was a great scuffle. Foot soldiers attacked the Indians, and horsemen ran them down and killed them.

Casteñada reported that the natives "spread throughout the country the news that the strangers did not respect the peace they had made, which afterward proved a great misfortune." Time after time the Spanish leaders broke their word, teaching treachery

*The cathedral in Ciudad Chihuahua, started in 1724 and built largely with a tax on silver
from nearby mines at Santa Eulalia. (Photographed on January 1, 1882.)*

147

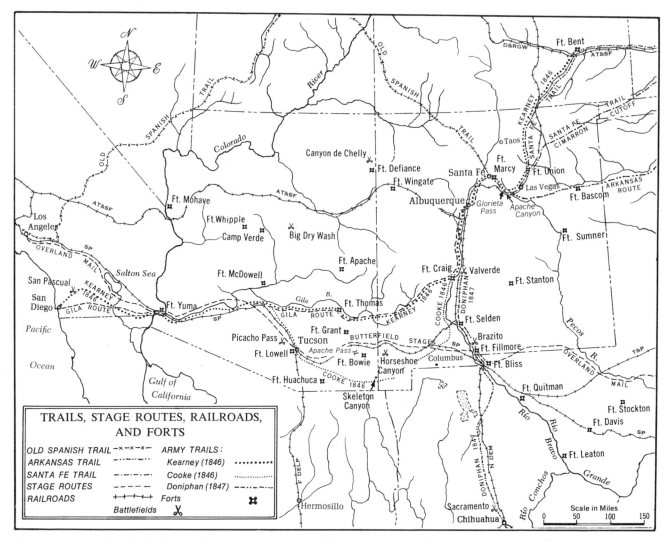

TRAILS, STAGE ROUTES, RAILROADS,
AND FORTS

OLD SPANISH TRAIL	—x—x—x—	ARMY TRAILS:
ARKANSAS TRAIL	—··—··—··	Kearney (1846) ········
SANTA FE TRAIL	—·—·—·—·	Cooke (1846) ···········
STAGE ROUTES	— — — —	Doniphan (1847) —··—··—
RAILROADS	+++++	Forts ⌘
		Battlefields ✂

Migrant mammals, including early man, found natural routes through the desert. Later explorers, traders, soldiers, stage drivers, and railroaders used many of the same routes.

to the natives and inaugurating four hundred years of sieges, battles, solitary killings, and mass slaughters. Whichever way the brown men turned, they found themselves in a difficult and dangerous passage between their primeval, time-tested, quiet pace and the tumult and violent change forced on them by the tanned white men.

Shortly after Oñate arrived in New Mexico, he assaulted a town of the Keres people, 1,500 persons in 200 houses in their almost impregnable Troy, a mesa 357 feet high—Ácoma. Apparently a small band of Spanish men had precipitated a bloody fight with some Ácoma warriors, who killed Juan de Zaldívar, the Spanish leader, and a dozen companions. A revenge party led by Juan's brother Vicente contrived to reach the top of the mesa, where they killed 600 to 800 Ácomans and captured 70 to 80 warriors and 500 or more women and children. They murdered some natives and threw their bodies over the cliff, hanged two Indians without cause, and burned the town.

At the trial of the captives in Santo Domingo, Oñate ordered that all males more than twenty-five years old have a foot cut off and be given twenty years

The high mesa pueblo of Ácoma, scene of Vicente de Zaldívar's assault in 1598.
(Photographed in 1904.) Enchanted Mesa is to the east, across a valley.

of "personal service"—slavery. All females age twelve or older were to be sold for twenty years of personal service. Two Hopis captured at Ácoma lost their right hands and were sent home as a warning to others. Several scores of young girls captured at Ácoma were delivered to the viceroy in Cuidad Méjico, who distributed them among convents. After dispensing this justice and teaching the infidels a moral lesson, Oñate turned to founding missionary districts and assigning a friar to each.

Spaniards like Oñate came from a Europe of caste and slavery, of almost incessant wars and cruelty. The

first to arrive freshly remembered wars against the Moors and the conquests of Granada, Mexico, and Peru. As time went on, their followers remembered the series of wars between their Holy Roman Emperor Charles V and King Francis I of France, wars against peasants and Turks, the Thirty Years War and other wars of the Reformation, wars over the Austrian and the Spanish successions, conquest and genocide in the Netherlands, the Napoleonic wars—wars—and the prolonged tortures of the Inquisition. It was this bloodthirsty occidental tradition of brutal, big-scale international intrigue and devastation, sanctioned by rhe-

149

Zuñi women bearing water jars, one with a gourd dipper, were photographed around 1901.

torical holiness, that the small nomadic nations and the city-states of the desert mesas and valleys were commanded to submit to.

While the Spanish military and administrative officers arbitrarily whipped, killed, hanged, burned at the stake, imprisoned, raped, and expropriated goods and lands, in the European tradition of war, they also unintentionally introduced diseases for which the Indians had no inbred immunity—tuberculosis, trachoma, measles, syphilis, whooping cough, dysentery, smallpox, and cholera. Some of these diseases reached tribes like the Pima even before actual white conquest and settlement.

In New Mexico the colonial government insisted that each pueblo elect a governor and made a silver-headed cane the symbol of the authority of this quasi-democratic leader. There were regulations that did protect Indians from the Inquisition as such, though not from its ideology. The Inquisition arrived in Santa Fe in 1625 in the person of Alonzo de Benavides. The Holy Office saw to it that one New Mexico governor was arrested and deprived of his property, and it ruined another governor and made him march barefooted through the streets of Mexico City, but it did not touch the age-old pueblos where "heathendom" survived alongside the newfangled Christianity.

The European priests undertook to convert and—by European standards—to civilize the aborigines. Though intelligence is relative and individual, the priests together with the secular colonists saw themselves as the *gente de razón*, the rational people, while the natives, as Fray Juan Díaz said, "lack rational civilization."

The Church with its architecture came to the sedentary tribes and, when it could, brought in nomadic tribes to settle at missions. Of necessity, the conquered pueblos and the agricultural and mission Indians learned some Spanish words and accepted, outwardly, the supernatural elements in the religion that the *gente de razón* pushed on them. They added Christian myths to their own. The Tewa people, for instance, already classified all human and spiritual existence into six categories, three human and three supernatural. An individual in his life cycle reenacted the tribal journey. The Indians accepted outwardly the forms of baptism, marriage, and communion. They accepted the saints and the *santos*, statuettes of saints, while still holding to their own gods, ghosts, and katchina dolls. Church and kiva shared the rites.

Since the padres suppressed all native religious activities during Lent, the Indians moved their mass public rituals up ahead of Lent. Originally the Tewa had planted all native crops after the vernal equinox. Now they learned to plant the exotic grain wheat earlier in the year, to allow for its long germinating and growing season and to have it ready to harvest before the insect infestations of August. They also learned to use beehive ovens in the Spanish style.

Besides wheat, the natives accepted a variety of vegetables, fruit trees, and where it would grow, the grapevine. They mastered horse and mule culture, and learned all the details of breeding, raising, and butchering the livestock that had been walked north.

As conscript laborers directed by the versatile missionaries, Indians learned to make sun-cured adobe bricks and kiln-baked bricks for structures. The gangs working to build churches learned to shape and use bricks for floors, walls, stairways, cornices, moldings, and domes. They learned to carve wood for doors, altars, icons, ox-carts, tables, and chairs—for all the wooden objects the fathers wanted.

The conquered—or occupied—Indian nations under

Jesuit auspices had to comply with sixteenth-century laws drawn up far away and increasingly long ago in Valladolid or Salamanca. *Las Siete Partidas* of 1576, for example, detailed the weekly schedule. Mondays and Tuesdays the Indians gave their working hours to communal industries, agriculture, and sheep and cattle raising. Wednesdays and Thursdays they worked for the padres at sheep and cattle raising, agriculture, industries, and educational activities. Fridays and Saturdays were days for the Indians. Sunday was for church.

This was the ideal, theoretical calendar. In practice, as Indian revolts made clear, the new regime not only violated the pace and direction of native life; it often led to virtual enslavement. This happened in Yaqui missions, where some Jesuits acted like feudal masters. It happened in the upper Rio Grande missions, where some Franciscans worked Indians hard at cotton-spinning looms or in dark, dusty mines.

Furthermore, in New Mexico and Nueva Viscaya two official systems meant slavery and debt peonage. The *encomienda* system gave the Indians to an agent who was to defend and convert them and in return get labor or tribute from them. *Repartimiento* distributed the Indians to work in settlements. Legal varieties of kidnapping and forced labor, concepts ancient in Caesar's time, were now functioning inside the rim of Spanish Christendom.

Indian women and girls did conscript work in the buildings of the great self-subsistent haciendas along the Casas Grandes, the Conchos and its headwater streams, and the Rio Grande. Men labored in the corrals and on the open range, and hundreds of other men, herded into mining camps, had to drill, shovel, carry ore in heavy leather bags while walking uphill on notched poles through the shafts, and suffer from silicosis and assorted bronchial and lung ailments. As a result of death, resettlement, or amalgamation, Indian tribes on both sides of the Sierra Madre Occidental began to disappear, the Conchos on the east, the Ópatas on the west. In the early seventeenth century, despite royal prohibition of slavery, slave markets began to appear in southern Chihuahua. Men and women—Tarahumaras, Tobosos, Sumas—were put up for sale.

No amount of sophistry could deceive the Indians. In 1846 Lt. J. W. Abert picked up a New Mexico

For two centuries this aqueduct carried water from Río Chuvíscar to Ciudad Chihuahua.

story. The white man said to the Indian, "You take the buzzard, and I take the turkey," or "I take the turkey, and you take the buzzard." The Indian replied, "You never said turkey to me once." But this dialogue does not catch the grim violence of the Three Hundred Years War.

RESISTANCE HAD TO BEGIN with the violent *entradas* of Guzmán and Coronado, the armed parties of Chambuscado and Francisco de Ibarra, explorer of Chihuahua. What natives who heard of it would ever forget the judicial decision of Oñate after the Ácoma affair? In return for killings and usurpations, broken promises and insults, Indians killed Franciscans, Jesuits, soldiers, colonists, and converted Indians subservient to whites. Then the whites called the Indians savages and treated them with increased savagery. In white history the chronicle of the redskins' resistance tends to receive minor space, as does that of blacks, but the tale is long. There was a bloody Taos rebellion in 1617. In Chihuahua, Conchos and Tobosos on horses sacked villages and drove the Spanish out of towns in the 1640s. Between 1648 and 1653 the Tarahumaras were in hot revolt, led by a small, gaunt patriot called Tepóraca. Together with the Tobosos they hemmed the Spanish in for a while at Tomochi.

151

Ruins of the massive Franciscan Mission San Gregorio at the Pueblo of Abó, New Mexico, built in 1646 and abandoned around 1675 because of Apache and Comanche hostilities.

In New Mexico, after a series of Indian conspiracies and sporadic outbreaks, the Spanish tried religious persecution of the Indian malcontents. In 1645 forty Indians near Santa Fe were flogged, imprisoned, and hanged for refusing to give up their faith. The result was another uprising. The Jémez and Apaches conspired, but the plot was discovered. Nine leaders were hanged, and the rest sold into slavery for ten years. Then Taos Pueblo schemed for a general revolt and outlined plans on a deerskin, but the Hopis refused to join in and the revolt was cancelled. In 1675 a tribunal found San Ildefonso Indians guilty of bewitching the superior of a Franciscan monastery; four were hanged, and forty-three whipped and enslaved.

Then in 1680 came a tremendous but temporary blow to Spanish prestige, the Pueblo Revolt. Its leader was Po-pé, a medicine man at San Juan Pueblo, whom the Spanish had chained, flogged, and whipped out of San Juan—for witchcraft. United, the northern pueblos killed four hundred or more Spaniards and besieged Santa Fe. They sent two crosses, one white and one red, to the governor inside the city walls. If he returned the white one and promised to leave New Mexico, the Spanish population could depart. If he

returned the red one, the Indians would massacre them all. The governor returned the red one and stayed on, though water and food became scarce. Early one morning the Spaniards sallied out, caught the Indians sleeping, and killed hundreds; but the next day the Spaniards completely evacuated Santa Fe and headed south. For twelve years they came no farther north than El Paso del Norte.

Victorious Indians washed baptized converts with soapweed and annulled Christian marriages, burned written records, destroyed missions, and filled up with rocks the mineshafts at Los Cerrillos. Santa Fe was an Indian capital until Diego de Vargas marched up in 1692 and the town submitted to him. To the north the Indians put up a stiff resistance. When Taos remained hostile, the Spaniards sacked and burned the pueblo, executed captive warriors, and enslaved women and children.

Inspired by the Indian victory of 1680, Conchos, Janos, Mansos, and Sumas formed a Chihuahuan confederation. They attacked churches, set fire to haciendas, and drove off cattle. Apaches pounced here and there, for their centuries of desert horsemanship and consummate guerrilla warfare had now begun.

152

Back and forth the killing went until both sides fell into the practice of assessing guilt by association, of assassinating casually, and of massacring by calculation. Kino reported one such feudlike sequence. For years the Spanish in northern Sonora had suffered theft of arquebuses, swords, daggers, saddlebags, saddles, boots, horses, and cattle. Suspicion pointed at the Sobaipuri Pimas. In 1688, according to Kino, the Spanish "unreasonably destroyed" their *ranchería* of Mototiacachi, beat fifty innocent natives suspected of thievery, and took twenty captives to be slaves in a mine. The day before Easter in 1695, forty or so Indians from the Pima mission at San Antonio del Oquitoa went to Caborca. They entered the house of Fray Francisco Xavier Saeta and killed him and his four servants. The governor of the army went to Oquitoa, killed a boy, beat an Indian woman, and took captive three little children he happened to meet. After burying the dead priest reverently in Caborca, the general led an expedition to catch the murderers. Many Pimas came to him, "both good and bad, to the number of more than fifty." They came with crosses and no arms. Criminals were among them and also friendly Indians who had helped much, traveling to hunt the killers. The soldiers killed all of the Indians.

"At the murders of so many innocents," Kino wrote, "for there were only five or six of the delinquents there, the relatives of the dead were aroused and stirred up to such a degree that after the garrison had retired or gone away, they burned the houses or chapels" of Magdalena and three other places, destroying all supplies, cattle, and horses. To punish this, a third expedition of 150 presidio soldiers and many friendly Indians went clear to the Chiricahua Mountains, where they found heaps of the stolen property and the spoils of a soldier recently captured alive after his three companions were killed. Owing to easy prejudice and no investigation, Pimas had been suffering for the deeds of Chiricahua Apaches.

In 1695 Théran de los Ríos was busy with three companies hunting down and killing Jocomes and Janos tribesmen, distributing captives among his soldiers. The following year a Chief Quique tried to stir up a general reprisal in northern Chihuahua and Sonora, but he was killed and ten of his associates were hanged.

There were endless raids and retaliations, treacheries and massacres by one side and then the other. Let a further sampling be enough. In 1699 and 1700 the Spanish were hunting down Seris to recover delinquents and apostates. In 1703 Janos, Sumas, and Apaches were pushing farther into Sonora. In 1751 the Pimas and Papagos rose up together in the Tubac area, murdered priests in Caborca and Sonóita, and drove owners and workers away from mines and ranches. Pimas and Seris were again in revolt in 1768 to 1770, and in 1777 the Seris revolted again. In 1781 Fray Francisco Garcés and scores of Spanish soldiers were killed in a bloody Quechan coup near Yuma.

What precipitated this slaughter? Fray Juan Díaz had predicted trouble from the Quechans, whom he saw as thieving and fickle, unless "our nation establishes itself at some points on these rivers." He himself was killed by Yumans in 1780, the year that Commandante General Teodoro Croix ordered "two pueblos of Spaniards in the territory of the Yuma Indians." In these military colonies the Quechans were voluntarily to seek conversion and work side by side with Spaniards. (These Indians kept resistance alive through two succeeding national regimes until defeated up the river, near the present town of Blythe, by Maj. Samuel Heintzelman, U.S.A., in 1852.)

By 1790, shortly before the first Washington administration began to make war on the Indians in Ohio, the official policy of the Spanish viceroy was frankly secular—do anything to keep the Indians quiet, or kill them. The Spanish military policy, as Spaniards saw it, had a steady measure of success. It produced bonanzas of beef and bullion. By force of arms the later Mexican government, joined in time by the United States, carried on the Europeanizing of the sandy subcontinent.

CHAPTER 13

THE COMING OF THE ANGLOS

the Spanish are Anglos (ie, white people—alt altho very cruel "people" more like devils)

*"Yanqui" expansion, Mexican retreat, and a treaty that
fixed the borders of the present-day Southwest*

DESPITE THE EXTERNAL PRESSURES from the central government in Mexico City and Madrid, and the internal pressures from native Indians, a regional European civilization developed and held firm. In Nueva Vizcaya and Nuevo Méjico and in Sonora, which sometimes acted like an independent nation, men carried on a medieval civilization. Environment dictated. Rivers and acequias held villages together. Men divided land into long strips which ran from riverbank upslope to the main ditch, or Acequia Madre. Most implements and household utensils and furnishings were made of wood. Homes and public buildings were in the Moorish style of Spain—flat roofed, mud-plastered, similar to the native pueblo style with its protruding beams because they were produced by the same type of natural setting and a parallel age-old pattern of life.

For most Spaniards, Mexicans, converted Indians, and *genizaros* (persons of mixed Indian ancestry, with additions sometimes from lusty masters), life meant family life, a simple economy, a brief education, trail-like roads, religious festivals, and domination by the priest, the governor, the commandante, and a rich family or two.

Early nineteenth–century Spanish officials and then the Mexicans who declared themselves independent of Spain faced in turn the international aggressions of Europeans and Yankees who sailed illegally into the ports on the long California coastline. Also, from the east came commercial probings by Louisiana Frenchmen, United States explorers or spies like Zebulon Pike, trappers, and traders. Former United States citizens seized a huge chunk of Mexico and set up the Republic of Texas, which produced a claim to New Mexico east of the Rio Grande and undertook to control the area.

After Texas joined the United States in 1845, the *Yanquis* pushed formidably against Mexico, whether the boundary was the Nueces River, as the Mexicans claimed, or the Rio Grande, as the Texans said. Thoughtful, articulate Mexicans, long sensitive to foreign agents, now feared for Mexican civilization. The budding struggle to halt *Yanqui* expansion was, as a Mexican wrote of Texas in 1840, a "war of race, of religion, of language, and of customs."

A year later the newspaper *El Siglo Diez y Nueve* *(19th c.)* saw Mexico as Catholic, generous, impetuous, and warlike and the aggressors as Protestant, calculating, businesslike, and astute. Mexicans knew what United States whites did to blacks, Indians, and Mexicans. They knew that the United States would defend slavery. They argued that in acquiring Florida the United States had insulted, cheated, and robbed the Spanish. Newspaper readers in Mexico City knew of the pejorative attitude toward Mexico and Mexicans in the New Orleans and New York journals. In response, the press and public opinion in Mexico City built up such pressure that the Mexican government was forced into a war for which it was not physically prepared.

Meanwhile the government of the United States, firmly led by President James Polk, of Tennessee, was bringing on a geopolitical war for which many citizens were not morally prepared. If the war was fought to extend the domains of chattel slavery, it failed, since

pages stuck together~ better to just tear 'em out?

*Water carriers photographed in January 1882 at the fountains in the Plaza de Armas,
Ciudad Chihuahua, where Doniphan's wild Missourians bathed in 1847.*

Doniphan's army marching southward across the waterless reaches of the Jornada del Muerto in southern New Mexico, before the surprise battle of El Brazito. See pic

the meager lands of the great interior deserts could not support the southern system. But it did fulfill the "manifest destiny" of the nation to engross a broad band of the continent from sea to shining sea. It did not fail to add to the American domain, as did the War of 1812, aimed at seizing Canada. It did not seize all of Mexico—a notion as old as young Aaron Burr and as new as some senators who debated the peace treaty in 1848. It gave the United States what the country had not acquired before and has not since— a huge, dry, sunwashed tract of true desert.

The most important battles of 1846 and 1847, those that defeated the armies of Gen. Antonio López de Santa Anna and that soon helped to turn "Old Rough and Ready," a general, into the President, took place south of Corpus Christi and near the Gulf: at Palo Alto, Resaca de la Palma, Monterrey, Buena Vista,

Cerro Gordo, Molino del Rey, and Chapultepec. It was a West Point war. West Point graduates directed the campaigns in the central war theater, fought the classic battles, and—without knowing it—trained for the next conflict. More than 160 young Mexican War officers, West Pointers, were to become generals, northern or southern, in the Civil War. At the same time in the northern Mexican deserts, frontiersmen and Missouri farm boys raised with squirrel rifles in their hands played hardy, significant roles.

AFTER THE UNITED STATES had declared war in May 1846, President Polk ordered Col. Stephen Watts Kearny, commanding officer at the western outpost of Fort Leavenworth and commander of the First Dragoons, to prepare an expedition to march on New Mexico and conquer it. A man of action and strong discipline, stern but courteous, inspiring respect, Kearny acted promptly. In June he had under way all sections of his Army of the West, which reached a total of almost seventeen hundred men. Among these were the First Dragoons; two companies each of infantry and light artillery; a party of topographical engineers commanded by Lt. William H. Emory; about fifty Indian scouts; an interpreter; a mounted company, the Laclede Rangers, from St. Louis; and Doniphan's regiment of 860 volunteers. (Polk had called on the governor of Missouri to furnish a thousand mounted volunteers. The men, who quickly signed up for a year, elected a frontier lawyer and fellow private, Alexander Doniphan, to be their colonel.)

More than fifteen hundred wagons jolted westward with the army, and there were hundreds of horses, thousands of mules, and more than fourteen thousand oxen intended for food, as in the days of Anza and Coronado. Later to come were the Second Missouri Mounted Volunteers and a force of Mormons being recruited among Latter-Day Saints camped near Council Bluffs.

Kearny's expedition crossed the plains on the Santa Fe Trail and by July 31 was concentrated across the Arkansas River from Charles Bent's fortified trading post. "The fort is crowded to overflowing," wrote Susan Magoffin. "Col. Kearny has arrived and it seems the world is coming with him." James Magoffin had arrived at Bent's after a sixteen-day buggy trip from Independence. With him were his brother Samuel and Samuel's young bride Susan, a faithful diarist. James Magoffin, a Santa Fe trader, married into a prominent Chihuahua family, had been the United States consul in Chihuahua and Durango, and a few weeks before had been talking with Senator Benton of Missouri, Secretary of War Marcy, and President Polk. Polk had given him letters and sent him to catch up with Kearny.

Kearny sent "Don Santiago" Magoffin ahead with Capt. Philip St. George Cooke and twelve dragoons, and a letter to Governor Manuel Armijo. Magoffin was to persuade Armijo not to fight and to bribe him. The letter told Armijo that Kearny came "as a friend & with the disposition and intention to consider all Mexicans & others as friends who will remain quietly & peaceably at their homes & attend to their own

affairs." It also said that he was determined to take possession of the country but that the inhabitants would be secure "in their Persons, their Property, their Religion."

Apparently, Armijo at first decided not to fight. Magoffin also somehow "reached" Col. Diego Archuleta, a man of patriotism and principle who was hot to resist the invaders. Kearny and his party made their way from Bent's over the difficult Raton Pass, through rough country, and on August 14 down into the irrigated valley of Las Vegas with its fields of waving corn. As Lieutenant Emory saw it, from a short distance the village "looked like an extensive brick-kiln. On approaching, its outline presented a square with some arrangements for defence." Kearny learned that a few miles ahead, at the next gorge, six hundred Mexicans waited to fight. He placed his camp for a mile along the stream and posted sentinels to keep hungry and jaded nags from getting into the unfenced cornfields.

Early on the fifteenth the army moved into Las Vegas. On the way officers from Fort Leavenworth rode up with papers promoting Kearny to brigadier general. At 8:00 A.M. the general was in the public square, where he was met by the alcalde and citizens, "many of whom were mounted, for these people," said Emory, "seem to live on horseback."

Kearny had the alcalde lead him up a rickety ladder to the top of one of the flat-topped, one-story houses facing the plaza. From there he spoke. His interpreter Antoine Roubideau translated the speech into Spanish. There stood the new general, a New Jersey man and a veteran of the War of 1812, fifty-two years old, a small, plain man with seamed cheeks and pale blue eyes. In a short speech he absolved the populace from allegiance to Mexico and put them under the protection of the United States. He guaranteed religious freedom and made the town authorities swear allegiance to his country.

Within the hour Kearny was leading his excited army toward the gorge and the six hundred Mexicans, but no one saw any Mexicans. "The men looked disappointed," Emory wrote, "and a few minutes found us dragging our slow lengths along with the usual indifference in regard to every subject except that of overcoming space." During the next couple of days Kearny received reports that Armijo, who had three

The city of Chihuahua (1882) dominated the royal road between Santa Fe and Ciudad Méjico.

We were there, 1968

thousand men available, was mobilizing for an armed stand at Apache Canyon nearer Santa Fe. These rumors were true, for though Armijo preferred to seem brave rather than to be brave, fellow countrymen had forced him to make preparations. But by the time the Army of the West reached the canyon, a tangle of brush and rocks and cliffs that could have been strongly defended, the Mexican army had evaporated. Armijo had fled Santa Fe and headed south. On the eighteenth Kearny marched into the capital without ever having fired a shot. His arrival was not a conquest but an occupation.

KEARNY, WHO HIMSELF had War Department orders to proceed to the coast and assist in the taking and organizing of California, ordered Col. Sterling Price to succeed him as the military leader in New Mexico, and he had special commands for Cooke and Doniphan. On September 25 Kearny and his First Dragoons left Santa Fe for a march down the Rio Grande. In southern New México he met Kit Carson and sixteen men headed eastward from Commodore Stockton and Major Frémont in California with dispatches for the Navy and War departments in Washington. He persuaded Carson to entrust the messages to others and turn back to guide him on the Gila River route to California.

On September 28 Colonel Price arrived in Santa Fe with the Second Missouri Regiment of Mounted Infantrymen. "Old Pap Price," a Missouri Democrat and tobacco broker, had been elected colonel by the volunteers. Lieutenant Cooke was busy in Santa Fe outfitting Mormons who had walked from Nauvoo, Illinois, accompanied by many women. Cooke and 350 Mormon men—the only battalion in U. S. Army history with all men of the same sect—were to find a wagon road from Santa Fe to California. They started out on October 19 with guides and Antoine Leroux, a mountain man.

Near El Paso they turned southwest and cut across a dry interior basin of the Chihuahua Desert. They passed the dusty bed of the Mimbres River and went on to the water sinks at Ojo de Vaca, on the trail from the Santa Rita copper mines to Janos. They traversed bits of scrawny prairie, shimmering dry lakes, and pale grasslands. Now and then in sandy washes they got water by digging; one isolated spring held only enough water for fifty animals. The guides missed Guadalupe Pass, and the Mormons had to get the wagons through precipitous rocky mountains by lifting wagons and lowering them by ropes or by taking them apart. Down at last into a broad valley, they passed by the ruins of the great Rancho San Bernardino, devastated by Apaches, and had to fight off bulls in longhorn herds gone wild. They went northward down the San Pedro River until they turned west to "Tueson," after which they had a grueling thirty-mile stretch without water on the way to the Gila River and the gentle, helpful Pimas and Maricopas.

But the worst lay ahead—getting the wagons west from the Colorado River to San Diego. The sand dunes and the scarcity of drinkable water in the northwestern Sonora Desert wore out men, mules, and horses, and put the men to the ultimate test. "I encountered extraordinary obstacles to a wagon road," Cooke reported, "and actually hewed a passage, with axes, through a chasm of solid rock, which lacked a foot of being as wide as the wagons." Cooke "made it almost a point of honor to bring the wagons through to the Pacific." He succeeded and was the first to bring a wagon train over the desert mountains.

By December 14 Doniphan was able to follow his primary orders, to march to Ciudad Chihuahua and there join forces with Gen. John Wool. Wool was to march inland from the Gulf and cut off northern Mexico. Doniphan's party, designed for speed, totaled 856 men and 85 wagons. But the party was slowed down—cluttered, even—by traders who had been delayed by the war. These commercial men, irrelevant to a military expedition, had 315 wagons of goods they wanted to sell in Chihuahua.

Doniphan's long march, compared then and later to Xenophon's anabasis, was partly a rollicking, undisciplined hunting party of companionship, card playing, and jest, together with a luxurious stay of wine, women, and song in El Paso del Norte. It was also partly an ordeal of waterless hardship and strain, as in the crossing of the Jornada del Muerto, a test of fortitude in the nineteenth century as it had been in the sixteenth, and in the sand dunes of Samalayuca—Los Médanos—and on south across sunbaked plains and passes where man and beast crowded to suck at muddy puddles. Several men died, one from bloating at a spring. Near Encinillas a careless soldier set fire to a field of dry grass that threatened to ignite the caravan.

The march was also partly war—two battles. At the Battle of El Brazito in southern New Mexico, a Mexican force of cavalry, infantrymen, lancers, and a howitzer drew up in a line two miles long. This force, commanded by Capt. Ponce de Léon, caught the Americans pitching camp. Doniphan ordered his men to form in line on foot. His order was "Prepare to squat." As they squatted the Mexicans fired, and the bullets went over their heads. Then, kneeling, they fired back with the same skill with the rifle that had enabled the Revolutionary Carolina riflemen to rout the redcoats at King's Mountain. They fired alternately, one group firing only when the other stopped to reload. The Mexicans wounded 7 volunteers but themselves lost 63 killed and 172 wounded, including their commander, who reported to his superiors: "*Americanos* do not fight as we do."

As the army approached Ciudad Chihuahua, it learned of Mexican preparations — redoubts, breastworks, and guns, under the command of Gen. José A. Heredia, on a hillside above the Río Sacramento. Heredia had 1,200 cavrymen, 300 artillerymen, 1,200 infantrymen, and 1,400 civilian volunteers with lances, machetes, and lassos. Sightseers were there to await the Mexican victory. But despite the Mexican superiority in men and emplacements, Doniphan won with unorthodox movement of his cavalry, which swung in from the side; with the careful sharpshooting of his Missouri frontiersmen; and with a speedy, mobile use of howitzers. He had the howitzers rushed into position near the Mexican line, and at a crucial time he had his men dismount and stampede forward on foot, sweeping up to the redoubts on the plain with hot gunfire. The United States losses were slight, the Mexican ones great in deaths and wounds.

The next day the Missourians marched into Chihuahua and camped in the plaza, bathed in its fountains, chopped down its trees for wood, and placed cannon facing the approaching streets. They were hairy with uncut beards and sunburned to brown and black. Their fringed buckskin jackets and homespun pants were torn and unkempt. Doniphan termed his men "rough, ragged, and ready." *Chihuahuenses* saw them as burros, but they were conquerors. Doniphan issued a proclamation declaring that the victorious United States laid claim to Chihuahua.

GENERAL WOOL was nowhere in sight, and no one knew where he was. Doniphan waited while the men grew restless. After he learned that "Old Granny Wool," more a disciplinarian and housekeeper than a fighter, was in Saltillo far to the east, Doniphan sent a dozen riders hurrying across the desert, moving at night to avoid detection, to ask for instructions. When rumors circulated that the riders had died, Doniphan talked things over with his men. Some lieutenants wanted to go on to Mexico City. Doniphan shouted, "I'm for going home to Sarah and the children!"—which spoke for most.

But on April 22 the riders returned. The regiment was to report to Wool. Off tramped the Volunteers for another long, hard, hot, dry, thirsty desert crossing, with occasional thunderstorms and drenchings. Once, Comanches attacked and ran off horses. Near the battlefield of Buena Vista, the finicky Wool reviewed them and formally praised them; a few days later General Taylor reviewed them at Monterrey, after which they moved to Matamoras and sailed for New Orleans. In thirteen months they had covered 3,500

A monument on the Arizona-Sonora boundary testifies to the epic achievements of Mexican and United States topographical engineers who surveyed the long international line through rough, arid terrain.

3500 miles. One soldier called the march "the most extraordinary and wonderful Expedition of the age."

THE WAR ENDED formally on February 2, 1848, in the suburban Guadalupe Hidalgo, north of Mexico City. The treaty was the work of Nicholas P. Trist, chief clerk in the State Department, an expert in the Spanish language, and husband of Jefferson's granddaughter. He was Polk's presidential agent, acting under secret instructions, yet he got involved in the intrigues of Polk's incompetent crony, Gen. Gideon Pillow. Even after Trist received a letter recalling him, he stayed to negotiate, for he was correctly confident that he could get a treaty on almost exactly the terms

Polk wanted. Trist failed to get Baja California, which would have meant a seaport for Arizona, but for $15 million he bought 530,000 square miles—New Mexico, Arizona, Utah, Nevada, California, and part of Colorado. Mexico ceased to be the fourth largest country in the world, and the United States became a continental power.

The treaty established the Rio Grande as the boundary as far as the New Mexico line, and then, using the latest map—Disturnell's—described the land line to the Gila, down it to the Colorado, and then straight across to a point south of San Diego. The treaty set up a commission to survey the long boundary, provided for sharing navigation on the Colorado,

Gila, and Rio Grande rivers and any railroad built on either side of the Gila. One article granted United States citizenship to Mexicans now established in territories previously belonging to Mexico and protected the property of Mexicans not established in the territories now in the United States. The new citizens had the constitutional protection of their liberty and property, and the free exercise of their religion. The United States agreed to use force to stop the incursions of "savage tribes" into Mexico. The United States agreed to prohibit the buying of Mexicans or of Mexican livestock or other property acquired by Indians inside Mexico.

Both nations took the boundary survey seriously. Ahead lay eight years of intermittent work to survey the Rio Grande and the arbitrary land boundary through forbidding terrain. One confusing problem that held up action was grave errors of location in Disturnell's map, which, for instance, put El Paso thirty-four miles too far north and a hundred miles too far east. The solutions included painstaking new computations of latitude and longitude, fresh map making, and a treaty arranged by James Gadsden in 1853. The United States paid Mexico $10 million for a tract of desert south of the Gila, a strip where the South hoped to see a railroad to the Pacific. Gadsden's treaty also cancelled the futile United States promise at Guadalupe Hidalgo to restrain the Indians from raiding into Mexico.

The completion of the international survey line, marked by stone monuments, was a frontier achievement, particularly for Maj. José Salazar y Larregui and William H. Emory, at that time also a major. The men of the international surveying parties faced irregular delivery of provisions, undependable water supplies, damage to delicate surveying instruments, and problems of triangulation, especially along the deep, winding, dangerous canyons of the big bend of the Rio Grande. They endured dust storms, uncompromising sun and heat — all the extremes of the deserts. On the one hand were floods at base survey points on the Colorado; on the other was a 240-mile stretch along the line between Sonora and Arizona in the organpipe cactus country with one known spring: Quitobaquito.

MEXICO MAINTAINED its sovereignty, and not until Porfirio Díaz assumed dictatorial powers in the 1880s would Yankee economic penetration begin. But New Mexico and Arizona were now Yankee provinces. The Treaty of Guadalupe Hidalgo had protected the Mexican–Americans in all their property rights. But Anglos coming in eager for land found the best acreages assigned to the holders of Spanish or Mexican land grants. Grants of as many as 50,000 acres seemed immoral to Americans used to sections of 640 acres or quarter sections of 160. A great land grab began— challenges to titles; land sales to pay taxes, legal fees, or debts; and squatting or violent trespass. Anglo owners replaced the *hacendados* of the old regime.

To a degree the few Americans who settled down in their new Southwest, far from their base of supply, adjusted to the regional life. They learned irrigation, built adobe homes with cottonwood ceiling beams, ate local food, spoke Spanish words, ranched in old ways, and more or less forgot about progress.

Prospectors and miners, ever active, and the timber cutters who came with them, meant economic revolution in the wilderness, as did land reclaimers like Jack Swilling on the Salt River and rowdies who assaulted and massacred Indians and stirred them to reprisals. And when the railroads steamed through in the 1880s the way was open to fast and violent change. The worst fears of the Mexican journalists of the 1840s would be largely realized as the culture of the American empire took its course southwestward.

PART FOUR

THE LEGACY
OF
PROGRESS

*At the turn of the century, smokestacks of copper
smelters alongside the Rio Grande at El Paso
symbolized progress and prosperity—not,
as seventy years later, environmental hazard.*

CHAPTER 14

MAKING AND HOLDING AN EMPIRE

*Trappers and traders, freighters and stagers, and troopers
along the Santa Fe–California Trail*

BEFORE THE TREATY of Guadalupe Hidalgo, the government, Spanish or Mexican, had law and wisdom on its side when it imprisoned trappers and other interlopers—like Zebulon Pike—who trespassed on the northern desert domain. They rode or tramped along its streams, they trapped the large, reddish-tan beavers, and they shot the bighorns for food. They respected the Indians only when they were useful or dangerous. Confident, quick to see possibilities of comfort and profit, capitalistic, and alert to the main chance, these pragmatic explorers were early working west from Raton Pass, Taos, and Santa Fe, down the branches of the upper Gila. Ever pushing westward, they found routes, located passes and oases, and sized up the strengths of Indian villages and Spanish-speaking garrisons. Some trappers crossed via the Virgin River, Las Vegas, the Mojave, and Cajon Pass to San Gabriel and Los Angeles, a route used by Jedediah Smith

Others used a southern route. In 1824 Sylvester Pattie, a Missourian, his son James Ohio Pattie, and others trapped along the Gila from New Mexico into Arizona. Beaver were abundant; the river was full of fish; grass was thick. Bighorns flocked within easy gun range on the hillsides. The trappers buried hundreds of beaver skins. Later, Indians took their horses and supplies, dug up the cache and "stole" the skins. At one time the seven trappers, starving, got so desperate that they ate a buzzard.

Two years later, while his father stayed to manage the Santa Rita copper mines, James joined a party of French-Canadian trappers. "I had a desire, which I can hardly describe, to see more of this strange and new country." Near the junction of the Gila and Salt rivers, Papagos massacred all but the leader and James Pattie. The two survivors met and joined a trapping party led by Ewing Young. They trapped down to the Colorado and then turned upstream. They caught as many as thirty beavers a night, especially in "lakes"—ox-bow lagoons of the river at low water. They met Mojaves and Hopis, who used slings as weapons. When they entered Santa Fe in 1827, Governor Armijo confiscated their year's catch.

Later in the year Pattie traveled to Sonora and the sea, and returned via Chihuahua. The exact route is unclear in his account, but his eye was as sharp for economic resources as for local talents. He praised the vaqueros' skill at noosing cattle and taming wild horses, and he admired the matadors. He liked the bottom land and the sugar cane farms near "Ymus" (Guaymas) and the level black soil along the Río Sonora; but with a gringo regard for modern efficiency, he commented on the awkward design of plows, hoes, and axes in shapes hardly modified since the days of the elder Cato. He preferred the Indians and Mexicans to the Spanish, as he spoke of "a people who have no saw mills, no labor saving machinery, and do everything by dint of hard labor." For Pattie, as for many other travelers, El Paso del Norte and the valley downstream was an oasis of wheat fields and vineyards.

During the winter of 1827–1828, the two Patties and a party trapped westward again. The Yumas were delighted to see them and, as in Anza's days, fell flat on the ground when the Patties shot off guns. The trap-

Fort Union, which from 1851 to 1891 protected parts of New Mexico, Colorado, and the Santa Fe Trail, is now a ruin guarded by the National Park Service.

165

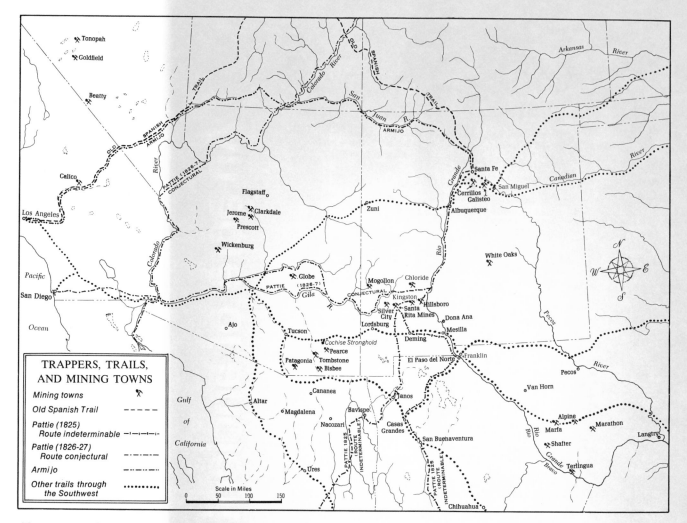

Trappers and prospectors on long migrations explored the new country with a passion. Where ores were rich, mining towns flourished, then died; only a few, like Bisbee and Cananea, still survive.

pers turned downstream, catching as many as sixty beaver a night, and sometimes raccoons, too. They marvelled at the dangerous bore as the tide rushed in over the low delta. They were in an area where whites were an almost unknown sight. Once Indians rushed upon them yelling and armed with clubs, bows, and arrows. The trappers made signs of friendship, and the Indians asked in Spanish who they were. "We answered *Americans,*" says James. "They repeated the name, asking if we were friends and Christians? To these questions we made a ready affirmative." All seated themselves on the ground and began a council of interrogation. The pipe was passed; the Indians dug a

hole and buried in it a war ax and all ill feelings.

Whole families now came up to the trappers, studying their red flannel shirts and their white skins. Some women made up to a very white trapper with fair, soft skin and blue eyes. They wanted him to strip himself naked so that they might explore him to see if he were white everywhere. He mildly declined. They went off and brought back a quantity of excellent dried fish and gave it to him:

"We persuaded him to oblige these curious and good natured women by giving them a full view of his body. He was persuaded to strip to his skin. This delighted them, and they conversed and laughed among themselves, and they came one by one and stood beside him; so as to compare their bodies with his. After this, as long as we staid, they were constantly occupied in bringing us cooked fish and the vegetables and roots on which they are accustomed to feed."

The trappers continued west over the desert, stumbled into the hands of authorities in Baja California, who arrested them, and landed in the San Diego prison. There the elderly Pattie died. The Patties were the third trapping party to reach southern California. Soon there would be Ewing Young, Kit Carson, and others.

The reports of trappers and their maps scratched on the ground or traced on hides aided the whole successive series of invaders—trespassers or military victors—from traders and troopers to stagecoach drivers and prospectors. Here and there, at the various rendezvous in the central Rockies or at the annual fairs in Taos, traders provided indispensable items. For much as the trappers knew about living Indian-style, close to the land, the game, the fish, they needed American and European technology. Their metal traps came from eastern factories; their flintlock long rifles and bullet molds from cities like Philadelphia; their axheads and "Green River" skinning knives came perhaps from Greenfield, Massachusetts; and their pipe tomahawks, like those of the Indians, often were imported from England. The market for their beaver pelts was the big cities, from St. Louis to London, where men wore tophats covered with fur. Wild though trappers seemed with their whang-leather saddles and their fringed, beaded bullet pouches, their hairy heads, and their outlandish dialect, they only served as the rough, exploitative edge of trans-Atlantic sophistication, killing beaver for distant dandies. When beaver hats went out of fashion in 1837, trappers began to face technological unemployment.

IN CONTRAST, the flexible and expedient middlemen, the traders, had more and more business as commerce in and out of Santa Fe grew steadily in importance. In 1829–1830 Antonio Armijo opened the first commercial venture westward over the route later called the Old Spanish Trail, from Santa Fe through southern Utah, and Nevada to Los Angeles and San Diego. It was a trail for mules, not for wagons. It was

"the longest, crookedest, most arduous pack mule route in the history of America."

Portions of the Spanish Trail were used by horse thieves herding stolen California horses eastward, by slave dealers who captured Ute women and children for sale as domestic workers, by official adventurers such as John Charles Frémont, and by Yankee residents of New Mexico leaving for California after the uprising of 1837. The Utah-California portion was later called the Mormon Trail. The diarists of the time had good words for Las Vegas—"The Meadows." A man noted in 1848 that Vegas meant a spring, grass, and "water enough in this rapid little stream to propel a grist mill. . . . And, oh! *such* water. It comes, too, like an oasis in the desert, just at the termination of a 50 mi. stretch without a drop of water or a spear of grass."

Eight years before Armijo started west from Santa Fe, William Becknell and four other men used pack horses to carry trade goods from Franklin, Missouri, westward to Santa Fe. When he returned home, Becknell tumbled a heap of coin on the ground to announce a profit of 2,000 percent. The following year Becknell and twenty-one others took the first wagon party westward, pioneering the Río Cimarrón cutoff route to San Miguel and Santa Fe. Becknell's wagon wheels rolling over the thick buffalo grass opened an era of commercial caravans and quasi-military expeditions, expansionist imperial politics sponsored by Senator Benton, defensive measures by Indians and Mexicans—a sturdy, economic penetration. Traders, not missionaries, were making a path for the conquering United States volunteers and troops of the later 1840s.

Within a few years the Santa Fe Trail, with variant cutoffs, ran approximately 775 miles from Independence, Westport, and Shawnee Mission to Council Grove, west along the Arkansas River, to Fort Dodge and Fort Mann, across the dry sixty-mile *jornada* to the Cimarron River crossing, Point of Rock in the extreme southeastern tip of Colorado, Camp Nichols in the extreme northwest tip of Oklahoma, the little buttes called Rabbit Ear, Canadian Crossing, La Junta, Pecos, and Santa Fe. Leaving the Missouri towns, highly organized and defended parties trespassed across immense plains defended in turn by well-armed, well-mounted Iowas, Pawnees, Cheyennes, Arapahoes, Co-

A high moment in the lives of hundreds of traders on the long trip west from Missouri:
the first glimpse of Santa Fe, capital of the Southwest.

manches, and Apaches, where water, wood, and shade were scarce, and where the livestock soon ate all the grass. Daily men faced broken axles, split axletrees, and horses driven half-mad by flies. Mosquitoes kept men awake all night. At river crossings the quicksand endangered man, beast, and wagon. And at the western end of the trail the traders faced arbitrary Mexican authorities who slapped on import taxes.

Santa Fe, goal of the Missouri expeditions and headquarters for the Americanization of the Southwest, was reached after eight to ten weeks. It opened the eyes of men from "the States." Here was a flat-roofed, one-story adobe town on a high plain, backed with forest and high peaks. The plaza was a confused marketplace shaded by a few ragged cottonwoods, a center

for throngs of people—gaunt, tobacco-chewing Missourians, Indians, soldiers, Spanish matriarchs wrapped in rebozos. Some young women smoked and flirted; others walked with glaring escorts. Mixed in were horses, mules, and strings of donkeys laden with towering packs of wood, fodder, and melons. Along the narrow side streets stood gambling halls. Dried meat and chili peppers hung from portals. At funerals bands of musicians, mostly violinists, marched rapidly along. At fandangos in homes people drank wine and brandy, and danced with energy and grace the Italiana or the Cuna, which was largely a waltz. At one such party Lt. J. W. Abert, a topographical engineer, studied the ladies draped in "stuffs most rich and skirts of monstrous width or fulness [sic]. While sitting down they

168

were wrapped in splendid shawls and gazed around the room with great complaisance, at same time smoking the cigarrito. These they make by rolling tobacco up in corn shucks prepared for that purpose."

Santa Fe people wanted goods that the St. Louis and Independence merchants delivered—shawls, handkerchiefs, hose, cambrics, looking glasses, cutlery, clocks, chairs, chinaware, rugs, chandeliers, candlesticks, guns, ammunition, steelyards, and anvils. Santa Fe had furs and two other things that Missouri traders particularly wanted. One was silver pesos; these became more common than United States dollars in Missouri, kept the state on a solid hard-money basis, and saved its banks from the dangers of fluctuation in the value of paper currency that troubled much of the nation. The other thing traders wanted was mules. The Missouri mule, a mobile commodity as profitable and famous in its day as the later Detroit automobile, originated as the Mexican jack was bred with the American mare, producing a mule larger and stronger than the Mexican one. Also, the American stallion and the Mexican jennet produced an offspring "superior" to the Mexican one. By 1860 the Santa Fe Trail had turned Missouri into a mule kingdom. The trappers caught out the beaver, but the New Mexico breeders never ran out of droves of mules, jacks, and jennets.

Even by 1840 the phrase "Santa Fe trade" was partly a misnomer, because Santa Fe was only in the middle of a trade, a hublike turning point in a far-flung enterprise. It operated southward along the old missionary and Oñate route to El Paso del Norte, Chihuahua, and on to Durango and Mexico City, which also received goods from the Gulf ports. From Santa Fe it operated eastward not only to Independence, but also from there by steamboat down the Missouri River to St. Louis, and from there up the rivers to Pittsburgh or down the Mississippi to New Orleans, and from there by ship to Philadelphia and to warehouses in Liverpool and Hamburg. The New Mexicans and northern Mexicans, reacting from centuries of colonial isolation, were eager for European rings, necklaces, cut glass, mirrors, writing paper, fancy dress stuffs, cologne, and champagne.

The international trade over the trail reached its climax in the 1840s. In 1846 some 363 wagons carried in a million dollars' worth of trade goods. The trade was a big business at the very moment when forces it had helped to create were about to end it with war. The trade had turned New Mexico away from Chihuahua by raising the standard of living. It had brought Anglos into the province and opened up routes for military invasion. It had poked a lasting hole in Indian control of the southern plains by killing the bison herds, commandeering the water holes, and stripping the cottonwood groves—a conquest by ecological destruction. It had fattened in every physical way the aggressive United States conception of a fated national transaction with destiny. The land of the Seven Cities of Cíbola would become American, and from them a road would lead to California, where golden cities would grow and tower in the sky.

ONCE PRESIDENT POLK had won his war and gained an empire of space and sun, the Santa Fe Trail—now a national road, a lifeline to new United States territory—supported a smooth, huge freighting business. There was heavy military freighting from Fort Leavenworth in eastern Kansas to Fort Union in northeast New Mexico. In 1849 there were about a thousand soldiers, or around a seventh of the United States Army, in New Mexico's Ninth Department. By 1859 there were two thousand, in sixteen outposts. In 1862 three thousand wagons with goods valued at forty million dollars moved into New Mexico—calicoes, shoes, flour, whiskey, musical instruments, even pianos, fire engines, and machinery and boilers for gringo mining operations.

Alexander Majors, the field man for the partnership of Russell, Majors, and Waddell, became the greatest freighter in the history of the trail. He set up careful rules for the mammoth caravans. There was to be no mistreatment of animals, not even any swearing, and no wagon trains camped together. His teamsters handled whipstocks ten feet long with buckskin lashes that they cracked like pistol shots, accurate on ox or snake. Only the railroads, the Kansas Pacific and the Denver and Rio Grande, Western, coming in the 1860s and 1870s, put the trail out of business. At the same time they put the age-old cultures of the pueblo Indians and Spanish villages into their greatest jeopardy yet.

By legitimizing American travel in the deserts, the Mexican War had opened up opportunities for fast

transportation. The discovery of California gold added an extra incentive to develop routes. In the early 1850s George Giddings, king of Texas stagecoaching, ran a mail route from San Antonio west past a series of army forts to Fort Davis, Van Horn's Well, on to Franklin (now El Paso), and north to Santa Fe. Giddings used the celerity wagon, or mud wagon, pulled by six mules, which he found functioned better in the desert than the Concord coach. Another firm, the Birch Company, ran stages between San Antonio and San Diego.

The most famous route was the one from St. Louis to Los Angeles and San Francisco that John Butterfield set up when he organized the Overland Mail Company in 1858. For three years, until the Civil War interfered, he had coaches running the 2,759-mile route in as few as twenty-one days. His stages forded the Pecos at Horsehead Crossing, went through the Guadalupe Pass of western Texas and past the salt lakes to Franklin, on past Fort Fillmore in New Mexico, Soldier's Farewell, Stern Springs in Arizona, Apache Pass—the most dangerous point on the entire route—Tucson, Maricopa, Yuma, Warner's Ranch, and on to Los Angeles.

At any time in the nineteenth and early twentieth centuries, stage travel in the West was more ordeal than adventure. Raphael Pumpelly, a mining engineer headed for the Santa Rita silver mines, described his trip in the fall of 1860 from St. Louis to Tucson. His journey was sixteen days and nights of continuous travel, riding backwards, with no rest at any time. He shared three seats with nine passengers. The riders on the front and middle seats faced each other, their knees interlocked. This means that each side of the coach had an extra leg, which dangled near the whirling wheel outside, or tried to find a place of support.

The heavy mail bags in the boot of the stage weighed down the rear and tilted up the front, so that the three front passengers, facing the rear, were constantly bending forward without support for their backs. Pumpelly's immediate neighbors were a tall Missouri man, his wife, and two daughters. The man was a border bully armed with revolver, rifle, and knife. His woman, a hag, dipped—"filling the air and covering her clothes with snuff." For several days the girls were "overcome by seasickness, and in this having no regard for the clothes of their neighbors." Hats kept blowing out of the windows and getting lost. There was danger of a Comanche attack, but nothing to do other than gawk out at the vast "republics" of prairie dogs. Pumpelly wrote that as the stage approached the Rio Grande, the "fatigue of uninterrupted travelling . . . was beginning to tell seriously on all the passengers, and was producing a condition bordering on insanity." People were flaring into angers and developing manias. While the stage jolted from El Paso west to Tucson, Pumpelly was lolling half-delirious. His neighbors kept jabbing their elbows into the ribs of his sprawling carcass. Painfully and amid hazards, he was conquering southwestern space, as were the soldiers of the army.

VICTORS TAKE on the problems of the defeated. The Mexicans, like the Spanish, had used a line of presidios to guard their borders from native Indian raiders. The winners of the Mexican-American affray had to send in an army to contain or suppress the same hostile Indians. From 1848 to 1890, until the Apaches were well subdued—a chapter in itself—forts went up to guard the road from San Antonio to Yuma and other roads at strategic points on the Pecos, the Canadian, the Rio Grande, and the Colorado rivers, in the Navajo country and especially in the several mountainous areas of the old Apachería, from Fort Stanton east of the Mescalero Apaches to Fort McDowell west of the White Mountain Apaches. The army was flexible; it founded, moved, and abandoned forts and camps as the need arose or ended.

Troopers stationed in the first federal forts, such as Fort Bliss and Fort Yuma, had immediate work after the gold discovery in California. Thousands of argonauts used the southern trails, including the road laid in 1849 from San Antonio past the Davis Mountains to El Paso. The *Houston Democratic Telegraph and Texas Register* said, "We think we may declare, without fear of contradiction, that the routes leading through Texas to California . . . possess advantages that entitle them to the most favorable consideration of the emigrant and the government." The routes opened up the region west of the Pecos with canyons of ash, oak, walnut, and bulging cottonwoods, grassy vales, and a few limpid streams, and also the bleak and sandy flats in interior basins of which one officer wrote: "It was a dreary sight to look upon the dull, wide

The abandoned headquarters building at Fort Davis, Texas, photographed sometime after 1907 but long before the National Park Service reconstructed it.

Formal army life during the era when soldiers guarded Anglo newcomers against the Indian raiders —probably Troops E and H of the Sixth Cavalry at Fort Stanton, New Mexico, ca. 1884–85.

waste around us; its parched barrenness, combined with the influence of a scorching July sun was enough to madden the brain."

The troops guarded the emigrant parties, the stagecoach lines, the United States mails, the local mines, and the trading towns. Detachments of men strung telegraph lines, patrolled the international border, or scouted for movements of Indians.

Forts in the Big Bend area, Forts Davis and Stockton, were near the Comanche war trail, down which Comanches and Kiowas rode, not only to raid Mexican villages and haciendas in Coahuila and Chihuahua, but also to plunder covered wagon parties heading for California. Fort Stanton, New Mexico, midway between Fort Bliss at the western tip of Texas and Fort Union in northeastern New Mexico, helped control the Mescalero Apaches, the sturdy people who liked to cut the central spike of the mescal plant into short

lengths and bake it for a day and a half in a deep pit before feasting on it.

FORT CRAIG, on the west bank of the Rio Grande at the northern entrance to the Jornada del Muerto, was a two-company post to protect westbound miners from the Navajo and Apache, and to guard the road between El Paso and Santa Fe. In 1851 Col. Edwin V. Sumner established Fort Defiance at Tsehotsoi ("Meadow Between the Rocks") amid hostile Navajos, with whom there was guerrilla warfare between 1858 and 1868. In 1861 the army abandoned Fort Defiance and moved the garrison to Fort Fauntleroy (now Fort Wingate), but in 1863 it reoccupied Fort Defiance, calling it Fort Canby. It was Col. Kit Carson's headquarters while he rounded up 8,500 Navajos, many of whom he marched to Bosque Redondo on the Pecos, where Fort Sumner soon appeared.

The hundreds of square miles of desert added to the United States by the Mexican War led the army and Congress to experiment with using camels for transportation. Varieties of dromedaries and Bactrians from several Mediterranean countries landed in two shiploads in 1856 and 1857, together with trainers and saddle makers. The army used them as beasts of burden in the party that surveyed wagon roads. Between May and October of 1857, the camel expedition crossed half the continent, from the Texas coast to San Antonio, to Fort Stockton and El Paso, Albuquerque, west across New Mexico and Arizona south of the Grand Canyon to Mohave City, and across the desert to Fort Tejon, on the far western rim of the North American deserts. The camels drank little; they ate most plants except grass; and they avoided sore feet since they lifted up their feet and put them down without any shuffle. On long distances, such as across Arizona on the Colorado Plateau, they did much better than mules. An officer in charge said, "The patience, endurance, and steadiness which characterize the performance of camels during the march is beyond praise." Wagon roads, congressional indifference, and the rise of pre–Civil War tensions ended the experiment. With roads, wheeled vehicles, and railroads in the offing, the camel had no utilitarian future.

JEFFERSON DAVIS and other southern leaders had backed the Mexican War and the Gadsden Purchase, official railroad surveys that gave ample attention to southwestern routes, and the camel experiment, as well. After secession, these same leaders sought to make the new desert territories, and California, too, part of the Confederate domain.

In 1861 Lt. Col. John Baylor and 600 Confederate Texans took Fort Bliss. Gen. H. H. Sibley and 2,300 men entered from Texas and at Valverde on the Rio Grande, near Fort Craig, fought and defeated 3,800 Union men under Gen. E. F. S. Canby. Sibley marched north and captured Albuquerque and Santa Fe but found no popular welcome as he had expected. When he headed through Apache Canyon, east of Santa Fe,

Union soldiers and Colorado Volunteers met him and defeated him. Nearby at Pigeon's Ranch, they captured his supply wagons. Of necessity he retreated.

In February 1862, Capt. Sherod Hunter and 100 Texas Confederate cavalry entered Tucson and continued on toward the Gila. At Picacho Pass, an open vale, they met a patrol of Union soldiers, part of the advance guard of the California Column. The troops skirmished. Three Union men and two Confederates died, and Hunter drew back.

Gen. James H. Carleton had trained the 1,600 men of the California Column—the First Infantry, California Volunteers—at barracks in Wilmington, California. After meticulous planning he had led them on a fully supplied, careful expedition across the desert—scouts going ahead to mark and clean wells—to Fort Yuma and beyond. He issued detailed orders to his officers: "Have your sabers very sharp, that they may readily cut through clothing. Cavalry recently mounted on California horses cannot use any kind of firearms with success. The men should practice dismounting to fight on foot a great deal." He was concerned about close fighting:

"If a rush is made by Texans on horseback with revolvers upon your cavalry while mounted, if the sabers are sharp I would recommend closing in with them as quick as thought. . . . In closing with cavalry against cavalry in hand-to-hand encounters on horseback, it is well to get your enemy in your power by cutting off his reins, killing his horse, etc. If your cavalry happen to be on foot and the Texans happen to be on foot, and attempt to make a rush upon your men with their revolvers, as is their custom, teach your men to use their side arms until the shots are exhausted and then the carbine."

Learning of Carleton's arrival in Arizona and Sibley's defeat in Apache Canyon, Hunter abandoned Tucson. When Carleton reached Tucson in June 1862, he proclaimed Arizona to be a United States territory under martial law. The column marched on eastward to reoccupy Arizona and New Mexico forts and help hold the Southwest for the conquering Union.

CHAPTER 15

METAL FEVER AND MONEY ON THE HOOF

*Mining and ranching—two ancient southwestern pursuits
of which fortunes and legends were made*

THE SKILLS IN MINING and metallurgy that came from Spain and flourished to the south in Guanajuato and San Luis Potosí became so inbred that Mexican men seemed almost to be born miners. The eye for valuable ore and the knowledge of how to dig it out, and transport it donkeyback, and convert it into bullion and coin—these opened mines and founded settlements on the cliffsides and shoulders of the Sierra Madre Occidental and in the canyons and valley bottoms from Alamos and Quitovac in Sonora to the Organ Mountains east of Las Cruces. Mexicans also found placers, as in the sands of the intermittent Río Altar or in the Ortiz Mountains of New Mexico.

It happened to be an Indian who discovered the rich copper mines of Santa Rita del Cobre in southwestern New Mexico. He told the Spaniard Lieutenant Carrasco in 1800. As first developed by Don Francisco Manuel Elguea of Chihuahua, the ore was so rich that workers carried it on pack mules and in wagons to Mexico City for reduction. There were long-lasting rich mines, too, in northern Sonora, as in the hills east of Tumacácori. But by and large in the Arizonan fringe of New Spain and then of the Republic of Mexico, mining was more prospecting than anything else as long as the Apaches rampaged, and at first United States mining was little or no better off.

There were discoveries in the 1850s, of copper at Ajo in Papago country and of gold placers on the Gila River upstream from Fort Yuma. The chief depot for mining supplies for northern Sonora and southern Arizona was Magdalena, "a parched confusion of adobe huts scattered over the slope of a barren hill like so many mud boxes." Magdalena, as J. Ross Browne saw it, also had its proud prefect and its poised women who carried *ojas*, earthen pitchers, on their heads. More important, it had common-man mining experts. After 1850, as before, it was Mexicans who taught Americans how to mine—how to pan stream sands, how to crush ores in arrastras or drag mines, how to roast ore in kilns, how to smelt silver in furnaces or extract it by mercury treatment in the patio process. Mexicans from villages and mines near Magdalena served as the principal working force in the Santa Cruz Valley after the Gadsden Purchase.

Yanquis led by Charles D. Poston settled on the site of the old presidio at Tubac (founded in 1752) while developing the Santa Rita, Heintzelman, Cerro Gordo, Patagonia, and other mines close by on the east. The silver lodes showed great promise and gave Arizona a reputation for silver production. In a prodigy of hard work by man and beast, two boilers—each weighing three tons—were freighted in 1,200 miles from Texas. One went to the Patagonia Mining Company.

At Tubac, Poston set up a "headquarters of civilization" that drew engineers and ladies of education and refinement. There were gardens shaded by acacias and peach trees. Deep pools in the Santa Cruz River, overhung by willows, became bathing places. Poston himself sat in the water and read newspapers. Everyone had plenty to eat from herds and crops in good bottom lands, wild game such as fat turkeys, and fancy imports such as Scotch whisky. By 1857 a thousand souls lived in and around the central hacienda. "We had no law but love," Poston later recalled, "no occupation but

*Headframe for the shaft of the U.S. Treasury Mine in the ore-rich Apache
Mining District in southwestern New Mexico, ca. 1900.*

The prefect of Magdalena, Sonora, in the 1860s —a symbol of authority and dignity.

labor. No government, no taxes, no public debt, no politics. It was a community in a perfect state of nature."

Under the laws of the Territory of New Mexico Poston was a syndic, or magistrate, and performed many marriages. When Father Mashboeuf, apostolic delegate of Bishop Lamy at Santa Fe, objected to these civil marriages, Poston prevailed on the bishop to add the sanction of the church to all the Carloses and Carlottas his marriage services had engendered.

At the Patagonia Mine, later called the Mowry, there was an almost model setup, a prefiguration of the company towns that grew up later in the century. There was a hacienda, a headquarters, and the mine itself. A visitor saw the houses of the elite, the quarters of the peons, the offices. He heard the hum of steam engines and flywheels; he smelled smoke from the mill and the charcoal pits, and the sulphurous vapors that whirled up from the smelting furnaces. He heard the clanking and smashing of the reduction works and the ax-chopping of the fuel woodcutters. Teamsters urged on the mules that pulled stolid wagons over rocky roads that were only twin trails.

After President Lincoln withdrew troops from the territory, there was the brief transit of the California Column, which eliminated Confederates, but there was no force to check hostile Indians or resentful Mexicans. The Apaches rushed in, raiding on both sides of the

new international line, knocking down the rock monuments, and Poston had to flee his oasis of exotic civilization. Once again Tubac became a ruin. While Nevada, California, Colorado, and other territories boomed in mineral production, while central Mexico continued to produce bullion, Arizona remained a kind of vacuum, one that sucked in, J. Ross Browne said, desperadoes from California and Sonora and Apaches from all over the Southwest.

During the Civil War Henry Wickenburg discovered the Vulture Mine—destined for a long life—in western Arizona. Then, one after another for half a century, important desert strikes took place—Prescott, Tombstone, Bisbee, Clifton, and Jerome in Arizona; Silver City, White Oaks, Cerillos, Galisteo, and Chloride in New Mexico; Beatty, Rhyolite, and Goldfield in Nevada; Calico, Bodie, and Panamint City in California; and Shafter in Texas. Men found silver at Shafter in the Chaniti Mountains in 1882 and mined it in miles of tunnels until 1942, when water flooded the mine. Other minerals—less glamorous than gold, silver, or copper—supported extensive workings, such as borax at Ryan in Death Valley, coal at Gallup, or mercury at Terlingua in the Big Bend badlands. The early discoveries each led to a rush, a new town, and a period of flamboyant affluence. The population, both of technical mining experts and of manual laborers, was likely to be dominated by immigrants. Western and southwestern towns were international phenomena. Later, a decline nearly always occurred in the mines and the vitality of the town, with a revival or two, and then ghosthood—followed sometimes by a sentimental touristic rejuvenation. Paralleling Central City in the Colorado Rockies or Virginia City in the Far West, Tombstone is a classic southwestern example.

IN 1877, WHEN TROOPS at Fort Huachuca were patrolling for aggressive Indians in the Huachuca Mountains, prospector Ed Schieffelin moved with them; but when they left the area, he stayed.

A soldier asked him, "Have you found anything?"

"Not yet, but I will find something some day," the prospector replied.

"Yes, you'll find your tombstone." The prediction proved to be literary or baptismal, not funereal, for Schieffelin lived out his days.

When he found two promising claims Schieffelin named them Tombstone and Graveyard. He and partners found float—surface rock—and traced it to an outcropping of ore worth a fabulous $9,000 a ton, and there they located the Lucky Cuss Mine and the Tough Nut, so named because it was hard to figure out the strike of the ledges.

Rising amid desolation, the town of Tombstone was booming in 1881, when it incorporated and became the county seat. Two years later it held seven thousand residents, and its surface real estate, laid out in rectangles, was worth more than a million dollars. A desirable lot measuring thirty by eighty feet, on Allen Street between Fourth and Sixth streets, was worth $6,000. Shanties that cost $50 to build rented for $15 a month. There were livery stables, stores, commercial (but not savings) banks, fraternal halls, shops for dark

suits and derby hats, and boarding houses like San Jose House—"Neat rooms with or without fire." There were the city hall, the county courthouse, a Chinese laundry, the C. S. Fly photography studio, Hart's Gun Shop, and the newspaper office for *The Epitaph*. In town stood the homes of the well-to-do. There were churches, though attendance tended to be meager. The reason for this, according to an old joke, was the balmy winter climate and the red-hot summers. Six months of the year heaven had nothing to offer; the other six hell had nothing to fear.

From the roof of the Grand Hotel or the Palace Lodging House amazed visitors looked down at the shafts, hoist works, and heaps of ore of the Vizina Mine, the Gilded Age, the Mountain Maid, or the Goodenough (which had the "Million Dollar Stope") —all in the very midst of town buildings. On the hill

This photograph of the Cliff Mine in New Mexico, probably taken in the 1880s, shows the tunnel, wheelbarrow, picks, and hand drills of a simple hand mining operation.

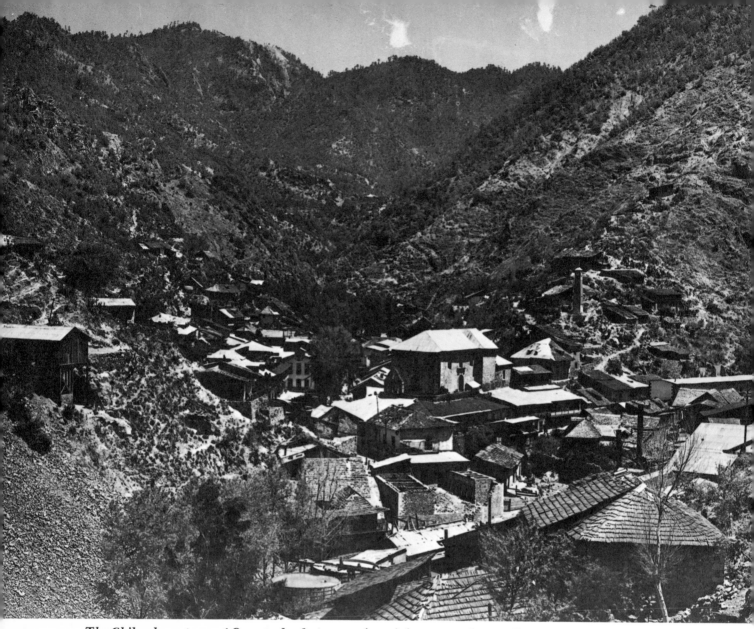

*The Chihuahuan town of Ocampo has been an active mining center since Indians
and Spaniards dug for gold and silver there in the eighteenth century.*

to the south were the Tough Nut, Contention, Lucky
Cuss, and other mines. The larger mines had extensive
wooden buildings, painted an Indian red. Inside were
handsome drafting and assay rooms and the desks of
the educated engineers and scientists necessary for
systematic and profitable underground mining. On the
outskirts of town were the workmen's huts and tents,
including tents with wooden doors and adobe chimneys. In one area stood an imposing set of wooden
buildings, the mule barns, a celebrated sight that all
strangers wanted to visit.

The basic labor of the town was underground, where
men worked every hour of every day digging out the

silver ore, which was blackish and resembled inferior
coal mixed with slate. Here was work for Mexicans,
immigrants from European nations, and Americans,
for the good wage of $4.00 a day for an eight-hour
shift or $3.50 for a shift above ground. Everything
depended on the production of the mines, which were
the sole reason for the town to exist.

Leisure hours followed the pattern long since set in
California and Nevada camps, with entertainment in
bagnios on the east side of town, at Blonde Mary's,
Dutch Annie's, or Big Nose Kate Fisher's, with gambling everywhere, and with alcoholic drinks in the two
principal hotels and at the Eagle Brewery, the Can-

Can Chop House, the French Rôtisserie, Alhambra, Maison Doré, City of Paris, Brown's Saloon, Fashion Saloon, Miners' Home, Kelly's Wine-House, the Grotto, the Tivoli, and at unnamed saloons. Cattlemen who brought in beef from Missouri or Texas wore wide felt sombreros and tailored clothing. At the hotel bars they were good for twenty to twenty-five dollars a day, and landlords found these easy spenders to be "perfect gentlemen." The leading theater, called the Olympic Opera House, then the Bird Cage, and later The Elite, attracted the leading itinerant minstrel-show and vaudeville entertainers of the era.

A visitor to Tombstone wrote: "From the hygienic point of view, whiskey and cold lead are mentioned as the leading diseases at Tombstone." Both went with the almost universal gun toting, especially by the rowdy element, which included cowboys who rustled cattle from nearby valleys in Arizona Territory and Sonora. It also included factions among officials supposed to keep law and order. In one faction were Deputy U. S. Marshal Wyatt Earp, City Marshal Virgil Earp, and "Doc" Holliday; in the other faction, backed by the sheriff, were two Clanton brothers and two McLowery brothers. The two McLowerys and one Clanton died in the celebrated gunfight in the O K Corral, commemo-

rated in Tombstone in 1970 with decaying, life-sized models on the very spot. After the Earp clan had fled to Colorado, a new sheriff, John Slaughter, pretty much put an end to crooked gambling, banditry, and rustling. He seldom took prisoners; instead, he chased suspects "clean out of the county." These suspects never re-appeared, anywhere.

In the late 1880's water began to fill the lower mining shafts. Expensive pumping equipment failed to solve the problem. The surface works of two big mines burned. By 1890 Tombstone was on the way to oblivion as a mining town, though new equipment after 1900 continued to work certain veins. But the place, as it advertises, was "Too Tough to Die." Then two books gave it a mythic aura and a sure-fire appeal to automobile tourists conditioned by decades of Western movies. The books were *Tombstone: An Iliad of the South-west* (1927) and *Wyatt Earp: Frontier Marshal* (1931).

LONGER-LIVED, STILL VIGOROUS after a century, and of vastly more economic importance, is Bisbee, which took the county seat away from Tombstone. Bisbee was crammed into the foot of a narrow, winding gulch in the Mule Pass Mountains. Like Tombstone, it was unlocated waste land until the 1870s, when the first

After the Civil War, Memorial Day parades were among the great annual events in mining towns, as here on Allen Street, Tombstone, within sight of the OK Corral.

Bisbee, lavish producer of copper for a century, as it appeared around 1900, before the smelters moved to Douglas. Today Bisbee is still a thriving, picturesque mining town.

notices went up, for the Copper Queen claims in particular. The camp grew slowly, for copper lacked the psychic magnetism of gold and silver, but there was a town by 1880. After mining engineers demonstrated how to mine and smelter copper ore and after eastern capitalists, including Phelps Dodge, had invested, the town grew to importance, drawing in prospectors and mining men from all over the world.

The town grew upward. Houses for thousands of people clung on stilts to the steep, rocky sides of the gulch for a distance of two miles. Down in the narrow bottom, twenty-mule teams pulled ore wagons, and ox teams pulled loads of mining timbers a foot square from distant sawmills in the Chiricahua Mountains. Men built large structures for smelters, and for decades the fumes from them killed most greenery in Bisbee, but after the stack of the Copper Queen Smelter in the new town of Douglas, miles away, was "blown in"—put to work—Bisbee began again to see the green of the cottonwoods, ailanthus, cypresses, and garden flowers that now give charm to the old, surviving city.

Badmen, rustlers, gamblers, and prostitutes drifted in from both sides of the border. Mexicans came north with burros and axes to cut wood for fueling household stoves and the early smelters, but the town built ethnic prejudice into its customs. Mexicans could not work underground, and Chinese were not allowed to stay overnight in town. Professional mine laborers came in from other western towns and from England, Spain, Ireland, Finland, and the Slavic nations.

Branching north from the center of town was Brewery Gulch, a lively core of saloons, dance halls, bagnios, boardinghouses, and fraternal halls. Rising around the sides and at the end of the gulch, reached by traillike lanes or steep wooden staircases, were tier on tier of working-class cabins, shacks, and tents. No one questioned the total vitality of Brewery Gulch. Likewise, for decades no one doubted its need for a good system of sewerage.

As an established mining town Bisbee came to be a community of working men with families, despite its bawdy side, normal for the era, and despite occasional lynchings, murders, shooting affrays, and acts of racial bigotry. One particular series of violent events, which links the history of Bisbee and Tombstone, is commemorated by a plaque in the Bisbee Library. The plaque, intended to honor Joseph Goldwater, was placed there by his great-nephew, Barry Goldwater.

On December 8, 1883, the stagecoach was due to bring from Tucson the gold for the monthly pay of the Bisbee miners. The gold would be put in the safe of the Goldwater and Castenada store. But miles to the north, near the railroad junction at Benson, a flash flood delayed the coach. Not knowing about the flood —no one in Bisbee did—or about the non-arrival of the coach, five bandits entered Bisbee Canyon. Three stood guard on Main Street while two entered the store. After finding no gold there, the men grew furious; they started shooting up the town and killed a woman and four men.

Months passed until the bandits were identified and caught. Also, John Heath (or Heith), a Tombstone faro dealer, was found to be the instigator of the holdup. He was tried and found guilty of second-degree murder. On February 22, 1884, fifty Bisbee men, displeased that the verdict was not death, rode horseback over the mountains to Tombstone and sent a man to the gate of the Cochise County jailyard, next to the O K Corral. The guard at the jail thought the man at the gate was the Chinese who brought the convict's breakfast, so he opened the gate. When the mob entered the jail, Heath said, "Gentlemen, I presume you are looking for me." The men took Heath and hanged him from a telephone pole on Allen Street. A coroner's jury declared: "We the undersigned, a jury of inquest, find that John Heath came to his death from Emphysema of the lungs—a disease common in high altitudes—which might have been caused by strangulation, self-inflicted or otherwise." The corpse was buried in Boothill Cemetery. The five bandits, found guilty of first-degree murder, were officially hanged in one drop in the jail yard.

MINING IS A SELF-TERMINATING activity. When men have taken out all the ore they can find or reached the profitable cutoff point of their technology, the enterprise ends. In contrast, ranching can be everlasting, since it deals in biological renewables—soil, water, air, grass, and livestock. Except for periods when the Apaches and their allies were in control, haciendas and ranches have been among the most steady post-Oñate habitations. The advancing Spanish and Mexicans carried north the techniques of handling livestock,

breaking in cow ponies, and using the tools, the devices, and the vocabulary that Spaniards and Moors had long before worked out in Iberia. North went the *chaparreras* of leather, the braided leather bridle, Chihuahua spurs with large rowels, metal and wooden blabs to wean calves, and branding irons. It was only a matter of time until Texans and other North Americans learned from the Mexicans and contributed the Colt frontier six-shooter and barbed wire.

In the eighteenth and nineteenth centuries, ranches in northern Sonora and Chihuahua were often principalities with fortified, defensible buildings. Hacienda San José de Barbicora, near the head of the Río Casas Grandes, for instance, was a great, straggling square of mud walls that enclosed living quarters, two patios, storehouses, a blacksmith shop, and adobe corrals and outbuildings—all built as if for long sieges. The Angel Trías holdings at Encillas and elsewhere were famous for size and wealth. Even more so were the seven or eight million acres that Don Luis Terrazas accumulated in Chihuahua in the 1860s and later. His men branded a hundred thousand calves a year. Nowhere in the United States, not even in Texas, did any ranch holdings come near such a size.

After the Treaty of Guadalupe Hidalgo enterprising Anglos founded ranches. Near Shafter, Texas, Milton Faver started a horse and cattle ranch on Cibolo Creek and called it Fort Cibolo. He built three quadrangular adobe fortresses, at Big Springs, Cienaga, and La Morita,

EXECUTION OF

DANIEL KELLY, OMER W. SAMPLE, JAS. HOWARD, DANIEL DOWD and WILLIAM DELANEY,

AT THE COURT HOUSE, TOMBSTONE, ARIZONA,

March 28, 1884, at .../.... O'clock p. m.

Admit Mr. H J Fisher

J L Ward

NOT TRANSFERABLE. SHERIFF.

Invitation to the hanging of five bandits who shot up the town of Bisbee.

The branding corral on the Ladder Ranch, New Mexico. Cowboys are variously roping, flanking, heating branding irons, and branding a calf.

to guard the edges of his Big Bend range, which he ruled like a grandee. After the Civil War newcomers like the immigrant Diedrick Dutchover started cattle or sheep ranches in the rainy, grassy Davis Mountains area, a million and a half favored acres of volcanic soil now used by about a hundred ranchers.

There were prosperous ranches in the Nogales region, in both nations. In the grassy, high Río Santa Cruz Valley were the Sopori Ranch, south of Tubac, and the Arivaca Ranch, east of it. Both of these, like hundreds of others in the border territories, suffered damage or destruction by Apaches during the Civil War.

Pete Kitchen held out as few ranchers did. His El Potrero Ranch was the best known pioneer ranch in southern Arizona during the 1850s and 1860s. He made his home a fort, a rallying point for travelers and pro-

spective settlers. He raised stock but specialized in grain, potatoes, cabbages, fruit, and hogs; his bacon and ham were famous in the Southwest. He employed many Mexicans and Ópata Indian laborers and used them to help him alertly and successfully fight off Apache raiders, even though his pigs were sometimes so full of arrows that they looked like "walking pincushions." The Indians learned to give Kitchen a wide berth—he had his own boothill graveyard.

After the Civil War, even though the Apaches continued to defend their lands for another twenty years, big ranching moved solidly into Arizona and New Mexico. Col. Charles Goodnight and his partner Oliver Loving blazed the Goodnight–Loving Trail from Fort Belknap, Texas, to Concho, Texas, west to Horsehead Crossing to the Pecos, up the west bank to Fort Sumner,

New Mexico, on north to Pueblo, Colorado, and to the cattle yards of the Atchison, Topeka and Santa Fe Railway.

John Chisum arrived in New Mexico at South Spring with ten thousand longhorns and established a ranch two hundred miles long, from the Texas line to Fort Sumner. He ran about eighty thousand head and became the "Cattle King of New Mexico." Near Deming was the Diamond A cattle ranch, one of a series that belonged to Haggin and Tevis, interstate operators. At Gila, New Mexico, the L. C. Ranch (Lyons and Campbell Ranch and Cattle Company), capitalized at $1,500,-000 under the laws of New Jersey, monopolized water rights in the vicinity and claimed a range of a million acres, on which they herded eighty thousand head.

In southern Arizona at Rancho San Bernardino, resuscitated, ex-sheriff John Slaughter controlled a million acres at one time and owned 100,000 cattle, 10,000 horses, and 5,000 mules. He bought cattle in Sonora, held them, and then shipped them by train to California. In the adjoining valley, Sulphur Springs, Col. Henry C. Hooker built his fortified Sierra Bonita Ranch, controlled a range thirty miles long and thirty miles wide, fenced bottom lands where he raised alfalfa and other hay, and became the cattle king of Arizona. He was a noted horse breeder. Visitors at Sierra Bonita in the period from 1870 to 1890 included John Muir, Frederic Remington, playwright Augustus Thomas, and Whitelaw Reid, editor of the *New York Tribune*.

The government bought herds to supply reservation Indians, and the mining camps were a market greedy for beef. William Cornell Greene, of the Greene Cattle Company, Cananea, Sonora, helped feed Tombstone and Bisbee. Once the railroads came, there was also the demand of distant city markets. The railroads meant the end of the hardy but gaunt longhorns—ancient desert creatures that had "all their meat up front, like the buffalo, and the public wants the steaks that come from the rear"—and the coming of the Herefords, standard to this day, a far superior beef animal.

Former Mexican owners lost out to the princely grandeur of ranches like the L. C. and the Sierra Bonita, and they lost out to gringos sometimes in their own country, as to William Cornell Greene or Sen. George Hearst, the mining magnate. Hearst got hold of a modest million acres in Chihuahua at fifty cents an

A ranch cook and his chuck wagon—the mobile kitchen and store for hardworking men on the roundups.

acre by arrangement with the dictatorial President Porfirio Díaz, who dispossessed Indians and peasants to consolidate the acreage.

The big owners of cattle—the financiers, the speculators—were in tune with the times. Acting like "kings," they dominated local government, dictated law enforcement, carried on range wars, and lived baronially. They gave lavish hospitality to their peers, resisted controls over the public domain, resented such competitors as farmers, sheepmen, coyotes, or mountain lions, paid the low wages of the era, and unknowingly abused land and water with headstrong overgrazing. In the Tonto Basin northeast of Phoenix, below the Mogollon Rim of the plateau country, a range war once lasted five years. It became a feud between two families, and before it ended, more than thirty cattlemen and sheepmen were dead.

Sheepmen shared the same nineteenth-century views. They saw the land, private or public, as a commercial commodity and its use as a commercial process. In New Mexico twenty families, sixteen of them *Hispanos,* owned three-fourths of the sheep. Southwestern sheepmen drove flocks to Mexico between 1821 and 1846, when the drives were profitable. From 1849 to the end of the 1850s they drove hundreds of thousands of sheep to the California gold camps, whose hungry miners paid high prices for mutton. Later they drove sheep past Taos, over the mountains, and eastward down the Arkansas River to the Kansas feed lots.

For stockmen, as for lumbermen, the end—profits—justified the means, whatever they were. In the metaphor of the period, such enterprisers were "making America." They were serving widely admired capitalistic purposes. They made money, sometimes paying dividends of 20 to 30 percent, they raised food and hides for people; and they gave publicity to the region.

The cattlemen's principal work force, the vaqueros or cowpunchers, performed the hard labor—the spring roundup of horses, the long summer roundup of cattle, or the winter roundup from water hole to water hole to find calves overlooked in the summer.

The roundups meant camping alongside the chuck wagon—the supply store and cookhouse on wheels that held the makings for meals and also everything else needed, from horseshoes and nails to tobacco and needles to mend torn clothing. Each man had a dozen or so horses, one to carry his bedroll, the others for work. The summer roundup meant the hot work of roping and throwing the calves, holding them to the ground, branding them, cutting a mark in the ear, and castrating. The air smelled of dust, dung, the smoke of the small fire that heated the branding irons, and the pungent odor of singed chair and scorched hide.

On cattle drives the men were on guard all night in shifts of three hours of circling, singing, and whistling. At four in the morning the cook yelled, "Roll out and roll up! Chuck!" Coffee was over the fire, beans were boiling. Inside the Dutch oven, buried in the coals, were bread and biscuits that cowboys said were "the world's best."

Men who punched for the big outfits periodically had to ride from line camp to line camp, finding stray cattle and herding them back inside ranch boundaries. The camps were log cabins or brush shelters roofed with sod and earth. Inside were a pair of bunks, a cook stove, a rough table, and supply of flour, beans, coffee, salt pork, and lick (molasses). The lone cowboy split some wood, cooked himself a meal, and climbed into a bunk. Cowboys and bachelor ranchers who cooked for themselves often had stomach trouble. They generally had too much chili in their beans, and they ate too much starch. "As a consequence," Jack O'Connor recalled, "they generally got potgutted in middle age and wore their pendulous bellies over their belts."

Cowboys were a wild, simple group—white, black, brown, or red—with a lore of their own, a swatch of songs and tales, and personal recollections of bears, wolves, lions, and storm calamities. A few, like William Bonney—Kid Antrim or Billy the Kid—achieved notoriety when they got involved in rustling or in range wars incited by competition for grazing rights on public lands, for water rights, or for government beef contracts for feeding either soldiers or Indians—or if they got involved in feuds.

A complicated feud started the five-month war in Lincoln County, New Mexico, with Billy among those on the side of J. H. Tunstall, rancher, merchant, and banker. On the opposite side were James J. Dolan, Lawrence Murphy, and others. A sheriff's posse that was on the Dolan side ambushed and killed Tunstall. Billy swore revenge. Tunstall's cowboys and Billy killed two members of the posse and ambushed and killed the sheriff, William Brady, and a deputy on the street in Lincoln. Then the two factions fought a battle in Lincoln, killing five men and burning a house.

Two years later the gang and Billy were in trouble for cattle rustling. Some were killed, but Billy was caught. A jury tried him and convicted him of killing Sheriff Brady. He was sent to Lincoln to be hanged on May 13, 1881. On April 28 he made a dramatic escape from the second-floor jail of the county courthouse by catching his guards off guard and killing them. A few months later Sheriff Pat Garrett traced Bonney to Fort Sumner. He surprised Bonney in the dark of a private house, fired two shots, and ended Bonney's career at the age of twenty-one. Bonney claimed to have killed a man for every year of his life.

This slim, quiet-spoken cowboy-outlaw, condemned as a murderer by public opinion at the time, has become the basis for a major tourist industry in New Mexico. People profitably commemorate every step of his career from Silver City, where his mother is buried; to Mesilla, where he once stood trial; to Lincoln, scene of his bloodiest tallies; to Fort Sumner, where he is buried with two fellow rustlers. Myth, journalism, the movies, and amoral hero worship have taken what one historian calls "the William Bonney of history" and created "satanic Billy," "saintly Billy," and "the American Robin Hood."

A vast roadless realm in the Gila Wilderness of New Mexico was the first area in the United States to be set aside as permanently wild.

*New Mexico cowboys and
Herefords on the rich grassland
below a timbered ridge.*

Sheep in a grassy desert swale near the ghost town of Bodie, California.

*Watered by summer downpours, the high desert ranges have been supporting
sheep and cattle industries since the sixteenth century.*

Reflections in a ghost-town window. Goldfield once claimed to be "the greatest mining camp the world has ever known."

After fifty years of boom and prosperity, Jerome closed down and began to weather and fall apart. Pause became collapse.

Goldfield, Nevada: The office of a mine abandoned in 1957 suggests the transience of material progress.

A poor Navajo, unadorned with jewelry, stands by his well-worn saddle; Echo Cliffs in the background.

Maria, celebrated potter of San Ildefonso Pueblo, exhibits some of her black-on-black ware.

This mesa is part of the sacred open space controlled by the Zuñi, a tribe carefully trying to reconcile respect for the primeval landscape with adaptation to Anglo technology.

The sky city of Ácoma, the pueblo brutally assaulted by Oñate's men, remains one of the astonishing city sites of the world, commanding terrain, sky—and imagination.

CHAPTER 16

CHANGE AND RESISTANCE

Red men's raids and white men's massacres; the Mexican
Revolution and folk hero Pancho Villa

CRAGGY MOUNTAIN PASSES and long, empty desert valleys loom as the scene of the three last, most protracted wars in the two nations—the official Mexican campaigns against the Yaquis, the United States Army campaigns against the Apaches, and the Mexican Revolution. To a remarkable degree the revolution was engendered and fought by men in the desert north, and one of its central events was an immense, hot, dusty hunt, as federal troops of both countries attempted to trap and capture the gusty folk hero, Pancho Villa.

For more than three centuries the most consistently powerful ethnic forces in the whole region were the agricultural Yaquis to the south and the Apache raiders to the north. No other tribes, not even the Navajos, so vigorously defended their territories from expansionist Mexicans or Anglos.

The Yaquis in their eight pueblos in the fertile lowlands of the Río Yaqui stood exposed to the conquistadors as early as 1529, and the Spanish word for conquest entered their vocabulary as *konkihta*. The ruthless Nuño de Guzmán entered the Yaqui Valley in 1533 and killed Yaquis, and Hurdaide came in 1610–1611, but each time the Yaquis stubbornly drove the intruders away. Then in 1617 they asked for Jesuits, received Andrés Pérez de Ribas and Tomás Basilio, and accepted baptism, training schools, and church rituals. There followed a century and a quarter of peace as the Indians adopted the metal hoe, the plow, horses and donkeys, and wheat. Their pueblos developed new village and military organizations and a new ceremonial calendar that blended the native religion with Catholicism. The

Yaquis learned to read and write in the Spanish way. When Kino began his work in Pimería Alta, he made the Yaqui towns his bases for supplies.

In the eighteenth century, when the smooth-working Jesuit regime began to disintegrate and church and state wrangled in Mexico as in Europe, Yaqui society fell directly into disorganization. In the 1730s Spanish civil authorities and a group of Yaquis accused a Jesuit of mistreating the Yaquis. A serious controversy arose that involved colonial officials in Ciudad Méjico, who were slow to settle the trouble. Yaqui factions developed, and in 1740 Yaquis were fighting Spanish soldiers. Calixto Muni rose to leadership of the rebels, but in a battle at Otamkawi ("Hills of Bones") Muni lost. The Spanish executed him, and the Yaquis had a hero.

During the Mexican war of independence, many Yaquis fought on the revolutionary side, but the new Mexican government sought to parcel out Yaqui land. Around 1825 surveyors appeared in Potam, Vicam, Rahum, and other villages. A Yaqui, Juan Bandera, who claimed to have had a vision of the Virgin of Guadalupe, organized resistance units. He preached an idea of Yaqui independence that dominated his people for more than a hundred years. He worked out alliances with the Ópatas, Mayos, and nearby Pimas, who all got caught up in the dream of a confederacy separate from Sonora. Although Bandera's soldiers often had only bows and arrows, they held out successfully until 1832 against the soldiers of the Sonora-Sinaloa government. The movement subsided but the aspiration did not.

Trouble mounted from time to time. After one disturbance Gen. García Morales burned up 450 Yaqui

Ruins at Cicuyé, now Pecos National Monument, were once a Franciscan church
of special beauty, large enough to hold all the people of the pueblo.

Navajo scouts in the 1880s. The army relied heavily on Navajo and Apache scouts during the decades of trying to suppress Apache "hostiles" who resisted Anglo domination.

men and women in the church building at Bacum. During the turbulence before and after Porfirio Díaz seized power, the Yaqui called Cajeme ("He-who-does-not-drink") became a power. From 1877 to 1885 he led the Yaquis, and for a time the Mayos, in a highly effective military organization. He waged border warfare against Mexican settlers, who had the backing of politicans and were pushing onto Yaqui lands. Cajeme replaced the old Indian tactics, the irregular guerrilla skirmishing that the Apaches never gave up. Instead, he fought the firm, fixed engagements prescribed by military science. After Díaz's *federalistas* finally defeated him at Buatachive, a fortified mountain north of Vicam, the Yaquis kept up a scattered resistance. Juan Maldonado, known as Tetabiate ("Rolling Stone"), organized the remnants of Yaqui power and waged a desperate, telling guerrilla campaign for ten years, until the Mexicans caught and executed him.

The Díaz regime did not let up on these stubborn people who identified with their ancestral place—the river, the valley, the uplands, the bordering mountains. Then, as before and later, the Yaquis held to their central belief in Our Mother, the land people live on. The Yaquis were indissolubly bound to their land. Contemptuous of such a notion, Díaz's soldiers herded

Yaquis off to haciendas, where they served as cheap labor. Favored Mexican farmers took their land. Yet guerrilla resistance continued into the twentieth century, as bands operated from water holes in the Bacatete Mountains. They raided as far north as Ures for food, keeping federal and Sonora troops on constant alert.

During the years 1900 to 1908, the governor of Sonora held hundreds of Yaquis suspected of crimes in the jails of Hermosillo and other towns, and shipped them out to any employer who wanted prison labor. Sonora officials took pay by the head for laborers they supplied to contractors. The central government used deportation as a means of trying to exterminate a culture. It shipped off many Yaquis as workers or as soldiers to most of the Mexican states, including Yucatan. Many Yaquis fled to the United States.

After Díaz resigned and moved to Paris, the deportations stopped. Some Yaquis joined General Obregón and moved with their families out through northern Mexico. Eventually some of these people settled in Ciudad Méjico; others formed permanent settlements along the railroad between Ciudad Obregón and Tucson. At the end of the revolution, the Río Yaqui population, about five thousand, was one-fourth of what it had been in 1800. The governor of Sonora, Adolfo de la

Huerta, and President Obregón started to rebuild the Yaqui culture and did reconstruct large brick churches. But already much of the good land lay firmly in the hands of Mexicans and North Americans, and the Yaquis grew dissatisfied.

In 1926 President Obregón claimed that the Yaquis showed hostility against him personally when he passed through on the train. He sent in soldiers, and there were skirmishes. Yaquis fled to the mountains. When they came down, after a military campaign, they were drafted into the army and sent to Vera Cruz, Ciudad Méjico, or elsewhere. It was a final dispersal. The government began a systematic military occupation along the Río Yaqui that lasted into the 1950s.

The Yaquis remained the last Indians in North America to be regarded by the white man as a serious military threat, though they were a non-militaristic, farming society. They are now a widely scattered group, with distinct colonies in two countries, especially in Guaymas, Hermosillo, Nogales, Tucson, Marana, and Guadalupe, near Tempe.

There are three or four thousand in the Arizona settlements. They have learned to survive amid the white man's cash economy and machine technology. Along the Río Yaqui they continue to be anti-Mexican, for Mexicans have seized their best lands and much of their upstream water.

And to a notable degree, everywhere they·have gone, the Yaquis have retained much of their ethnic distinctness. They preserve the culture that evolved during the peaceful days of Jesuit occupation. Some hold to the mystical insights and visions reported in Carlos Castaneda's *A Separate Reality* and *Teachings of Don Juan: a Yaqui Way of Knowledge*. During Lent and Holy Week there are the activities and ceremonies of the Judases or Pharisees, led by Pilate with a red flag and the Horsemen or Spanish *caballeros* led by a blue flag. In October by truck, car, or special train a quarter of the population of the Río Yaqui pueblos and other thousands from Sonora and Arizona colonies, plus many Papagos and Pimas—four to five thousand in all —converge on Magdalena for the three-day fiesta of San Francisco de Assisi.

The Yaquis' name for themselves is *yoemem*, meaning "persons, we, the human beings." Others are not quite people, and the Mexicans are *yorim*. Similarly, the Pima call themselves *O-otam*, "men, or people," and the Navajos' own name is *Di-neh*, "the people." The Apaches, too, though called derogatory names by whites, term themselves *N'de* or *Dine*, "the people." As for ancient Greeks, all others are barbarians.

THE VARIOUS APACHE groups preceded the whites in overrunning the grasslands and deserts from the Great Plains to western Arizona and well down into Mexico. What the Spanish called Gran Apachería was 750 miles east and west by 550 miles north and south. Early in the seventeenth century Apaches were stealing horses and becoming master riders. By century's end the Spaniards were busy trying to defend their frontiers from the galloping invaders. In 1693, for instance, Gen. Juan de Retana, guided by two old women, led a force from interior Chihuahua to the Rio Grande against Apaches based in the Chisos Mountains. For a century and a half border war was a Spanish worry.

An important start in controlling Apaches was made under Jacobo Ugarte y Loyola, governor of Coahuila and then of Sonora between 1769 and 1782, and then Commandante General from 1786 to 1791. Applying the policy of the viceroy, he made separate peaces with Apache tribes, exploiting discord in Apachería, offering Indians a choice between extermination or peace. He sent out military expeditions to keep distant bands off balance and welcomed Indian allies, which meant that Indians would kill Indians.

Once Mexico gained its independence, however, and cut back on support for the presidios, Apaches renewed their raiding and looting. During the war of 1846–1847, when northern Mexico had no defenses, the Apaches swept in with impunity, boldly invading towns, laying waste the haciendas, taking captives, and running off whole herds of cattle and horses. The Mexican frontier was theirs for the taking. Their standard of living reached its era of climax. At a time when most Indians were losing their territories, the Apaches, as George Kendall wrote in the 1840s, were retaking land from Mexicans and presenting "the singular anomaly of a tribe of aborigines increasing in numbers and in such wealth as the Indian most covets—horses and arms, trinkets and finery."

After the Guadalupe and Gadsden treaties, United States forts tried to continue the tasks of earlier pre-

Revolutionary leaders, left to right: Tomás Urbina, Pancho Villa (in eagle-backed chair), Emiliano Zapata, and Otilio Montana, around 1914, before Villa had Urbina hanged for hiding loot from bank robberies.

sidios, with some success though against the great odds. But Congress appropriated too little money. The entire Southwest held only a dozen Indian agents and about three thousand soldiers, who faced some thirty thousand Apaches. The United States had armaments and West Point training, but the Indians had knowledge of guerrilla tactics and survival amid drought.

Lt. Col. Philip St. George Cooke led an expedition against the Jicarilla Apaches, Col. Thomas T. Fauntleroy against the Utes and Jicarillas in the San Luis Valley of Colorado, and Col. B. L. E. Bonneville against the Gila Apaches. In effect, however, the army could not substantially control the Apache people, who

thrived on the booty brought right under their noses by trapping and prospecting parties, traders' wagons, stagecoaches, and argonauts heading for California. Mexico, torn by the struggle between Santa Anna and liberals, could not stop the Apaches in motion south of the border.

Apache-white relations took a plunge for the worse in early February 1861, at Apache Pass. Lt. George N. Bascom and soldiers from Fort Buchanan ineptly attempted to trick and arrest Cochise, the Chiricahua chief, for a child kidnaping he said other Indians had committed. The Cochise delegation came into Bascom's tent under a flag of truce to parley. When Bascom said he would hold the Indians captive until the boy was returned, Cochise slit the tent and escaped. Bascom held the other chiefs and hanged them; in return Cochise had white captives killed and mutilated. Bascom's blunder started a twenty-year war. Within sixty days 150 whites were killed, and Bascom's duplicity eventually led to the death of 5,000 whites.

After the federal government withdrew its troops in 1861, Arizona and Sonora experienced total war. For hundreds of miles there were vacant houses, crumbling adobe buildings, herds of scared cattle gone wild, and roadsides marked by impromptu graves of white men, many of whom had been tortured. In retaliation whites broke their word and massacred families of innocent Indians, made bridles from hair of scalped Indian victims, decorated the bridles with teeth knocked from the mouths of living women, poisoned Indians with strychnine, invited Indians to gift giving and then blew them up with gunpowder, and shot any Indian at sight. "Shoot um," said an early miner near Prescott, "shoot um, damn um, shoot um; don't wait for um to beg off." Following a practice used before the war with the United States, Governor Ygnacio Pesqueira of Sonora, a mine owner, offered scalp bounties.

The United States Army, led generally by men trained to respect an enemy, had both successes and failures as it undertook to reconquer the Southwest from natives as from the interloping Confederates.

On July 15, 1862, a detachment of the California Column led by Brig. Gen. James Carleton was camped in Apache Pass. They were ambushed by five hundred Chiricahua and Mimbreño fighters led by Mangas Coloradas and Cochise, who were behind the stone breastworks that commanded the water hole. Only mounted howitzers that spewed twelve-pound shells routed the Indians. After this battle Carleton ordered Fort Bowie built at the entrance to the pass.

Later in the year Carleton, now commander of the Department of New Mexico, sent Col. Kit Carson and the First New Mexico Volunteers to subdue the Mescalero Apaches. By early 1863 Carson had succeeded, and the captives moved to a new reservation on the Pecos River at Bosque Redondo (Round Grove of Trees). Later the Mescaleros fled and turned to raiding, until persuaded in 1871 to settle at the Fort Stanton agency, from which they escaped periodically.

During the wars of the 1860s and later the beleaguered whites left in Arizona Territory appealed for more and more military protection. Meanwhile, ranchers such as those of the Chiricahua Cattle Company fortified their buildings and even put parapets above the roofs. In 1871 a bloodthirsty band of Tucson whites took matters into their own hands. They rode northeast and descended on Camp Grant like a mob. Near there a band of about three hundred Arivaipa Apaches led by Eskiminzin had surrendered to Lt. Royal Whitman and were encamped under his protection. On April 30 the Tucson party fell on the camp and killed more than eighty-five adults, mostly women, and carried almost thirty children off into slavery. Many non-Indians approved of the massacre, but it slowed down the efforts of the federal peace commissioners. This was a time when the government was ending the practice of signing treaties with Indians and setting up a permanent reservation system.

Soon afterwards Lt. Col. George Crook took command of the Department of Arizona. Thomas J. Jeffords, a stageline operator, and Gen. O. O. Howard persuaded Cochise to settle on a reservation at Sulphur Springs, west of Apache Pass.

BUT OTHER APACHES were on the loose. Crook converged men on the Tonto Basin of central Arizona. On December 27, 1872, Capt. W. H. Brown, with two troops of the 5th Cavalry and thirty Apache scouts, surprised a band of more than a hundred Yavapais at a cave deep in the recesses of Salt River Canyon. The band refused to surrender and a fight began. Some of Brown's men shot their carbines at the roof of the cave and deflected a deadly fire at the defenders. Other men rolled boulders over the cliffs above and down to crush the "defiant enemy of civilization." The army finally killed sixty to seventy-five human beings—their most striking victory in the long history of wars in the Apache homeland. Soldiers who got into the cave found a writhing mass of wounded humanity and captured thirty women and children.

In April of 1873 the Indians made peace at Camp Verde. The Indian Bureau, with help from energetic agent John Clum, collected most of the Arizona and New Mexico Apache bands at the San Carlos agency on the Gila. But trouble built up here and elsewhere because quarters were crowded and unhealthful and, unlike Clum, most agents were corrupt and inefficient. The agents doled out meager beef and fare, and traders sold inferior whiskey to the Indians. Civil and military authorities disagreed; white settlers kept encroaching on Indian lands. Indians who had been raised to roam resisted the attempt to turn them into farmers and destroy their tribal way of life. Dissident Apache bands, no more willing than the whites to change accustomed ways, continued traditional pillaging the length and breadth of the plateaus and lowland deserts.

In 1879 Chief Victorio, with Warm Springs and Mescalero men, struck in western Texas, southern New Mexico, and Chihuahua. Citizens of Silver City, New Mexico, offered $250 for every Apache scalp. Texas Rangers and sheriffs' posses cornered Victorio's band, but the Indians escaped. Columns from Fort Davis and other Texas posts marched a total of 90,000 miles in a largely futile pursuit. In early August of 1880, Gen. Benjamin Grierson and troops from Fort Quitman and Eagle Springs defeated Victorio at Rattlesnake Springs. Two months later Mexican troops trapped him in Chihuahua and, in a final battle, Victorio was killed.

Followers who escaped, led by Nana—an aged, rheumatic chief—holed up in the Sierra Madre. Later they joined forces with Geronimo (Goyathlay or Cow-a-ar-tha—One Who Yawns). After the death of Cochise in 1874 Geronimo had grown to command of the Chiricahuas, who had been moved to a parched reservation adjoining the San Carlos agency, near Fort Apache.

In 1882, after bloody fights to the north that involved White Mountain Apaches, Geronimo and a band of Chiricahuas jumped the reservation and fled to the Sierra Madre, from which they descended to raid in northern Mexico and southern Arizona. Since the two countries had signed a pledge of cooperation in tracking down Apaches, General Crook sent into Mexico several detachments of Apache scouts, commanded by white officers. They returned the Geronimo band to San Carlos.

But in 1885 Geronimo, Natchez (son of Cochise), old Nana, and 190 others headed for Mexico again. They eluded United States cavalry sent to intercept them in Mexico and raided the border all summer. In four weeks, during November and December, one small band of eleven Chiricahuas traveled more than 1,200 miles, wore out 250 horses, killed thirty-eight people, were twice dismounted, and escaped intact into Mexico. But once again Crook's Apache scouts finally located Geronimo and his band and persuaded them to confer with Crook, at Cañón de los Embudos, Chihuahua, on March 25, 1886. They surrendered. On the way to Fort Bowie the Indians went on a mescal spree and escaped, riding across the border to the Sierra Madre.

The newspapers, the public, and officialdom assailed Crook, who was replaced by Brig. Gen. Nelson A. Miles. Miles erected twenty-seven heliograph stations on high peaks for rapid communication and organized large "pursuing commands" to replace detachments of Apache scouts. In the summer of 1886 troops pursued Geronimo through the trailless, hot gorges of the Sierra Madre. At a camp near Skeleton Canyon in the Guadalupe Mountains Geronimo surrendered for the last time and ended his career. With him at the end were fewer than two dozen men and their families.

THE SUN-DRIED TERRAIN that supported heroes (or villains) like Juan Bandera or Cochise produced their twentieth-century counterpart, the poor boy Doroteo Arango, who grew up among outlaws, took the name Francisco ("Pancho") Villa, and galloped into the history of the continent. He was heavy set and dark skinned. He spoke the language of the peon of northern Mexico but could neither read nor write. Whether bandit, revolutionary reformer with an agrarian program, commanding general, governor of Chihuahua, or quasi-president of Mexico, he chose to see himself as a champion of the common man. He was used, he said, to the "long struggle with the exploiters, the persecutors, the seducers." He was full of "anxiety and hate."

Certainly he played a spectacular role during the revolutionary decade of the 1910s when Sonora and Chihuahua men—Francisco Madero, Venustiano Carranza, Adolfo de la Huerta, Alvaro Obregón, Plutarco Calles, and Abelardo Rodríguez dominated in war and politics. Then, as before Díaz, there was turbulence, betrayal, and assassination, with Villa caught in the midst of it and often highly visible. Like several of the other leading *insurrectos* or *revoltosos* he appeared often in El Paso, especially in South El Paso, called "Chihuahuita" (Little Chihuahua), where the Sheldon Hotel was in many ways the capitol of the revolution.

In early May of 1911 Villa's troops and those of Pascual Orozco gathered to assault the federal troops defending Juárez. The *insurrectos,* with bandoliers of cartridges hanging heavily across their chests, camped on the banks of the river across from the El Paso smelter. War was next door to the United States and in plain sight. In three days of unorthodox sniping from rooftops and of knocking their way through adobe walls, whole city blocks at a time, the peon army took Juárez and accepted a formal surrender. Stray bullets had crossed the river, killed five El Pasoans, and wounded fifteen others.

Two years later Villa captured Juárez again and also cities far to the south—Lerdo, Gómez Palacio, Torreón. "I was now a Revolutionary man who won battles for the people. Did that make me a bandit?" He had received American support and was careful in his treatment of United States citizens. Villa broke with many of the other revolutionaries, including Carranza, who had become president after a series of double dealings and assassinations.

When Woodrow Wilson recognized the Carranza government and sold it arms, Villa felt twice wronged. With strong peasant support he began to act like a war lord, plundering at will in Chihuahua and Sonora. He declared that he was for punishing the political and religious rulers "who betray the cause of the poor." When Carranza began marshaling an army to move against Villa, the United States let Carranza use the Southern Pacific tracks to move General Calles, troops, and arms from El Paso to Douglas. At Agua Prieta, twin city to Douglas just inside Mexico, Calles laid down an artillery barrage and machine gun and rifle fire that defeated Villa and also sent leaden showers into Douglas.

In hopes of provoking the United States against Carranza and unhorsing him, Villa resorted to harsh violence. One day in January 1916, a band of Villistas stopped the train at Santa Ysabel, Chihuahua, pulled off seventeen miners who were United States nationals, and killed sixteen of them. Then shortly after midnight on March 9, after careful spying, Villa and 1,000 men charged across the border into the little burg of Columbus, New Mexico. They surprised 200 troopers of the 13th Cavalry and spent hours in shooting, pillaging, pulling rings off women's fingers, and burning buildings. They killed eighteen Americans — townspeople and soldiers — and wounded another eighteen or so. When more cavalry troops appeared on the bleached horizon at dawn, the Villistas galloped south, leaving twenty-five to thirty dead on the streets. An army pursuit column broke through three rear-guard defenses and killed another seventy-five of Villa's men.

Villa's armed invasion of the United States, the first external one since the War of 1812, stirred Wilson into a dusty, futile, undeclared war, a deliberate invasion of Mexico made presumably with Carranza's permission. Brig. Gen. John J. Pershing—"Black Jack"—of Fort Bliss had to organize the Punitive Expedition. Using hard-tired trucks (that broke down), open-seater biplanes (that could not rise over the desert ranges), and mule pack trains (slow but sure), Black Jack's wide-ranging cavalry and infantry columns, led by such officers as Lt. George S. Patton, marched almost the whole length of Chihuahua. His men skirmished with Villistas and even fought against Carranza forces, who killed a dozen Americans at Carrizal and captured twice as many. Villa, master of forced marches, unexpected appearances, and untraceable disappearances, kept himself and his main troops out of sight.

After many months of futile patrolling, Pershing and his Punitive Expedition returned to the United States, but Villa looted on in Mexico. Villista bands crossed the river to raid Texas settlements and ranches in the Big Bend, pillaging, burning, killing, and being killed. In 1919 Villa made peace and retired to manage a model farm. Four years later, near Parral, he was ambushed in his automobile and machine-gunned to death.

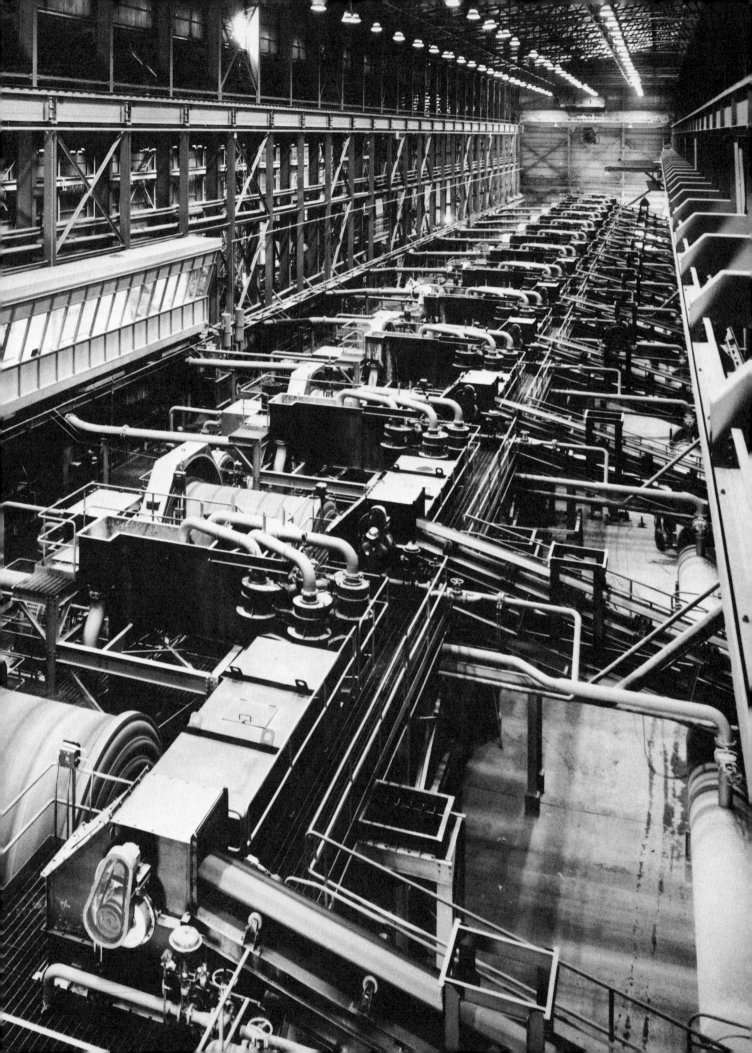

CHAPTER 17

TWENTIETH-CENTURY BONANZAS

Company towns and real estate booms—where big-scale operators have made fortunes from the land

EARTH'S CRUST determines. When lodes are rich but small, and veins peter out, a mining town has a short, often rowdy life and is lucky to exist until a census year. When lodes are big and deep, even if low in value per ton of ore, the camp grows into a town that lasts for decades or centuries, becomes the talk of international investors, subsidizes corporate superstructures, and puts ambitious men into the United States Senate. In the nineteenth century, when prospectors worked by hunch and stockholders gambled on the future, some towns were gaudy "helldorados" that declined in a decade or two to ghosthood and legend. In the twentieth century the typical mining center is a company installation, or company-dominated town, or simply a mine near a town. It is owned by a monolithic corporation, fully advised by geologists and engineers who decide by calculation not chance, for owners who are investors, not speculators.

Hundreds of southwestern mining towns had their day in the sun—Hillsboro and Shakespeare in New Mexico; Terlingua and Shafter in the Big Bend; Pearce, Dos Cabezas, and Charleston in Arizona; Searchlight in Nevada; Greenwater and Randsburg in the Mojave. Contention City, a mill town on the trickling San Pedro River, where the ores of Tombstone were reduced, flourished for about ten years. The town was industrious, not contentious. It supported a population of about two hundred men—some with wives and families —who worked at the Grand Central, Head Center, and Contention mills, and drank at the Dewdrop and Headlight saloons. Two stage lines brought passengers daily from Tombstone and the Southern Pacific at Benson.

From 1880 to 1888 there was a post office. Today, only a few fragments of adobe wall remain among the creosote bushes and coarse grasses that have regained the terrain. The town is only a memory in the files of the *Arizona Daily Star:* "Reportedly, somewhere above the townsite are traces of a cemetery." The dead have buried the dead.

As a productive town, White Oaks, New Mexico, like Tombstone itself, lasted about twice as long as Contention City. A desperado escaping from a Texas jail accidentally found the ledge that became the Old Abe Mine and produced more than three million dollars in gold. The Old Abe and other mines led to a stampede, and men nailed together a town for about two thousand persons, among them the politican H. B. Fergusson, father of two important writers; Albert B. Fall, an unscrupulous lawyer, later a senator and a scandalous member of the Harding Cabinet; and Emerson Hough, the popular novelist who wrote *The Covered Wagon.* At the Little Casino Madam Varnish, known for her slickness, dealt poker and faro.

But after 1900, with mine production dwindling, the town began to fall apart. The Exchange Bank, the hotels, the saloons, the stores—many of them two stories high—turned into gaunt ruins. Boards peeled loose. Brick buildings such as the schoolhouse were locked up, vacant. Adobe walls washed away or were roofed with sheet metal that rusted. In place of merchants' signs were warnings KEEP OUT or DANGEROUS—KEEP OUT. Thistles, yuccas, and cholla cactus reclaimed the sidestreets and lots. The intermittent creek that ran through the town gullied during showers.

The Phelps-Dodge concentrator at Tyrone. The control room overlooks the ball mills, where crushed low-grade copper ore gets ground to the consistency of flour.

One elaborate, red-brick mansion continues in use in White Oaks; its rooms are eleven feet high and its outside corners trimmed in stone. A few retired people now live in resurrected houses or in trailers. Cedarvale, the cemetery, holds family plots and interments from the 1890s to the 1970s. Like most dead mining towns—but unlike the present Tombstone or Calico, which have been resuscitated and fabricated for tourists—White Oaks is an unexploited, honest relic of a town that never intended to outlast its lode.

Towns larger and more important than White Oaks finally died if mining was the sole reason for the community and the mines flooded or petered out. In southern Nevada, Goldfield, "the greatest proven gold-mining district in the world," had its day between 1902 and the early 1920s. Even Jerome, Arizona, which lasted more than half a century, reached a terminus.

A few towns had natural advantages that enabled them to live on and even to grow. Silver City, New Mexico, 6,000 feet high in the Pinos Altos Range, has survived the ups and downs of mining booms, Apache raids, and floodwaters to become a modern town that attracts retired people from smoggy Southern California, serves as a commercial center for ranches, mines, and tourist resorts, and houses Western New Mexico University.

BISBEE'S LONG HISTORY embodies the complete shift from the individualistic frontier to modern corporate control. In the early twentieth century numerous companies owned the mines in Bisbee, the most important mining town in Arizona and one of the copper centers of the world. But consolidation was going on. The Calumet and Arizona Mining Company acquired the Irish Mag Mine. Later Phelps Dodge bought the Calumet and Arizona, and became by far the leading employer in town. Phelps Dodge owned the largest mine, the Copper Queen, the largest hotel, the hospital, the department store, the library, and other enterprises. It was "The Company." Below Bisbee's Brewery Gulch, out in an open valley, The Company built an attractive subdivision called Warren.

Phelps Dodge had labor policies that were good for their day during the period from 1900 to 1933, but along with Calumet and Arizona, and the Shattuck-Arizona Copper Company, Phelps Dodge had a silent hand in the most famous illegal episode in the city's history, a *cause célèbre* in 1917, when the sheriff and vigilantes kidnapped more than twelve hundred striking members of the IWW Metal Mine Workers' Industrial Union, put them in cattle- and boxcars, and summarily deported them across the state line to Columbus, New Mexico—in flat-footed violation of their constitutional rights.

Even as Phelps Dodge was planning major developments in Bisbee, such as the Sacramento, its first open-pit mine there, the firm was trying an experiment in total-community creation of a mining town at Tyrone, New Mexico. The company owned all the property and did all the planning. It employed Bertram G. Goodhue, designer of homes in New York and later of the Panama-California Exposition in San Diego, to plan the buildings and houses. He chose an appropriate Spanish architecture, and in 1915–1916 a beautiful model town appeared amid a mountain valley of live oak, piñon, juniper, and scattered cacti. Carefully laid out, making the most of arcades and the latest in comfort and luxury, Tyrone had a deluxe arrangement of civic center, shops, clubs, school, bank, theater, company offices, hotel, staff housing, hospital, homes for Mexican workmen, garage, warehouse, post office, and railroad station. The company store was "the Wanamaker's of the desert." The library held five thousand volumes. Everyone agreed that Tyrone was unique—there was no other town like it in all the world.

But unfortunately for all concerned, the copper mines, with conventional tunnels and shafts, soon proved unprofitable, and the company halted operations in 1921, after five or six years of work. For some years thereafter a skeleton crew kept the mines open. Some residents stayed on, and artists and writers rented homes, as did commuters from Silver City. From time to time the company tore down a building and fenced off portions of the town to discourage visitors. Tiles fell, stucco warped off, boards replaced broken windows, but the architect's bold, strong forms, his arcades and modulated spaces gave the ghostly townscape a special grandeur.

The only thing wrong with Tyrone was a lack of rich ore, for as a planned town—its artistry excepted—it represented a growing practice. The early camps, such as Bisbee or Jerome, grew up spontaneously, haphaz-

The model mining town of Tyrone around 1920, with the railroad depot and Phelps Dodge buildings around the plaza, the school in the right background, and company-owned housing on the far ridge.

ardly, like hillside towns in ancient Tuscany and Greece, but twentieth-century company-owned towns were laid out in advance like Roman army settlements. In 1900 "Rawhide Jimmy" Douglas and John Slaughter, the rancher and ex-sheriff, platted the city of Douglas to go with the prospective Phelps Dodge smelter. They provided for electric lights and power, gas, telephones, a water works, an ice plant, sewerage, and streets so wide "that 20-mule teams could turn around in the middle of the block." In 1911, Ray Consolidated planned for Hayden to be the "model town of Arizona" with its business and residential sections, underground sewerage system, street lighting, and graded thorough-fares—and a shanty town for the Mexicans.

A more recent example is San Manuel, planned and built by Magma Copper during the 1950s in the San Pedro Valley. It is a complete town, with residential districts, shopping centers, schools, public library, and hospital. Six or seven miles away elaborate plants and equipment at San Manuel Mine bring up the copper and molybdenum ores from a thousand feet and more beneath the surface, where workers mine by under-cutting a layer of ore, deliberately caving it in, then breaking it into pieces and bringing it to the surface.

Since five hundred million tons of ore await under-cutting, San Manuel can expect to last for generations.

Company towns, fully planned or not, have been a solution to the lonely isolation of many deposits. Such towns are needed in out-of-the-way places like Eagle Mountain, where Kaiser Steel Corporation built a town for its workers and executives at the first important iron mine in California. Company towns have provided minimal housing, services, and recreation for immi-grants, mostly single men at first, and later for their families. Sometimes they have exploited the worker by overcharging him at the company store—mining the miners. "I owe my soul to the company store," a popular song put it. Towns like Trona (American Potash and Chemical Company) in the Mojave have lost in dubious paternalism and gained in democracy as good roads and automobiles have ended their isolation.

One-payroll towns like Silver Bell (American Smelt-ing and Refining Company) or Santa Rita (Chino Cop-per, then Kennecott Copper) are expedients. They are not normal American towns any more than mining is a self-perpetuating activity that deals with a permanent, renewable resource. Proof is what happens to buildings as the mines expand. Tyrone failed first because of the surface ores, but open-pit techniques later made the lode profitable, and in 1967–1968 the owners, for sound commercial reasons, demolished the town and began a deep, open excavation like those at Bingham Canyon, Utah, at McGill, Nevada, and elsewhere in the coppery West. Goodhue's model community, sophisticated, and imperially conceived, became a gigantic, terraced hole in the earth's crust, marvelous in its geological way. Technology and economics had conquered esthetics and the arts. The ghost town lived on only in the ectoplasm of camera negatives.

The Warren subdivision, elegant in its day, is now encroached on by man-piled hillocks and mesas of overburden and debris. Little South Bisbee, a cluster of houses, slowly dies like a drained and dried-out reservoir, surrounded by waste rock that cuts off all the horizons. Residents come home on a road that passes through a tunnel under mine wastes.

Let no one shed a tear. The demise of towns and suburbs, like the building of new, up-to-date ones, goes with the transience of American life, especially on the frontiers of expendable bonanza resources. With technology progressive, the demise especially accompanies developments that make it profitable to mine ore with only 2 percent, or 1 percent, or even 0.5 percent of useful content. This is a great contrast to the past. In 1906, for example, the Shattuck-Arizona Copper Company confined its shaft-and-tunnel operations to deposits that yielded an average of 17 percent.

The open-pit mine, useful for iron at Eagle Mountain, coal at Farmington, New Mexico, and elsewhere for minerals such as boron, gypsum, perlite, and sand, has been the making of Big Copper in the Southwest—at the Santa Rita mines, now about 170 years along, and in fourteen major pits in Arizona, including Ajo, Morenci, and Mineral Park near Kingman.

In Bisbee, a century old now, the Campbell and Warren shafts still probe down—currently 3,200 feet—to where men mine peacock bornite, iridescent in purple, yellow, or golden; but the particular glory of the town is the Lavender Pit. Before stripping operations began in 1951, men moved 191 buildings, relocated 3,200 feet of highway, and built a concrete ditch to channel off water from surrounding mountain sides. About 250 feet of useless, leached-out caprock were removed and

dumped around Warren and on toward Mexico. Then heavy drills, electric shovels, and sixty-five ton trucks began the task of winding down inside an ever more immense and deep bowl. Eventually there will be a hole over a thousand feet deep. It is low-grade quartz monzonite porphyry that gives the cavity its value and its varicolored sides—reddish pink, greenish, or cobalt, with greenish-blue streaks and yellow-green patches. Like other coppery glory holes this technological crater is vastly more stunning to see with its trucks curving up and down, its machinery humming, rattling, and throbbing, than the immobile meteor-made crater—600 feet deep and 4,000 feet across, now weathered and dull near Flagstaff.

Southwest of Tucson in the Pima Mining District, over a hill from the ornate, staid, arbitrarily placed townhouses of the Green Valley subdivision, three mining companies are at work in five new open-pit mines. The Sierrita Pit of the Duval Corporation is working with ore that has an average copper content of only 0.35 percent and a molybdenum content of 0.036 percent, yet each year the mill will produce profitably 65,000 tons of copper, 13 million pounds of molybdenum, and 500,000 ounces of silver. During the predicted life of the property, the company expects to excavate one billion tons of overburden and ore, which is twice the tonnage excavated for the construction of the Panama Canal.

A few miles away the Twin Buttes pit of the Anaconda Company, according to expert judges, is "probably the most highly automated mine in the world." A network of conveyor belts, one of them 8,300 feet long, removes the ore from the pit. Control towers route the ore as needed to the crushers or to stockpiles.

Corporation operations are far from the simple panning of a placer miner sloshing creek, sand, and gravel in a pan. They are a complex of rotary drills, electric shovels with nine-cubic-yard dippers; the receiving hopper and pan feeder of the primary crushing plant and conveyor; the intermediate crushing plant with its pan feeders, a coarse metal screen called a "grizzly," an intermediate crusher and conveyor; the fine crushing plant with more bins, screens, and a fine crusher; and the big concentrator plant with its conveyor, tripper car, ore bin, water supply and reagents, ball mill, classifier, and flotation works. There is also

UTAH ARCHITECT

Number 55   Winter 1974

View from Mill, looking north.

Looking west from top of ore bins.

Iron boxes.

Drain detail, iron boxes.

View of Mill, looking south.

OLD TINTIC STANDARD REDUCTION MILL
—IN WASATCH

All concrete

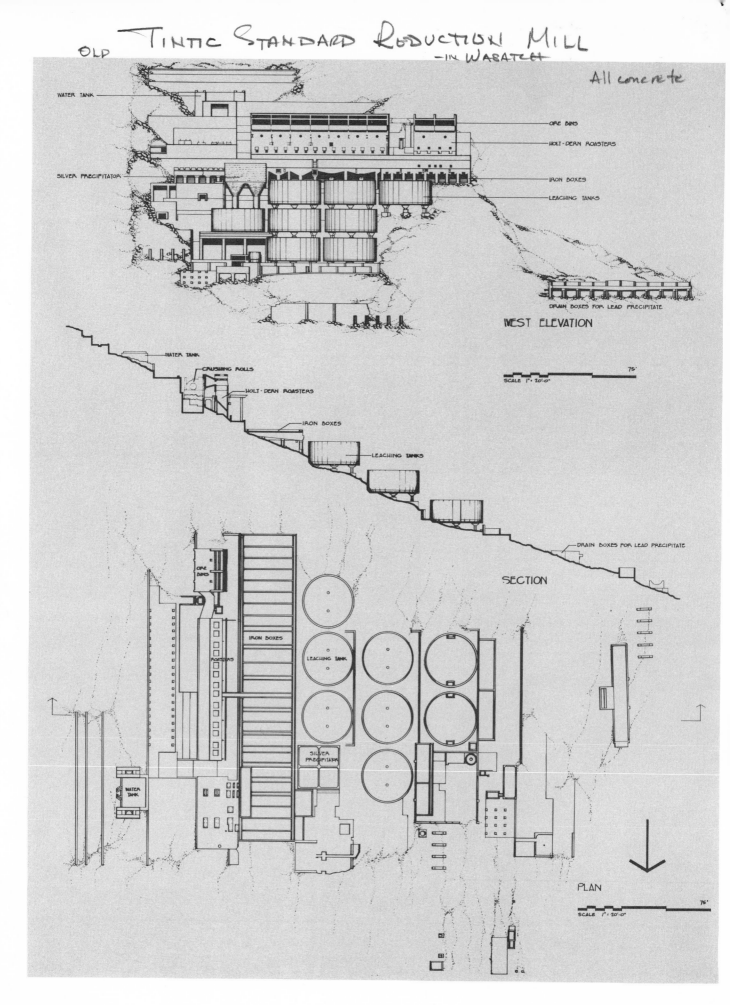

WATER TANK

ORE BINS

HOLT-DERN ROASTERS

SILVER PRECIPITATOR

IRON BOXES

LEACHING TANKS

DRAIN BOXES FOR LEAD PRECIPITATE

WEST ELEVATION

SCALE 1"·20'-0"   75'

WATER TANK

CRUSHING ROLLS

HOLT-DERN ROASTERS

IRON BOXES

LEACHING TANKS

DRAIN BOXES FOR LEAD PRECIPITATE

SECTION

ORE BINS

IRON BOXES

ROASTERS

LEACHING TANK

SILVER PRECIPITATOR

WATER TANK

PLAN

SCALE 1"·20'-0"   75'

the smelter furnace, where lime and silica are added in reverberatory furnaces, the slag on top is taken away for the sump, and the matte (copper) is taken to the converter for more heating and a separation of more slag from the blister copper. The blister copper goes off to the anode furnace, where the metal is cast in fifty-pound slabs called "anodes" and is ready to go to the refinery in El Paso or elsewhere.

Uranium had its boom after World War II, and Grants, New Mexico, became "the uranium capital of the world." Carlsbad on the Pecos produces 85 percent of the nation's potash. Boron, California, produces most of the nation's borax. Coal mines near Gallup have produced for railroads, smelters, refineries, and homes, as have mines at small towns, often company dominated, near Albuquerque and Santa Fe.

In the richly mineralized states south of the border, as in those north of it, exploration goes on and new mines come into production. The Mexican National Comisión de Fomento Minero and both Mexican and American firms are readying open-pit mining near La Caridad in eastern Sonora. Elsewhere, such as at old Alamos, Santa Bárbara, Chiapas, or Aldama, government and private enterprise are opening up deposits of copper, lead, zinc, silver, and uranium.

In the deserts geological wealth beneath the surface matches geological scenery of mountain and canyon. New techniques like making Bouguer gravity maps reveal deposits such as a gigantic salt dome thousands of feet deep in the west end of Salt River Valley, near Luke Air Force Base. It contains from fifty to a hundred times as much salt as Great Salt Lake. This bonanza of salt will go into softening water, curing hides, and feeding cattle. After the salt has been dissolved and pumped up to crystallize in the sun the cavities remaining will serve to store natural gas.

THE EVOLUTION IN MINING from the chance beginnings of Tombstone and White Oaks to the premeditation and intricate technology and financing of Magma Copper Company (wholly-owned by Newmont Mining Corporation) or Duval Corporation (a subsidiary of Pennzoil United, Inc.) has its parallel in the rise of casual, small towns into modern cities with elaborate budgets and planning commissions. Carl Hayden, born in Tempe in 1877, who represented Arizona in Congress

from 1912 to 1969, and Jack O'Connor, a novelist and journalist who was born there in 1902, both later recalled a little town of horses and buggies, livery stables, teamsters, and wagons; of playing in the river, walking the railroad bridge; of blacksmith, old-timers, Maricopas and Pimas who peddled mesquite wood from house to house; of chicken yards, outhouses, neighborhood gossip; and of hunting along the riverbanks or at ranches outside of town. What they recalled is an American small town with Arizona local color, before the first world war and automobiles changed everything.

That simple Tempe is now a real estate bonanza. It boomed from 24,000 citizens in 1960 to 62,000 in 1970. It now merges without identity into the Phoenix metropolitan area of 800,000 persons or more with a million in sight. Like the other Salt River Valley metropolitan cities—Tucson to the south and Yuma, Albuquerque, Roswell, and Las Vegas, Nevada—it has gone through all the stages familiar to Americans elsewhere. With its teachers' college transformed into a university, Tempe has become a cultural center, while the larger cities have risen strikingly as commercial, financial, social, and manufacturing or recreational centers. With growth in population, regional features have declined under the steady impact of the standard national culture of the service station, movie theater, shopping center, franchised restaurant, and big-scale subdivisions. These symptoms of accepted material progress have come because the towns have had water, space for expansion, striking scenery, and strategic position on well-traveled routes. Location has determined their success.

LOCATION HAS ENABLED El Paso, Texas, which is inextricable from the former El Paso del Norte (now Juárez), to become the typical modern city in the Southwest. It lacks the centuries-old, authentic charm of Santa Fe, the swank of shopping districts in metropolitan Phoenix, or the Hollywoodized glamor of Palm Springs. It does have a huge Mexican population, diversified industry, and a modernized frontier army post, Fort Bliss. It has a bona fide sister city just across the river, and together the two constitute the biggest, busiest, and richest international metropolis between Detroit and Cape Horn. El Paso, as its newspapers attest, is at once interested in Texas—though most of

Tyrone today, an open-pit copper mine rumbling with 85-ton trucks, a 10-cubic-yard electric shovel, and to the rear, a 12-inch electric rotary drill rig.

Texas is far from it—in New Mexico, and in Chihuahua. No other southwestern city is so involved in Mexican affairs. Many El Pasoans commute to work in New Mexico, just as many Mexicans cross each day to labor in El Paso. Here, at the lowest pass across the mid-continental mountains of the United States, prehistoric and historic traffic has moved in all directions.

As shown by Owen P. White, the city's breezy first historian, or C. L. Sonnichsen, its jaunty, scholarly historian today, El Paso's story is an integral part of the greater story of Spanish exploration, the settlement of New Mexico, the Pueblo Revolt of 1680, the growth of Juárez, the Chihuahua Trail; the Apache wars, the coming of American explorers and traders, the Mexican-American War; the era of wagons, stagecoaches, and railroads (which changed the city's face from adobe to lumber and brick); the tough post–Civil War days of badmen, cattlemen, and sheriffs and of shootouts in streets and saloons; the rivalry of Albert B. Fall and Albert J. Fountain, the lawyer who was hard on rustlers; the gilded age of big saloons like the Gem and of famous parlor houses like Tillie Howard's on Utah

Street; and the development of the city as a commercial center for mining and ranching in four states. The story is of the long struggle between legitimate businessmen, churchgoers, reformers, cultured people, and good citizens on the one hand and, on the other, gamblers, confidence men, madams, gunmen, and cutthroats. There came to be an elite Victorian society that prized honorable behavior, took duty seriously, and ordered fresh smilax from California to decorate their homes for parties. El Paso was tied closely into the operations of Mexican revolutionaries, the border traffic in Prohibition liquor, the burst of Ku Klux Klan activity in the 1920s, and the development of water conservation the whole length of the Rio Grande.

In the recent twentieth century its power has grown with new factories, busy banks, the expanded activities of Fort Bliss, air and freight traffic, a mounting set of tourist attractions, and growth of a university that exchanges teachers with the University of Chihuahua. And its prestige has grown with the fame of resident artists and writers and the golfer extraordinary, Lee Trevino. Geography, the international line, and economic trends have made El Paso the commercial capital of an immense area.

IN EL PASO, as in Phoenix and other cities, redevelopment programs downtown are a response to the outward sprawl and the leapfrog rise of shopping districts and self-centered suburbs. The desert's most famous such suburb is Scottsdale. In 1940 it was too unimportant a village to get into the admirably catch-all contents and index of *Arizona: A State Guide;* even in 1960 it held only 10,000 persons. But in 1970 it epitomized explosive affluence. Scottsdale had almost 67,000 residents and about 7,000 horses, which had right of way over cars.

In Paradise Valley is the most prestigious of Scottsdale hostelries, the big Camelback Inn, terraced on a hillside and built in Pueblo style, landscaped with lawns and flowering plants. It quietly symbolizes luxury. Nearby, often behind rustic rail fences and amid spacious grounds, are big homes banked with bougainvilleas and other colorful vines and shrubs. Elegant modern-style homes perch on the southern slopes of Squaw Peak and on the rocky sides of Camelback Mountain. Flatland Scottsdale boasts handsome new homes, a new civic center with lagoon and swans, and a shopping center along Scottsdale Road that is Madison Avenue's imitation of the Old West, an idealized Western movie set.

This brand-new commercial district is called Old Town Scottsdale. It has artist-designed rustic street signs, arcaded sidewalks, gaslights, palm trees, flower beds, and many fastidious shops with goods priced for rich customers in the market for jeans, cowboy hats and boots, Indian rugs, baskets, and pottery. The shop that sells leather jackets smells richly of leather. Several galleries sell paintings and sculptures by southwestern artists. There are excellent indoor restaurants and also patio restaurants, where patrons eat outside by tinkling fountains. The shops on one curving street, Fifth Avenue, specialize in imports from foreign countries—India, Mexico, Norway. . . . There is a landscaped courtyard where visitors can sit and both watch and smell a fountain that is perfumed. The entire Old Town has a synthetic quaintness and a real expensiveness that delight many residents and tourists.

Scottsdale's plush motels, such as Executive House

Arizonian, and its guest ranches arrange for horseback rides in adjoining fragments of desert, for chuckwagon breakfasts, or for evening steak fries. There is an American Heritage wax museum. Frank Lloyd Wright's Taliesin West is open to visitors, as is Paolo Soleri's studio, where visitors buy metal and cast ceramic bells. There are a prodigality of swimming pools and eight golf courses. For the special good life in the sunny, warm "winter" season, this genteel outpost of Back East ranks with Palm Springs, the outpost of coastal California, and year around it is a quiet contrast to the Las Vegas Strip with its entertainment and gambling. All are remarkable social flowerings of the desert, spreading below startling desert mountains and alongside authentic desert flora.

More or less guiding the Scottsdale bonanza is the Scottsdale Planning Commission. When Kaiser Aluminum and Aetna Life and Casualty jointly bought the 4,236-acre McCormick Ranch in 1970 and hired seventeen experts to plan a community of thirty-five thousand persons, the plan had to fit into the Scottsdale master plan. The Kaiser-Aetna project means a whole new business, residential, and recreational community inside Scottsdale, which itself is a similar commune inside greater Phoenix.

This new bloom spot of glamor, like present Scottsdale, will be a place of suburban residence and a prime winter resort and tourist center. Its two main designers, Victor Gruen and Associates of Los Angeles and Environmental Planning Consultants of Tempe, propose estate homes, row houses, and offices and stores, as well as a complete school system, an equestrian village for the horsey set, a lake, and a network of pedestrian, bicycle, and horse paths. Behind such a conversion of a ranch into a deluxe town, as the planners note, is the decline in Arizona of mining and agriculture as economic bases and the increasing importance of tourism and winter homes—and of electronic and aerospace industries. After all, the biggest private employer in the Salt River Valley is Motorola. Ore and soil rank lower in dollars attracted than scenic space and sun—provided there is water.

SCOTTSDALE, PRESENT AND FUTURE, is a product of private affluence. Los Alamos is a product of the biggest lode of all, the United States Treasury. In 1946, when the newly created Atomic Energy Commission replaced the army there, it planned and constructed a model federal city. The long mesas fingering out from the Jémez Mountains made zoning easy. Several mesas were for the laboratories; one was for public buildings and an unobtrusive shopping district with one store of each kind (there was no liquor store). There were small signs and big parking lots. Several mesas went to residences, and one mesa became a golf course kept green with recycled sewage water.

The AEC replaced the shacks, hutments, and expansible government trailers of the Manhattan District with permanent buildings, the central Los Alamos Scientific Laboratory, special buildings for physics, radiochemistry, occupational health, the Van de Graaff accelerator, the rolling mill. Cryptic road signs, clear to professional insiders, pointed to BETA SITE, HP SITE, WA SITE, or RD SITE UHTREX. The AEC landscaped where the army in its hurry had merely bulldozed pines to wasteland. A fancy new hospital arose, as well as the credit union and the Museum and Science Hall for visitors.

The Commission provided wide streets, lofty bridges over the arroyos between mesas, and high metal crossways for pedestrians, especially children. At first the government was the landlord. Later it sold lots and homes to residents and gave the area to New Mexico to be a separate, small, special county. A handsome county and city building appeared at the civic center. In the sturdy log building that once housed Los Alamos Ranch School for Boys at Otowi, New Mexico, art exhibits took place and a chamber of commerce began to function. Each August there is a Los Alamos County Fair with traditional competitions in horticulture, cooking, clothes making, and artwork. The town has no billboards.

A product of federal largesse, Los Alamos today is an attractive town, crammed with Ph.D.s and other literate and often liberal-minded citizens very much pro peace and ecology. It is rather like a model college town that houses an institute of technology. It has attractive schools, many churches, and curving residential streets shaded by elms, ashes, and native pines. The homes have wide green lawns, forsythias, weeping willows, and in summer banks of hollyhocks, dahlias, marigolds, gladioluses, and petunias. Lusty crabapple trees bend heavy with fruit. It is a pretty town with the look of new subdivisions in Flagstaff or of the older federal city, Boulder, Nevada, built to go with the building and maintenance of Hoover Dam. Like Boulder, which has always banned gambling, Los Alamos with its verdant campus quality seems to be a place apart from the state it is in. Its architecture is unrelated to New Mexico traditions, and its activities are a contrast to those of the nearby pueblo of Santa Clara or of the Spanish towns across the Rio Grande Valley. It is a favored Anglo, middle-class, intellectually elite town, green from luxurious use of scarce New Mexican water, high toward the blue sky amid a splendid western setting, the Jémez range, and with a view to the east of the distant Sangre de Cristo Mountains. Close by, easily reached by car, are a commercial subdivision, White Rock and Pajarito Acres, Indian and mission ruins, ski areas, fishing reservoirs, camping country, a sportsman's shooting range, and the amenities of Santa Fe.

Out of sight over the Jémez peaks are the remains of "the world's largest crater," and though the professor-scientists of the local laboratories plan devices that make large craters in Nevada and may someday make them in foreign cities, the town itself is gently unaware of death. Hidden away in forest is the Guaje Pines Cemetery. Sometimes during summer thunderstorms enormous streaks of lightning—wide, straight, more powerful than all the voltage of New Mexico—gleam from the heavens to the Jémez peaks. For moments the pummelling of thunder replaces the roar of machinery in the laboratories, where men study to master nature and augment the nation's hegemony in a world of equally strong-willed competitors.

At the base of Casa Grande Mountain in the rugged Chisos range of Texas is the main lodge of Big Bend National Park.

The Chapel of the Holy Cross contrasts with natural red sandstone temples in Oak Creek Canyon, south of Flagstaff.

Overleaf: Hikers amid spruce-fir forest at one of the Latir Lakes in the Sangre de Cristo Mountains, lofty watershed of the Rio Grande and the Pecos.

One of the architectural masterpieces of Kino's Pimería Alta: Mission San Xavier del Bac near Tucson.

The old designs: corn-and-squash necklace, a black pottery sugar bowl, a silver spoon and earrings—all handcrafted by Indians of the San Juan pueblo.

The new jewelry: this coral necklace departs from traditional designs but typifies the craftsmanship of today's finest Indian artisans.

Kachina dolls are replicas of gods that live on the mountains and come down for ceremonial occasions.

A Taos man flenses a deer hide during the process of tanning. Near him is a ladder descending into one of the pueblo homes.

Indian dress and pottery mural, located on the wall of Maisel's Indian shop in Albuquerque, dates back perhaps a hundred years.

CHAPTER 18

THE GOOD LIFE

Sun-drenched tourism, health, and retirement, from the
first Harvey House to Sun City and the Las Vegas "Strip"

THE 1880|s WERE a great turning point in the history of the Southwest, for with them came the end of major Indian fighting, the rise of big mining and cattle enterprises, and the opening up of a marvel-filled region to tourists and new residents. Most crucial of all, the decade brought the Southern Pacific eastward from California via Yuma, Tucson, and Deming to El Paso and on to San Antonio and New Orleans. The Atchison, Topeka, and Santa Fe, building westward from Kansas City, linked Las Vegas to Lamy and Albuquerque; from there it went both southward to Deming and a junction with the Southern Pacific, and westward via Gallup, Winslow, and Kingman to Needles, Barstow, and either Los Angeles or San Francisco. The Denver and Rio Grande built southward from Colorado, and the Mexican Central worked southward from Juárez to Ciudad Chihuahua and Ciudad Méjico. After the Santa Fe acquired the Sonora Railway and also connected from Kansas City to Chicago, it had a through line from Lake Michigan to the sea at Guaymas. The Southwest was tied solidly to world trade and travel.

The railroads offered travelers a vast, grand new area to visit, gasp at, and write home about. The Santa Fe, in particular, advertised and shaped the development of the lands of enchantment, for it ran through or near the most extraordinary scenery of the region. In 1901 its spur line to the south rim of the Grand Canyon confirmed its hold on the supreme outdoor spectacle.

In the notable evolution of the Santa Fe, a particular and enduring force was Frederick H. Harvey, a poor English immigrant who became the master hotel and dining-room man on and alongside the Santa Fe tracks. From the late 1870s until his death in 1901, he gave a distinguished quality to food and dining service at Santa Fe stations and resort hotels, and on dining cars. The Irish linen and English silver, the high-salaried chefs, savory dishes, fresh fruits and vegetables, the choice of wines and specially blended coffee, the decor of rooms, the courtesy—all were the work of this meticulous planner and relentless inspector.

He developed large bakery ovens at Las Vegas, New Mexico, a division point. He kept a special refrigerated boxcar shuttling between California and Missouri, taking Kansas City meat westward and fresh produce from Los Angeles eastward. Along the way his own farms produced eggs, butter, and milk. He had Yaquis in Guaymas catch green turtles that he kept in tanks at Hotel Montezuma, a spa near Las Vegas, until the time came to kill and serve them to fastidious patrons.

One of his achievements was the corps of waitresses. He used newspaper ads to recruit eastern and midwestern girls: "Young women, 18 to 30 years of age, of good character, attractive and intelligent." Expertly trained, chaperoned in dormitories, hundreds of these Harvey girls gave the Southwest a table service it had never before seen. They, as much as the cuisine, drew customers to the Harvey-run Santa Fe hotels such as the El Ortiz in Lamy, El Navajo in Gallup, Fray Marcos in Williams, and Casa del Desierto in Barstow. Harvey's hotels became more than touring centers. They became social centers and match-making bureaus. Though the new girls promised not to marry for a year, Harvey had

The Las Vegas Strip, middle-class gambling oasis of lavish nightlife and daylife, is
glitteringly imposed atop the springs and meadows of the historic Spanish Trail.

217

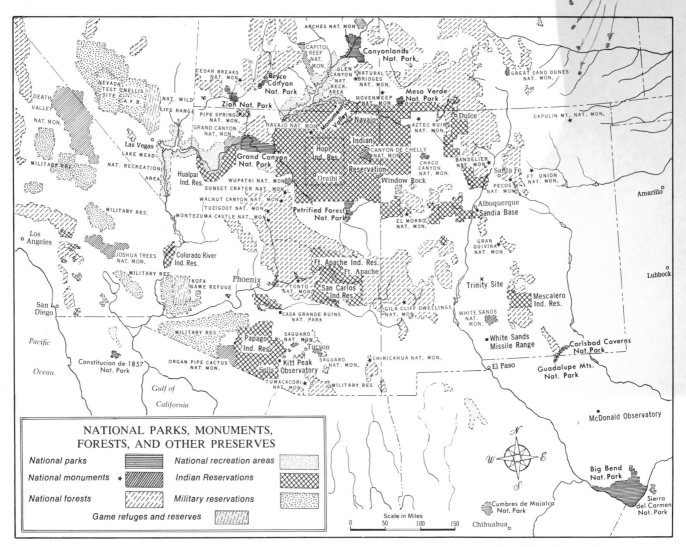

No region in North America has more special-purpose reservations to protect aboriginal peoples, ruins, scenery, wildlife, forests, recreational waters, and outposts for military science.

to relent again and again, for he and the railway had imported this feminine bonanza into the wifeless masculine desert wilds. Perhaps a thousand babies were named Fred or Harvey or both.

From 1884 on, Harvey was using Indian motifs on the walls of eating places. He encouraged Indians to keep native skills, and he displayed and sold their wares. He urged architects to build stations and hotels in an appropriate style. He gave flavor to the Southwest and glamor alike to Indians and the railway. He was a positive force for both Indian and Anglo civilization—for informed tourism at its best.

The era of elegant railroad travel lasted until World War II. Meanwhile, from around 1915, the automobile had gradually been leading tourists into the deserts, on the pioneering southern route, the Ocean-to-Ocean Highway, and later on the numbered state and U.S. highways. By the 1930s tourists were bringing more income into Arizona than all its mines were bringing up to the surface. After V-E and V-J days the building of interstate highways and the boom in air travel made the Southwest deserts available to vastly more people than the trains had long before. Tourism became the leading business in New Mexico.

Back in the 1880s Henry Brown of Santa Fe, photographer and publisher of stereopticon slides for sale

ew Otero S&L
Raise 6 Flags
...ctronically

...aLSENBURG, Colo.—Elec-
...cally operated flagpoles will
feature of the seventh of-
...of Otero Savings and Loan
...ciation, now under construc-
...in Walsenburg for opening
...winter.

...ero Savings — founded in
...ch...unta, Colo., in 1890 with a
...ch in Denver at 8980 E.
...pden Ave. that opened in
...1st 1973—traditionally
...s each morning over all of
...offices the six flags which
...flown over the years in
...east Colorado — the ban-
...s of Spain, France, Mexico,
...Colorado and the United

...rle C. Carpenter, Otero's
...dent, said electronic con-
...will raise the flags auto-
...cally each morning at the
Walsenburg office and
...them at dusk.
...er Otero Savings offices in-
...three in Colorado Springs
one in Pueblo.

...shops, expressed the varied ...larly the Atchison, Topeka, ...having taken possession of ...anta Fe Trail," tourists, ...men will find ready means of ea... ...lmost inaccessible country; a...ero Savings...consisting of beautiful scenery... ...s, Indian pueblos, cave dw... ...endid agricultural and gra... ...health, also, will be greatly b... ...oft and mild atmosphere of t... ...of its health-giving mineral wa...

Brown sp... unknowingly for the auto an... ...he outlined the permanent a... ...nd sun.

DURING THE ... aca, the newcomers had ... ...al details to notice or write ... ...t the army topographical en... ...n the 1840's, men like Frémont, ...bert, were literate, well informed, and res...ive to the landscape. Explorers like John Wesley Powell, archeologists like Adolph Bandelier, and journalists like George Wharton James began a rich tradition of extolling the visual wonders of the Southwest. With publicity and time, with the paved road ending the myth that the desert is impenetrable, and with the sanctification of areas as national parks, the deserts have increasingly gained in reputation as an assemblage of stupendous scenery.

There are the 1,700-foot canyons of the Rio Grande, which defied the early boundary surveyors; the White Sands, the world's largest gypsum dune field; Carlsbad Caverns, enormous yet delicate; the Chiricahua Mountains, fantastically eroded; Death Valley, that beautiful exhibit of natural extremes and oddities; and the Grand Canyon, a chasm full of mountains. Just now being opened by a railroad line is the deep Barranca del Cobre—Copper Canyon—in the Sierra Madre between Ciudad Chihuahua and Los Mochis. Matching the geological wonders are the adaptations of wild plants and animals, in their natural state, wherever men have let them survive, or in special collections such as the new Carlsbad Zoological–Botanical Gardens State Park or the Arizona–Sonora Desert Museum, set in a sajuaro forest a few miles from Tucson. There, amid native surroundings, visitors see a variety of living insects, reptiles, amphibians, birds, and mammals, including

Of the Harvey Houses one rhymester wrote: "We all couldn't eat without 'em but the slickest thing about 'em/ Is the Harvey skirts that hustle up the feeds." (AT&SF station, Deming, New Mexico, 1913.)

Tourists seek out the ruins of prehistoric Paquimé (now Casas Grandes, Chihuahua), once a large city of plazas, three-story buildings, ball courts, pyramids, and a complex irrigation system.

dwarf Sonoran deer and river otters.

Finally, the desert Indians, especially in the pueblos, are a great attraction. Scores of prehistoric cliff dwellings and pueblo ruins, from Pecos National Monument to sites in the Grand Canyon, win a steady patronage of serious tourists delighted to find ruins that date back to the ninth century or earlier. Chihuahua has not only the Casas Grandes ruins at Paquimé, but nearby in Cañón Garabato are 900-year-old cliff dwellings where an artistic, agricultural civilization flourished. Mexican and United States tourists already visit here, and the Mexican government may make it a national park to rival Mesa Verde in southwestern Colorado. The whole prehistoric complex stands open near Los Alamos in Bandelier National Monument—cave dwellings, pueblo foundations, ceremonial caves, and ancient trails.

Since the 1870s fascinated visitors to the Southwest have watched Indian ceremonial dances, with their stylized movements and thumping rhythms. Army personnel at forts and camps used to need entertainment, and wagon loads or carriage loads of officers and wives, visiting congressmen, and important guests attended dances such as the snake dances of the Hopis, the rain dances of the Zuñis, or the corn dances of the Santo Domingos. Later the Indian Detours of the Santa Fe took busloads of tourists to the dances. Automobiles

brought in sightseers, who by their very numbers impaired the quality of the event they were observing.

The national movement to conserve human history flowers in the state and national parks and monuments that preserve what little is left of ancient Indian history and of non-Indian history since Coronado. The 1906 Act for the Preservation of American Antiquities made possible, for instance, Gran Quivira National Monument, which President Taft created in 1909. Three centuries before, Indians had abandoned the town that Oñate in 1598 called Pueblo de las Humanas, where later the Franciscans had to abandon two seventeenth-century missions.

Restored or preserved ruins like those at Fort Davis, the Territorial Prison at Yuma, the mission churches downriver from El Paso, or the Hubbell Trading Post near Ganado on the Navajo Reservation—these help the serious tourist with imagination to get away from the tedious, sign-covered commercial present and into the contrasts and variety of the past.

The same is true of responsible historical museums in Santa Fe, Juárez, Tucson, and other cities, on campuses from Hermosillo to Alpine, and at state and national parks such as White Sands, New Mexico, and Tubac State Park, Arizona. One architectural museum, Pioneer Arizona in the Verde Valley north of Phoenix, brings together actual historic buildings.

Demolition—urban renewal—in the name of progress has destroyed old, distinctive downtowns in numerous cities. Out-of-the-way towns in Mexico like Ures, from which Anza made his first California expedition, remain virtually intact from an earlier age. New Mexico draws hungry tourist crowds to Old Town in western Albuquerque and to Old Mesilla, each with a famous restaurant. So far, though crowds, automobile traffic, and new highways threaten it, Santa Fe—old, busy, and charming—remains the best preserved and most vital historical survival in the region. It has bent with the centuries but has escaped "renewal." It modestly offers its plaza and Governor's Palace, its narrow streets, free from gridiron uniformity, its Indians seated on arcaded sidewalks vending jewelry and pottery, its fonda, or inn, on a site where there has been one fonda or another for perhaps three hundred and fifty years, and its San Miguel Chapel, the oldest church in the United States.

THE FLATLANDS AND UPLANDS of the two-nation deserts have long attracted hunters eager to shoot elk, antelope, deer, bear, bighorns, and wild turkeys. Although overhunting and land development have depleted wildlife, fishing—once a minor activity for most tribesmen and Anglos—is now a thriving recreational sport in the hundreds of new man-made streams called irrigation canals and in the man-made lakes on rivers from the Conchos to the Colorado. Exotic species, planted in appropriate water (warm or cold), grow long and fat amid sunburned rock and sand—channel catfish, northern pike, walleyed pike, perch, bass, German brown and rainbow trout, and landlocked Kokanee salmon from British Columbia. In Lake Powell, astraddle Utah and Arizona, fishermen have evolved new techniques to catch bass, which are near the surface, and trout, which prefer the colder water below twenty feet. The new desert waters are a miracle of fishes provided by technology and federal bureaucracy.

In the less populous days of Henry Brown, the stereopticon man, the health seeker was more conspicuous than now. Easterners and Californians with bronchial and lung disorders, many a tubercular who needed to flee damp coastal air, and many an asthmatic who had inhaled too much industrial and coal smoke used the railroads to reach recommended spots where clean, dry

air, cold or warm, promised relief or cure, comfort or longevity. Albuquerque, Santa Fe, Ruidoso, Tucson, Palm Springs, and Hot Springs, New Mexico, developed colonies of "lungers." Ailing friends of ranchers, lingering as guests, served among the pioneering patrons in the dude ranch business. Many a health seeker recovered and became an active citizen in ranching, business, teaching, politics, or law.

With the growing popularity of transcontinental automobile travel, many among the tourists from the coasts and the Midwest saw the sundusted Southwest as a place to spend each winter or to live when retired. While many poor Mexicans looking for work moved to the border cities, a migration of retired Americans looking for respite and recreation—and domestic help—moved toward the same spots. The towns and spas have grown steadily during the present century, and after World War II there was a boom of in-migration that led to the invention of a new kind of city.

A few miles from Phoenix on a former ranch, two former carpenters, Del E. Webb and "Jake" Jacobson, developed the first big retirement community in the region, Sun City. It was what real estate writers call a "total-town project oriented to leisure." It pioneered in the Salt River Valley the idea of large new settlements of persons fifty years old or older who are interested primarily in play. In 1960 its opening anticipated the market for early, well-heeled retirement and rapidly achieved a resounding success. In 1963 Sun City had a population of 4,500; in 1970, 14,000; in 1971, 17,000; 30,000 is predicted for 1980.

In its homes, duplexes, garden apartments, and patio houses, all one story high, there are no permanent residents under age eighteen. In 1970 buyers had their choice of six different house plans; and since parts were interchangeable, there were twenty-four choices in all. No. 62A, for instance, was the "Rosemary"; No. 62B was the "Cochise." Among the patio house plans there were three choices; among duplexes, sixteen. Since the climate makes lawns hard to maintain, many front yards are layers of natural rock or of gravel painted green, red, or brown, placed on top of hidden tar paper (to suppress weeds). Except for schools and a cemetery, Sun City is a complete town with banks, hospitals, churches, medical buildings, shopping centers, country clubs, a nursing home, an amphitheater, and a Howard

THE GREAT SOUTHWEST

—118

Johnson restaurant. The outdoors still gets hot, a hundred degrees or more, but everything inside is air-conditioned, and no one lives far from one of the five elegant swimming pools.

The corporation intends to have "a warm, neighborly, and attractive atmosphere," and it succeeds with its citizens, who give the appearance of being more homogeneous, unified, and contented than most Americans. One reason is the development company's plan to help people avoid rocking-chair retirement and random senility, and instead to "get wet to the neck" in hobby and club work and quiet sports. Sun City has generated more than one hundred twenty-five civic and hobby organizations, four recreational centers, professionally equipped arts and crafts centers, and ample facilities for tennis, lawn bowling, or billards, as well as exercise equipment and miniature or full-scale golf. Thriving Sun City draws its residents from all the states and several other countries, but especially from Illinois, Michigan, New York, California, and Arizona itself.

Such corporation-engineered suburbs, planned for everything but work and politics, have begun to surround Phoenix, Tempe, and Mesa, and combine with other city growth to threaten the agricultural base of the state. There are Litchfield Park, a development started in 1964 by Litchfield Park Properties, a subsidiary of Goodyear Tire & Rubber Company, to replace the long-staple cotton fields opened during World War I; Carefree, a community of plush homes located on streets with names such as Never Mind Trail and Lazy Lane; and other communities in the planning stages or under construction. Fountain Hills, a retirement city, will have a fountain (the world's highest) that jets a single stream of water 560 feet into the evaporative ambient air. In the stretch south from Phoenix to Tucson and the border at Nogales are the touted preliminaries of real estate developments, among them one that "will include facilities for almost every conceivable outdoor sport."

To the west, on the Arizona waterfront, on one of the Colorado River reservoirs, lies Lake Havasu City, founded in 1964 by McCulloch Properties, Inc., a wholly-owned subsidiary of McCulloch Oil Corporation. After acquiring state lands, Robert McCulloch founded his city by forming Lake Havasu Irrigation and Drainage District, which became the city's government, providing water and roads. A company brochure shows a rapid rise in capital investment, assessed valuation, population growth (to eight thousand in 1971), business establishments, homes, public school students, and so on.

Sloping desert, bulldozed bare and turned into lawns, rows of palm trees, curved streets, and homes and shops —all far apart (separated by lots held on speculation)— stand as evidence of a real estate boomtown. There are Lake Havasu Marina; the Nautical Inn resort hotel and water sports center; Lake Havasu Hotel, with a waterfall slanting down its roof; a golf course; a green, neat civic center with fountains; and a Science and Industry Park that has factories for chain-saw cutter bars, portable welders, gyroplane and minibike engines, and fishing lures. There is also a printing firm with a full-color, high-speed press.

The corporation makes much of McCulloch's purchase of a London bridge completed in 1831. It has low arches, extends for a thousand feet, and contains 130,000 tons of granite. Dismantled piece by piece and freighted to Lake Havasu, the bridge now crosses a machine-dug inlet of Colorado River water.

Far more modest in material development than Lake Havasu City is Truth or Consequences, New Mexico, terraced along the north side of a bend in the Rio Grande. Hot Springs, New Mexico, acted on a proposal made by Ralph Edwards, radio and television producer and Hollywood "personality." As the tenth anniversary of his Truth or Consequences radio program approached in 1950, he announced that if a town in the United States would change its name to the name of his show, he would stage his tenth anniversary in that place. In a special election the citizens voted 1,249 to 295 to rename the town. Edwards came and staged the affair— and he did more. He began coming every year, and the little health and retirement resort, still a small town, became widely known. It was no longer one of the thirty-three United States towns with "Hot Springs" in its name.

Twenty-two hot mineral baths offer sweat baths, colonics, massages, and other health treatments. Hot Springs National Bank claims to be the only bank in the nation with its own hot mineral bath. More than one hundred fifty motels, mobile home parks, and trailer parks provide for the clients, mostly elderly, who find the air (pure), elevation (4,200 feet), humidity

Sun City's Lakeview Recreational Area offers mini-golf, sailing, and fishing. Beyond, amid new houses, are old palms brought in horizontally and re-erected at decorative angles.

(normally 10-15 percent), dryness (7 inches of rain a year), average temperatures (46 degrees in winter, 77 in summer), and sunshine (318 days a year) to their liking.

An elite way to visit the Southwest, established long ago at big spreads like the Sierra Bonita Ranch, has come down through the era of dude ranches, now called guest ranches, which thrive outside Tucson, Wickenburg, Victorville, and other desert towns. In winter they draw patrons from east and west. No one can deny the pleasure and luxury of fashionable guest ranches with their fancy but western bedrooms, dining rooms and cocktail lounges, patios, pools, flower beds, corrals, horseback rides, and cookouts, all in benign weather, while St. Paul and Chicago shiver, Los Angeles chokes on smog, and Miami sweats in high relative humidity.

When the visit becomes permanent or semipermanent, the fancy home often becomes the landmark. For some it is the second or third home, or the headquarters for travel during retirement.

There are such homes in Santa Fe or Sedona, south of Flagstaff. Fanciest of all, with famous or fabulously wealthy inhabitants, are homes and estates in the Paradise Valley–Scottsdale section near Phoenix and in the Palm Springs complex of towns. Like Phoenix, Palm Springs attracts industrial magnates, but in particular it attracts arts and entertainment celebrities such as Frederick Lowe, Raymond Loewy, George and

David Hearst, Jack Benny, Liberace, Bing Crosby, Bob Hope, Gloria Swanson, and Debbie Reynolds. Their homes are among the sights of the town even when they are hidden behind walls, oleanders, and clustered palm trees. *Palm Springs Magazine* gladly pictures the doings of the glamor set at the Racquet Club, the Tennis Club, the Canyon Country Club, and the Thunderbird Country Club.

The swimming pools, the ultramodern architecture, the lush landscaping of Palm Springs, Palm Desert, La Quinta, and other oases lie between wild sand dune country to the east and towering chocolate-brown mountains to the west, dominated by forest-topped Mount San Jacinto. The elegant tone of the town is caught in its spacious civic center. One of earth's most stunning views from an airport is the ground-level view from the lobby westward to the civic center and to San Jacinto towering up and up for more than eleven thousand feet to its rounded summit, white with snow in winter.

Relentlessly, despite Mexican laws designed to keep outsiders from buying or controlling Mexican land, Californians have pushed southward into Baja California, acquiring second homes or weekend cabins along the coast from Costa Azul southward past Rosarito and toward Ensenada. The Arizonans, hungry for a western seashore Gadsden couldn't buy for them, are

*Navajo Lake—15,000 acres of dammed San Juan River water east of Fruitland and Aztec, New Mexico—
is a popular fishing place, although the fish are notably contaminated with mercury.*

developing a series of beachheads for villas—on Bahía de San Carlos near Guaymas, at Bahía Kino, a lonely, windswept curve of sand west of Hermosillo, and at Puerto Peñasco, hardly more than sixty miles from the international boundary. Rocky Point, an old volcano, separates the port town of Peñasco from a long, white beach where Phoenix, Tempe, and Tucson people are building estates. Technically, it is Mexicans—*prestanombres*—who own the sand lands, but American partners are the engineer, land developer, and manager. Arizona officials have cleared the subdivision for advertising and sales in Arizona.

THE NORTHWESTERN METROPOLIS of the region, Las Vegas, busy night and day, has its own specializations, with its gambling, its restaurants, its lavish and expensive shows, droves of car and plane tourists, visible

call girls, and its corps of disguised Internal Revenue Service tax detectives.

Fortune has favored this one-of-a-kind tourist stop, which one newspaperman calls a "spotlighted oasis green with money." It is near the canyon where Hoover Dam became a famous sight. It has had an abundance of ground water since the days when the wet meadows were a major camping place on the Spanish Trail. It is on the Union Pacific Railroad, which long took pride in its passenger trains, and it straddles one of the main east-west transcontinental highways. It is on the routes of leading airlines, with more than two hundred fifty commercial flights there daily. It is within an easy drive from opulent, free-spending Southern California. It is a major beneficiary of the wide-open gambling bill of 1931 that set Nevada apart from the other states.

The Las Vegas "Strip" is two miles of flashing neon

alongside wall-to-wall motels and sixty-six gaudy gambling palaces, which often are combined with huge hotels that poke into the sky. At night the lights dim the moon. Reflected in the sky on a dark night they are a luminiscent landmark for fifty miles. The free-standing illuminated sign in front of the Frontier Hotel is about fifteen stories high; at night jet pilots sight it when they are a hundred miles away. The Flamingo, Thunderbird, Caesar's, Sahara, Landmark, Sands, Stardust, Riviera, Tropicana, and others, which attract big investors like Kirk Kerkorian or Howard Hughes, offer such entertainers as Phil Harris, Dean Martin, Carol Channing, Sammy Davis, Jr., Mitzi Gaynor, Buddy Hackett, Marlene Dietrich, or les Folies Bergères.

Buildings in Las Vegas are designed to stimulate gambling. All entrances lead directly to casinos; seats and phones are likely to be in the rear of casinos, not in lobbies; decor is exciting to the senses and likely to be red; and ceilings are low in order to accentuate the tables. The temperature is completely comfortable, 67 degrees in summer and 72 in winter. Each kind of game is strategically placed in the rooms, with slot machines adroitly scattered everywhere. Sound, whether music or hubbub, is kept at a steady, exciting level, whether attendance is sparse or the room is jammed tight. There are no clocks, but there are plenty of drinks and handsome men and women in one role or another.

Rooms, meals, and shows are no longer inexpensive, as they once were before inflation hit, but by offering big-scale, big-volume, show-biz gambling to the American middle class and by building up a convention business. Las Vegas enterprise has made a triumph of artifice and novelty. It is a calculated Machine Age caravansary where well-insured people can happily take chances with their expendable income.

Of all the desert cities Las Vegas has most concentrated, capitalized, and glamorized its entertainment. Its fellow towns give pleasure by means of events of all sorts, from old customs to contrived public relations gimmicks. State and county fairs have origins solidly

in the past, as have religious festivals like the fiesta of San Francisco de Assisi in Magdalena and the *luminarias* in Rio Grande towns. On Christmas Eve there are miles of lighted candles inside little pots or boxes or paper bags folded and filled with sand. These outline garden walls, entry walks, porches, the tops of houses, ramparts, and curbs.

Chambers of commerce and kindred business interests are behind livestock shows, rodeos, bullfights in the big Mexican border towns as in the Plaza Monumental of Juárez (*"La mas Comoda y el mas Prestigio en la Frontera"*), the Gold Rush Days celebration in Wickenburg, the annual date carnival with its Arab motif in Indio, or the Big Surf in Tempe, where machinery creates an artificial wave for persons who want to surfboard amid creosote bush and cholla. A Socorro, New Mexico, golfing match tees off from a 7,000-foot mountain. Ruidoso Downs, isolated in a mountain valley not far from the rich oil men of "Little Texas" (southeastern New Mexico), promotes itself as "Home of the world's richest horse race—the All-American Futurity."

El Paso, ambitious to attract conventions and tourism and to persuade visitors to "Stay Another Day," has entered the lists of January 1 tournaments. It stages a Sun Carnival with an elaborate New Year's Day parade, dancing in the streets, Sun Carnival Art Show, Sun Carnival Symphony, Sun Carnival Rodeo, Sun Bowl basketball tournament, and a climactic Sun Bowl football game.

Public bureaus in Utah, Nevada, and Chihuahua have ready-to-mail packets of tourist information. In Arizona the Travel Information Section of the Department of Economic Planning & Development, with its booklet *Amazing Arizona: You Can Always Expect to Enjoy the Unexpected,* and the Highway Department, with its multicolored *Arizona Highways,* represent boosterism at a high level of proficiency. Equally adept is the Tourist Division of New Mexico's Department of Development, which puts out *The Land of Enchantment Where the Fun Never Sets.*

225

CHAPTER 19

THE RED MAN TODAY

Indians' continuing struggle to preserve the old culture and gain their share of the good things of the new

NEWSPAPER READERS and businessmen were astonished to learn one day in March of 1970 that a tribe of Apaches had put up two million dollars in cash to back a Hollywood film. It was a Western called *A Gunfight*, starring Kirk Douglas and Johnny Cash, in which two Texas gun-slingers down on their luck agree to a shootout for pay. There would be a grand finale in a bullring. The film was to be made in New Mexico and Spain. In quickly making a telephone contact with the Hollywood producer, Ronald Lubin, and then arranging to supply the money, the Jicarilla Apaches who number 1,779, beat out MGM, United Artists, and other prospective lenders—an act that Lubin found to be "aggressive and marvelous."

In order to avoid dipping into their portfolio of thirteen million dollars in investments, the Jicarillas borrowed the two million from banks, where their credit was excellent—in contrast to that of some film studios. They would get the first two million of the film's profits and a quarter of the profits thereafter. The picture shows no Indians, but financially, as tribal president Charlie Vigil said, "This is one round where the Indians are going to win."

When the film had its premier in Albuquerque in May 1971, five hundred Jicarillas sat in the audience—whole families, from the elderly down to three-year-olds—along with Lubin and associates and the United States Indian Commissioner. As the curtains parted, the motion picture began, showing a brilliant sun rising over a stark New Mexico landscape. A man on horseback rode into view. The first credit appeared: "The Jicarilla Apache Tribe of American Indians Presents

'A Gunfight'." The audience burst into applause.

They clapped for good reason. Apaches—Apaches, mind you, heirs to three hundred years of white hostility, to the French association of the word *Apaches* with criminal gangs in Paris—Apaches had shed the old image. They had competed successfully with giant corporations. They had invested big money and now stood to make a handsome profit on the world market. They had been the angels bankrolling glamor, a Hollywood movie, distributed by Paramount, that featured famous performers and would be widely viewed in the United States and Europe.

This peaceful Apache coup was the most dramatic and sensational Indian success to date. It called attention not only to the Jicarilla community but also to the new relative affluence of many southwestern tribes, though most certainly not of all.

THE DESERT AND PLATEAU Indians survived the army's physical control of the period from 1848 to the 1880s and the period of Protestant missionary thought control that began when the government handed the schools over to the sects. Generations grew up torn between the old and the new, lingering confused as they confronted sectarian teachers, white ranchers, dam builders, anthropologists, miscellaneous trespassers and pillagers, tourists, crooked traders, and often the officials of the Indian Bureau itself.

But from the Hoover administration on, especially under Indian Commissioner John Collier during the New Deal, the tribes came to possess a new sense of tribal organization and self-determination, of rights

A meeting of the Navajo Tribal Council. The Navajo Nation, the biggest group of native peoples in the United States, faces crucial economic and social problems as it grows and develops.

227

for Indians and of self-respect for Indians and their culture. A 1924 law had given Indians nominal citizenship in the United States and their state of residence. Indians first received draft calls during World War II; the right to vote came in 1948. But as the Commission on Civil Rights reported in 1961, the status of Indians continues to be more complex than that of non-Indians. The tribes have certain inherent sovereign powers, for they were here first. Conquest by the white man ended their external powers but not their internal ones. In the relationship between an Indian and his tribe, the United States Constitution and civil rights laws do not apply. The courts and Public Law 280 have repeatedly defined the status of Indian tribes as dependent sovereigns, subservient only to the federal government. They have a status greater than that of the states themselves. Any substantial change in the affairs of a tribe requires the consent of the tribal government.

Learning of this independence at a conference on "Arizona Indian people and their relation to the state's total structure," an Arizona civic leader cried out: "Beautiful! Indians have a better go at self-determination than a God-fearing, taxpaying citizen of the so-called dominant society. They are in the driver's seat."

Indians are subject to federal legislation and are covered by many special federal laws. In matters such as welfare, education, and taxes, Indians find themselves caught between the state and the federal governments. Legal decisions vary from state to state as to a state's right to collect income and sales taxes from reservation Indians. The Arizona Court of Appeals says Arizona may collect taxes. Certainly Indians pay sales taxes when they buy off the reservation. They also pay severance taxes on oil and gas, and federal income taxes.

In short, an Indian is a tribal member. He is a "ward" of the central government. He is a United States citizen with most of the same rights and privileges of other citizens. He is a member of a racial minority, with one advantage over the Negro—he can go home again or he is already there. No state can seize tribal property.

The former possessors of the continent by right of prior occupation now have only their reservations, on lands once thought by whites to be relatively valueless but now seen as immensely valuable for numerous resources that include space itself. In New Mexico and Arizona, Indians now loom as important landlords.

Just the same, on reservations big or small, Indians live constantly endangered by federal bureaus, federal judges, and private corporate interests with tricky leases to offer. Navajo rights to Colorado River water are jeopardized by the Bureau of Reclamation. Recently the Bureau of Land Management gave to the state of California control of 1,500 acres of valuable Mojave Indian land, and legal technicalities denied the Mojaves their day in court. In the late 1950s the Agua Caliente Indians of Palm Springs, through a land settlement in the plush desert town, came into an annual individual income of around twenty-five thousand dollars. Then the Bureau of Indian Affairs permitted state officials to declare nearly two-thirds of the tribe's members incompetent to manage their own income. Trustees who were appointed began pocketing an average of one-third of the proceeds from the Indians' land. The scandal that broke smirched lawyers and judges alike.

Indians have problems more basic than crooked California trustees. The thriving Navajos need more land. Owing to overpopulation, there is underemployment, as among Taos and Santo Domingo Indians. The Navajos, Hopis, and many others must seek seasonal work on ranches or in towns, and there are Indian colonies all along the Santa Fe and Southern Pacific lines. Among Navajos there is much malnutrition, protein deficiency that impairs the mental growth of children. Among adult Indians, as among non-Indians, there are problems that come from personal dislocation and loss of identity. The suicide rate among Indians is many times the national average—three to ten times, depending on the tribe. The alcoholism rate is also high. In arrests for drunkenness the Indian rate is three times that for the general population, a figure that indicates in part the attitude of policemen toward Indians. In Flagstaff the radio carries Hopi-language commercials for cheap wine.

Of Gallup, self-styled "Indian capital of the world," an Indian anthropologist says, "There are more bars and places to get liquor in Gallup than any place else I have heard of, and bartenders sell drinks to people already drunk." The town of 16,000 persons has twenty-six bars and its own bottling plant for inexpensive wine. The local jail holds only sixty drunks, and often there are scores more in town, who swamp the Gallup Indian Center and a warehouse room maintained by a Roman Catholic charity. The Navajo Legal Aid Service helps as it can and advocates a rehabilitation center to replace either the old jail or a new 250-person prisoner center now being proposed.

In general, the federal government provides poor hospital care. Indian Health Service hospitals are decrepit and crowded. Indians have one of the lowest health levels of all United States population groups; they die from preventable diseases long under control among others. Perry Sundust, chairman of the Phoenix Indian Medical Center Advisory Board, like Representative Morris Udall, was critical when President Nixon held up a $1 million sum voted for additional patient care. Sundust said the president had "ignored the fact that these sick people will remain sick without adequate care. . . . Indians are treated like third-rate citizens."

As a whole, Indians in the United States, as in Mexico, rank among the nation's poorest citizens. Unemployment is ten times the national average, and annual per capita income is half the national average. Even for the Jicarillas the average per capita income is $2,200, which is below the national figure. The Laguna Pueblos average $3,600 per family; the Navajos, $825 per capita. Forty-two percent of all Indian children drop out before the end of high school; most who start college drop out, and the suicide rate for Indian teen-agers is three times the national average.

Clearly, among Indians, as among Chicanos, blacks, and whites, too, all is not well. Yet improvements and help have been coming. In the 1930s the Rural Electrification Administration took electricity to the Indian villages, and Indians joined rural America in using household appliances—radios, washing machines, power pumps, refrigerators, and televison sets. Indians acquired cars and trucks. Antennas sprouted on rooftops. To get cash for these things, Indians looked for jobs. While some moved to cities like Chicago and Los Angeles and lost their culture, others remained in the villages and built up the physical standard of living while continuing the old cultural and inner life. As the executive head of Zuñi Pueblo says, Indians are now on their way to being assets to themselves, their states, and their country.

The University of New Mexico has a Minorities Cultural Awareness Center, and in the School of Law

Robert L. Bennett, an Oneida, directs the American Indian Law Center. The university's Native American Studies program helps the individual adjust to college, gives courses to help him return to the reservation, and offers courses to all students on Indian history and culture. The University of California at Los Angeles has Monroe E. Price and others teaching Indian law and seeing to it that Indians do fully get their day in court. On their reservation Navajo leaders hold seminars to discuss the details of Indian problems and prospects.

In the general revolt against the Anglo middle-class establishment, friends of Indians have rallied on many fronts. Advocates of the Tigua Indians in El Paso have urged Texas to provide the Tiguas with land for housing and medical and educational facilities. The proposal includes putting a museum at the site of the original 1682 Tigua Pueblo in Ysleta, where Indians can make and sell pottery and other wares. It also calls for excavating an old pueblo, abandoned around A.D. 1400, near Hueco Tanks in the desert between El Paso and the salt lakes to the east.

INDIANS TODAY have become increasingly vocal in numerous ways and under various circumstances, not in the old tradition of war whoops, but in the current one of civil protest. Ácoma and Laguna parents have reported to federal officials that the Grants school district has misused public funds in "discrimination against Indians and poor people." Indian women in Sandoval County, New Mexico, have protested against the reluctance of Anglo fellow citizens to let Indians register to vote. When the Inter-Tribal Indian Ceremonial took place for the forty-ninth time, in 1970, a band called "Indians Against Exploitation" picketed the affair and called for giving control of the ceremonial to Indians or closing it down.

Louis Rodgers, director of American Indian studies at Navajo High School in Ramah, New Mexico, has urged that the Ramah school and the Rough Rock Demonstration School get rid of Anglo educators: "If education is going to be Navajo and directed with Navajo interests, everything and everyone that is not Navajo-thinking should be eliminated—from instructors to administrators, from curriculum to textbooks, in particular, history textbooks. Even Anglos with the

Plants like this one of __General Dynamics__ at Fort Defiance, Arizona, provide jobs for Navajo workers.

best of intentions," Rodgers said, "remain as a symbol of suppression and oppression."

A speaker at Navajo Community College said, "Go home, missionaries. You've got plenty of work to do on your people. We don't need you here. . . . [We] have our own values . . . our religion." Daniel Deschinny of Window Rock spoke with scorn and cynicism: "I don't think the whiteman is interested in the idea that Indians should become whitemen. The whiteman is interested in the natural resources the Indians have on their reservations."

At Northern Arizona University in Flagstaff, which lies close to big reservations, students in the Alliance of Concerned Native American Students have demanded that Indian minds plan the Indian Studies course and write their texts, and that Indian voices do the teaching. The students' position is that only an Indian can give the Indian point of view, which will benefit white students and help Indians cope with post-graduation difficulties. In 1971 Navajo upper-classmen objected to a course called Navajo Blessing-way Ceremony because the teaching of a sacred ritual in a public classroom is an invasion of religious privacy. In Los Angeles at the Southwest Museum, a seemingly pro-Indian institution, young Indians successfully demanded the total removal of an exhibit of ancestral bones dug from a sacred burial.

Indians have attacked the stereotyping of themselves in stories and films. They object to having frontier Indians says "Ugh" or utter sounds that translate as

"Many pony soldier die." A committee of the American Indian Historical Society examined three hundred textbooks and supplementary volumes used in public and Bureau of Indian Affairs schools. They found insults, scorn, and omissions. The best of the books, they concluded, treat the Indian as only a footnote to American history.

Indians have invaded Western movie locations and picketed theaters to protest unfair caricaturing of Indians. They made Hollywood producer Jerry Adler change the name of *Nobody Loves a Drunken Indian* to *Flap*. Responding to the new Indian angle, Arthur Penn's *Little Big Man* is pro-Indian.

Dr. Cecil Corbett, minister and educator, a Nez Percé married to a Navajo, has said that there are some common cultural characteristics of Indians that are virtues on their reservations but do not serve them well off the reservations—a lack of competitiveness, strong kinship with family and clan, and a casual attitude toward material things: "These are usually looked up as 'Indian problems' by Anglos, and by some Indians, because they make it difficult to thrust the Indian into the dominant white society. Now, however, people are pointing out that the white society itself doesn't function too well. And some experts are predicting that it won't work at all as technology, automation and information force us into a new kind of world."

I NDIANS ARE NOT ALONE in asserting the superior features of their society. Southwestern whites, who once looked down on Indians, confusing a white-caused culture of poverty with indigenous Indian civilization, now confront self-assured, trained Indians, sometimes wealthy, backed by public law, and sustained by a tradition of cooperation and respect for the gray hairs of maturity and wisdom. There is among Indians a tradition of long talk followed by general agreement—the very thing, as Erna Fergusson has pointed out, that the United Nations seeks to attain. The whites who now take a new, positive look at Indian society face deviation and rebellion and commune-ism among their own long-haired children and a widespread, multifaceted disillusionment with material and competitive values in the whole growth-economy of advertising, salesmanship, planned obsolescence, and self-centered, private-home life, busy keeping up with the Joneses and the installment payments.

Also, Anglos now smell, hear, taste, and see the brute evidence that they are destroying their natural environment in the name of personal freedom, private ownership, and dollar profit. Indians with a philosophy of tribal ownership have a viewpoint that is ecologically respectful of Mother Earth. Many tribesmen oppose development of their lands. The Papagos, for instance, are not just interested in making money from copper mines; they also want a properly balanced land use for the tribe's future. Some Navajos view with doubt the Fairchild electronics plant at Shiprock, which provides a thousand jobs but mostly to women, turning the men into babysitters and urbanizing a people with a nomadic past. Why be like the Anglos with their progress?

Such astute Indians tell a story.

An Anglo saw a chief who sat fishing beside a stream.

"Say, chief, why don't you leave this and make something of yourself?"

"What should I do?"

"Well, you could go and get an education and study and get a degree."

"Then what would I do?"

"Then you could go to work and be productive, and if you fulfilled your responsibilities well, in several years you could retire."

"Then what would I do?"

"Go fishing."

The story holds a general truth, but in a thousand specific ways Indians *are* active in maintaining or improving their status. Shoshone and Paiute Indians are working to reclaim Coso Hot Springs from the 2,100-square-mile Naval Weapons Center in the western Mojave Desert—for at least five thousand years Indians have bathed in those springs. The Santo Domingos have turned down a large timber company that proposed putting a multimillion-dollar pulp mill on their bank of the Rio Grande. With help, the Taos Indians have pushed through Congress a bill that returns to them 48,000 acres of forested mountain that includes Blue Lake, a sacred shrine and the source of their water supply. In 1971 the Fort Apache Indians announced they would close their huge reservation to

Anglo hunting and fishing unless the government passed a law that would curb abuse of land and damage to wildlife.

Indians also have pressed for payment for land seizures. In 1971, for example, a federal Indians claims commission recommended that the United States pay $27,190,000 to the Papagos for land taken from them by reservation lands drawn in 1916, for minerals extracted since then, and for other damages. The land seized is the surface of the towns of Ajo, Gila Bend, Nogales, and Tucson.

Many tribes, especially those with ample land, are improving their lot. The Jicarillas were four hundred poor persons in 1940. Their respectable bankroll today is the result of land ownership. Incorporated, with $15 million in assets, they lease almost half of their reservation to oil companies, who give them three-fourths of their annual income of $2 million. Most of their other income is from the sale of hunting and fishing licenses, from a motel and shopping center, a cattle sales barn, logging, an elk farm, and a factory that assembles electronic components. By an agreement with Energy Conversion Systems, Jicarillas assemble stainless steel cooking pans. The Jicarilla have revamped Dulce to make it an up-to-date town with office buildings, a post office, a bank, a grocery store, a motel, and a restaurant.

The Mescalero Apaches are successful in cattle and lumber, and they have developed a ski resort on Sierra Blanca peak. Their civic center holds tribal offices, a motel and restaurant, and a retail store that offers handicraft for sale. There is a hillside subdivision of small homes, approached by paved streets. Near Globe the San Carlos Apaches, though mostly cattlemen organized into five associations, have developed the Globe–San Carlos Industrial Park. One firm, Hydrionics Carbon, uses local oak and juniper wood to produce activated charcoal, used for filtering in the manufacture of sugar, wine, and beer. The plant, which gives off no smoke or other pollutants, also produces acetic acid and wood alcohol.

On the million-and-half-acre Fort Apache Reservation, the White Mountain Apaches, with a net worth of $160 million, are in cattle, lumbering and also tourism. They have the largest privately owned recreation area in the West, with twenty-six well-stocked trout streams. They have created the biggest cold-water lake in Arizona and a large ski resort. Many young Apaches go away to college and jobs, but, as Eddie Jojola pointed out, "There's a strong come-back —a strong feeling that they want to return to their homeland."

The Navajo Nation of 129,000 persons, a population growing five times as fast as the United States population as a whole, has a reservation four times what it was in 1868, with $200 million in assets from oil, gas, uranium, and coal deposits. It owns an industrial complex, a shopping center, a college and a scholarship fund, a helium plant, an $8-million sawmill in the Chuska Mountains, and the largest singly owned stand of yellow pine in America. It has a stake in a project that will irrigate 110,000 acres and employ 8,000 men. It charges fees for entrance to Monument Valley Navajo Tribal Park and to Lake Powell Navajo Park. It holds the Navajo Tribal Fair each September, with racing, barbecueing, dancing, cooking, and baby contests. Navajo rug and jewelry makers command an international market. The leader of two-year Navajo Community College, Carl Todacheene, wants the graduates to go on to four-year institutions and learn the skills that the tribe needs in planning public works, giving medical care, growing food, managing water, repairing cars and other machinery, and managing stores, laundries, and other service businesses. Some Navajos even argue for separate statehood.

The pueblos, which sometimes have limited acreage, have made numerous economic adjustments. Santa Clara has opened a long, beautiful canyon to camping and fishing. Laguna, with royalties from uranium, has made prudent Wall Street investments— its headmen read the *Wall Street Journal*. Sandía builds steel furniture for the Post Office Department. Zia numbered twenty-five hundred persons in 1598, was

down to fifteen families three centuries later, and is presently up to around five hundred persons. The men herd cattle, and the women make a polychrome pottery with bird figures and terraced or wavy patterns. Jémez keeps it language and customs very much alive. Its basketweaving is on the decline but its bright-colored pottery is in solid production. Many Jémez people work for the Forest Service or at Los Alamos. Isleta, near Albuquerque, profits from a public recreation area with fishing and camping facilities. It leases half of its community center to an electronics factory.

The Zuñis built their own water system in 1954 and have sewer, electricity, and gas systems. They have a 4,800-foot paved and lighted airstrip and an Ampex factory that employs 135 persons. They have a new tribal center that houses Zuñi Craftsmen's Coöperative, where there are 400 full-time silversmiths, weavers, and makers of fetishes—stylized snakes, bears, and kindred creatures. A shopping center and supermarket are planned. All these are material things outside the pueblo. Inside is a way of life that stays properly hidden from the non-Indian observer.

All of this is part of a highly diversified development plan that will eventually turn Zuñi into a modern New Mexican town. According to Robert Lewis, executive head of the pueblo:

"It will be a modern community of which the state can be proud, but it will differ from other towns in that it will still be uniquely Zuñi. It will remain the only place on earth where the Zuñi language is spoken, the only place on earth where the Zuñi religion is practiced, and the only place on earth where the themes of Zuñi culture find expression in the art forms and crafts of the people. . . . [We] will expand our participation in the life of the state, contributing our full share to its future development, but at the same time we will remain distinctively Indian."

Navajo Dam
H.T. Person
helped get
it built

With the Trinity explosion of July 16, 1945, the Atomic Age with all its implications came alive alongside the Jornada del Muerto.

Have pic of Boy tho

The new high-rise skyline of Albuquerque, the aggressive economic capital where U.S. 66 crosses the Rio Grande. The Sandia Mountains are in the background.

Phoenix, the bustling metropolis that is reclaiming the Salt River Valley from agriculture, as seen at sunset from Squaw Peak.

well!

El Paso, key highway and railroad junction and commercial center, which joins Juárez to form an international city that commands the Chihuahuan Desert.

hmmm...

Arizona's elegant Fifth Avenue in fashionable Scottsdale adjoins streets of brand-new Old West shops.

In Grapevine Canyon: Death Valley Scotty's Castle, financed by a Chicago insurance man and now an alluring tourist attraction.

237

Copper smelters near Winkelman and Hayden in the sajuaro region of Arizona.
Smoke and fumes are no longer seen as the banners of progress.

The Mohave Power Plant in Nevada, designed to use
Navajo coal to generate power for distant cities.

Spillway and control towers at Hoover Dam,
the first major dam on the Colorado.

meaning 2. 1

CHAPTER 20

FINE ART AND BIG SCIENCE

Artistic forms that have Indian and Spanish roots;
awesome technology that is distinctively American

CULTURALLY THE MOST COHERENT communities of the last five hundred years of North American desert history are the pueblo villages of 1530. They combined architecture and urban design, allowed for both private and public life, and made for contented living. They had integrated arts and crafts, dances and rituals, economic and religious systems that had lasted for centuries. They consciously respected the environment and existed as a balanced part of the total ecological system.

Newcomers speaking Spanish or English have altered the original cultures and the settings that held them, yet the remains continue to be the most interesting and durable elements in the scene. The Hopis, Zuñis, and Rio Grande pueblos possess the Southwest's longest-lasting, strongest, and most artistic of civilized traditions.

Second historically, as Roland F. Dickey makes clear in his *New Mexico Village Arts,* is the culture of descendants of early Spanish colonists, whose styles of architecture, household furnishings, religious carvings, paintings and painted borders, and tools give residual charm to Chihuahua and New Mexico.

The individualistic Americans are a weak third, despite their wealth in dollars, possessions, and relative size of population. They have imposed themselves on the land and imported bits of heterogeneous culture from Europe, Asia, Africa, and elsewhere in the United States. A constructive minority of Americans however, have encouraged Indian and Hispano artists to create and recreate in their ancestral idioms.

American and European archeologists, such as the earlier Bandelier or the later Edgar Lee Hewitt, studied the Indians as architects and artists. Charles F. Lummis and fellow writers publicized the pueblos and encouraged native artisans like Maria, maker of black pottery at San Ildefonso, and her successor, Rose Gonzales. It was Lummis, a friend of Theodore Roosevelt, who coined the name *Southwest* and urged the slogan "See America First." Before World War I painters were discovering the area, especially New Mexico. Today there are perhaps more producing artists per capita in New Mexico than in any other state. In its great days of carrying passengers, the Santa Fe Railway hired Mary Jane Colter to copy on dishes the conventionalized birds, animals, monsters, and insects that appear on the pottery of the prehistoric Mimbres people, whose balanced, colored decorations equal those of ancient Etruscans and Greeks.

Creative writers responded to the pull of the upper Rio Grande towns, the Navajos, and the California deserts. Scores of popular writers have worked or reworked southwestern frontier materials—the Apache wars, cowboy life, mining booms, Mormon settlements. For more than a century strong scenery and the faces of native peoples have attracted master photographers.

Archeologists and historians, writers, and artists continue steadily to examine the region, with the most yet to be done with the Mexican strip from Baja California eastward into Coahuila. Painters, sculptors, and craftsmen are numerous wherever collectors and free-spending tourists congregate, in Palm Springs, Scottsdale, Sedona, Old Town in Albuquerque, Taos, Juárez–El Paso, or Santa Fe with its Canyon Road, a

Highly sophisticated astronomical facilities atop Kitt Peak are dominated by the even higher
Baboquivari Peak, sacred to the Papagos as chief abode of the god Ee-Ee-Toy.

winding riverside lane with dozens of shops, studios, and workshops for pottery, paintings, drawings, purses, trays, books, and other items.

There are annual cultural events such as the three-day Firebird Festival of Arts, sponsored by the Phoenix Art Museum in the Civic Center, the Indian Market in the Santa Fe Plaza, or the extraordinary Santa Fe Opera, which each summer brings singing stars from the world around to its two-month series of grand operas given in its outdoor opera house on a hillside away from town. The 1971 season was its fifteenth.

The artistic vitality of the region shows itself in architecture, bulkiest and most three-dimensional of the arts. Conspicuous throughout the Southwest are admirable adaptations of traditional style. Many buildings in the Mission style have large, semicircular arches, low-pitched tiled roofs, parapets, smooth-plastered walls, balconies, and towers or turrets capped by domes or pyramidal tiled roofs.

More elaborate in style is the Spanish Colonial Revival. Again there are the red-tiled roofs with a low pitch, but there is ornamentation around the doors and windows. Columns or pilasters flank the doorways, the balconies have railings of wrought iron or wood, and windows have grills (rejas), of iron or wood with turned spindles.

The Pueblo style, native to New Mexico and Arizona, appeared in California in the 1890s. In New Mexico it had its Anglo beginning in 1905 in a building at the University of New Mexico. The style set the motif there and the university has grown into "a gigantic academic pueblo" with adroit functional adaptations and a distinctive appearance. Pueblo style means massiveness and no arches; buildings are of adobe or of materials made to look like adobe. The walls have blunt angles and look battered. Roofs are flat, and there are stepped-up roofs for upper stories, as at Taos Pueblo. Beams (vigas) project to irregular lengths. Homes in New Mexico employ this simple, sturdy, impressive, indigenous style, as do hotels and motels all over New Mexico and Arizona. The Albuquerque airport, built in 1966, adapts Pueblo to the requirements of an aviation terminal.

Some homes and office buildings are modernistic, as are banks and department stores in Phoenix and Tucson or Luhrs Tower in Phoenix, designed by the Trost brothers of El Paso. The influence of Frank Lloyd Wright shows in buildings such as the Phoenix Art Museum, designed by Alden Dow. At his studio in Scottsdale Paolo Soleri advocates Neo-Expressionism—sweeping curves and arches and vaults in many forms.

Colleges and universities contribute increasingly to the cultural life of their towns. The University of Texas in El Paso, with its Bhutanese architecture, the state universities in Albuquerque and Tucson, both with busy presses, and the two former agricultural colleges that now have become New Mexico State University and Arizona State University—all are expanding their liberal arts and artistic offerings. The University of Nevada at Las Vegas, once a few classes offered in a high school building, is now a full-fledged institution with 6,500 students in special fields, such as performing arts, ecology, and hotel administration.

IN 1894 PERCIVAL LOWELL, at his observatory on a hill in Flagstaff, began his studies of the planets, especially Mars. He pushed the rise of astrobiology as he examined the ruddy deserts of Mars, the channels, the severe climate, and the dark areas that could be mosses or lichens. He argued for the existence of life on the red planet. In the cold, clear atmosphere of Flagstaff, 7,200 feet in elevation, he demonstrated that a small instrument in good air will show much more than a large instrument in humid, overcast air like that of Paris. Lowell's data, assembled between 1894 and 1916, stand up under the latest techniques of astrophysics and will help the National Aeronautical and Space Administration plan its scheduled manned Mars landing sometime around A.D. 2000.

While experts at Lowell Observatory were looking into space, Professor Andrew E. Douglass of the University of Arizona was probing backwards in time and providing archeologists in the Southwest with a precise calendar that goes back to 273 B.C. Douglass pioneered dendrochronology—dating by tree rings. In wet years trees grow more before slowing down and depositing an annual ring. In drought years they barely grow at all, and annual rings harden close together. Working backwards from cross sections of living trees in years of known weather records, Douglass matched the overlapping tree-ring record in beams or timbers in Anglo, Mexican, Spanish, pueblo, and

Taos Pueblo, a focal town in New Mexico history and one of the great sights of the Southwest, is a supreme example of native Pueblo architecture.

prehistoric cliff dwellings and in the charred embers of ancient campfires.

Arid lands have long interested scientists because of the dramatic visibility of the geological history and the special adaptations made by wild living things. In the 1880s and 1890s Dr. C. Hart Merriam of the U.S. Biological Survey noted the layers of biological differences from one elevation to another, from the bottom of the Grand Canyon to the top of the San Francisco Peaks, and developed the concept of North American life zones. And as Mexicans and North Americans now crowd into the deserts, scientists are

particularly busy, either studying nature before it is irreversibly destroyed or studying procedures that will support human life in denatured, million-automobiled cities. Foundations are behind some of the research; so are state agencies and the federal government.

In Arizona there are biological study stations at El Portal, southwest of Lordsburg and near the Chiricahua wilderness, and south of Tucson in the Santa Rita Range Reserve. There is also the Southwestern Arboretum near Superior. With sums from the National Science Foundation, as during the International Biological Program, scientists in the Committee on

Desert and Arid Zones Research study all the kinds of ecosystems in the desert. They investigate the life processes that involve higher plants, vertebrates, invertebrates, microorganisms, and aquatic organisms, as well as matters such as temperatures, the movements of waters and salts in the soil, and the processes of evaporation.

In several areas Forest Service researchers experiment with prescriptive burning to simulate natural fires and avoid the buildup of litter for occasional great conflagrations. At range experiment stations experts study the use of grass and water on cattle range lands. The Soil Conservation Service works out means of rescuing eroded land. In Chihuahua Dr. Martin H. Gonzales directs investigations at La Campana Livestock Experiment Station.

In western Texas the state Water Development Board, the U.S. Air Force, and the Bureau of Reclamation experiment with cloud seeding. They distribute silver iodide to produce the freezing of water droplets in clouds, which releases heat and may in turn make the clouds grow and produce rain. NASA and its Mexican counterpart cooperate to use aircraft and satellites in taking infrared photographs and using other remote-sensing devices. These enable men to study underground water systems, geological formations and ore bodies, plant diseases, the condition of crops, and the species of plants growing, such as marijuana. The cooperative Mission Screwworm keeps at the task of eradicating the screwfly and its larvae, destructive to cattle herds along the Mexican borderlands from Texas to California. In the summer of 1970 aviators of the mission dropped 670 million sterilized male screwflies in the active program of biological control. Arizona men have pioneered in a similar sterilization program to control the pink bollworm. Thus local economic concerns push men toward wiping out species that nature provides a place for in the great chain of being.

THE HIGH, CLEAR HEAVENS of the great deserts have for decades played a mighty role in big space exploration, nuclear science, and war—hot or cold. To a notable degree the nuclear age is physically a southwestern product, a result of the huge, almost unpopulated spaces, mostly government owned, and of the

transparent skies, once the realm of the Great Spirit.

"During recent years," as the National Science Foundation discreetly says, "the growing importance of scientific research to the national welfare has given rise to new activities and agencies within the federal government." One result is the complex of facilities for astronomical research at Brookhaven National Laboratory, New York; Green Bank, West Virginia; Boulder, Colorado; at the Cerro Tololo Inter-American Observation center in Chile; and at Kitt Peak National Observatory, Arizona.

The Kitt installation, founded in 1958, perches atop a mountain 6,875 feet above sea level, just inside the Papago Reservation. An association of universities operates the complex for the National Science Foundation. It was put here because of absence of dust, fog, airplane vapor trails, smog, industrial smoke, and city lights at night. Adjacent to a series of special telescopes for stellar studies—from sixteen to eighty-four inches—is the world's largest solar telescope of its kind. This device, dug deep into the rock of the mountain, makes possible a variety of detailed studies of the magnetic field of the sun, of sunspots, flares, granulation prominences, the light spectrum, and other solar phenomena. The findings at Kitt Peak lead to equipping rockets with special optical equipment. Aerobee rockets launched from White Sands, New Mexico, carry Kitt Peak spectrographs and other equipment to the outer atmosphere. A scanning spectrophotometer flown on an Aerobee 170 vehicle in 1968 investigated the ultraviolet spectra of stars in the constellation of Orion. At ninety-five miles up a camera inside the nose cone took x-ray photographs of the sun. In the planning stage are large telescopes automated to operate for years from outer space. A 150-inch mirror telescope is nearing completion.

At Kitt Peak the once "pure" science of astronomy is now potentially reddened with the blood of human beings, for astronomy is part of the competitive military-space program of the Pentagon. And in older southwestern observatories men work with a stepped-up urgency that star study did not have in the days of Bruno and Kepler or Percival Lowell. At Lowell Observatory on Mars Hill, astronomers use computers to scan the sky to determine for practical purposes the size, mass, composition of specific stars, the distance

~Santa Fe—ABQ

from earth, and the movement in space. At the University of Texas McDonald Observatory in the Davis Mountains, astronomers with grants from NASA are studying the surfaces and atmospheric characteristics of the planets of the solar system. In early 1971 their 107-inch mirror, part of the world's third largest telescope, made laser contact with a reflecting prism that the Apollo 14 astronauts had placed on the moon.

Although studying natural objects in space is a major enterprise, there are installations, too, for sky-watching artificial objects out in international space. The U.S. Air Force runs an electro-optical facility on the mountain top at Cloudcroft, New Mexico. There military and civilian scientists use highly complex electronic equipment, an IBM computer, a 48-inch reflector telescope, and a camera that takes two hundred photographs per second. They photograph distant satellites, even though these streak from one horizon to the other in from twenty to forty seconds. The object is to solve some of the problems involved in photographing very distant objects. By diplomatic arrangement the United States has placed a Space Capsule Tracking Station in Sonora between Navojoa and Ciudad Obregón; it observes astronauts as they pass over. The Goldstone Tracking Station near Barstow in the Mojave has huge dish antennas that not only watch men in the sky but also measure the size and structure of quasars (energy sources) and radio galaxies.

Scientific activities more obviously interlocked with military preparedness and training take place at Albuquerque's Kirtland Air Force Base, a research and development center, and the Atomic Energy Commission's Sandia Base with its Special Weapons Project. Holloman Air Force Base has the Air Force Systems Command at Alamagordo, near the White Sands Proving Ground; and there are Walker Air Force Base at Roswell; Fort Huachuca, Arizona, headquarters of the Defense Department's Strategic Communications Command; Luke Air Force Bombing and Gunnery Range in western Arizona; and the great chunks of California desert occupied by the Marine Corps Training Center north of Twentynine Palms; the Air Force Flight Tests Center at Edwards Air Force Base north of Lancaster; and the Randsburg Wash Test Range and the China Lake Naval Weapons Center, where thousands of scientists and technicians live in isolation.

Most important of all—forces in the shaping of history—are the activities of the AEC at Los Alamos and elsewhere in its dispersed domain. Applied science in the whole region, the nation, and the world reached a climactic period during World War II in the temporary army camp shacks of Los Alamos.

Here, amid pine forests and stunning vistas—in a secret town reached by outsiders (even by Franklin D. Roosevelt), only by means of P.O. Box 1663, Santa Fe— J. Robert Oppenheimer and an extraordinary group of fellow scientists and technicians carried on research, devised, and partly assembled the first atomic bomb. The Los Alamos Laboratory, known as Project Y, was the crucial center of the nationwide research and development program called Manhattan Engineer District. It involved intricate coordination with laboratories in Berkeley and Chicago, and radically new plants in whole new cities, Hanford, Washington, and Oak Ridge, Tennessee. After strenuous researches, after facing multifarious problems and a horde of unknowns, the scientists realized that they had to test an actual nuclear detonation.

They chose an empty site on a ranch astride the old Jornada del Muerto; Oppenheimer called it Trinity. There was a trial run on May 7, 1945, with a hundred tons of TNT and an interspersing of fission products. The big test came two months later.

After elaborate secret movement of materials, provisions for observation and measurement, and for safety for scientists and technicians, the first plutonium bomb was ready for implosion at Trinity. Carefully assembled, the bomb lay at the top of a high steel tower. Oppenheimer, Vannevar Bush, Enrico Fermi, Edward Teller, Ernest O. Lawrence, and other scientists arrived, as did Gen. Leslie R. Groves, director of Manhattan District.

Came the predawn hours of July 16, 1945. The result of three years' work and two billion dollars in expenditure could possibly soon set the atmosphere on fire and extinguish all life on earth. No one knew for sure what would happen. General Groves had brought psychiatrists to calm the scientists, but now psychiatrists were trying to calm each other. Since the skies were rainy, the test was postponed several times, but shortly before 5:30 A.M. the world's first nuclear countdown began.

At the final count of zero a point of light became a

Overleaf: An eagle's view of Los Alamos: left, residential district; center, civic and business district; right, scientific laboratories; beyond, Rio Grande Valley.

small sun, the steel tower completely disappeared into microscopic bits, and a huge incandescent column spewed over and engulfed the desert in light as no noon sun ever had done. The center of the fireball was perhaps four times as hot as the sun's center and ten thousand times as hot as the sun's surface. A multicolored cloud surged up eight miles, evaporating the clouds in its path. Earth trembled. A pressure of a hundred billion atmospheres pushed down, creating a huge, sloping crater, melting a layer of earth into greenish glass, lumpy with holes—trinitite. A security guard sensed doom: "Jesus Christ! It's got away from the long-hairs." Twenty miles away on Compania Hill, Ernest Lawrence shouted, "It works! It works!" Near Albuquerque, 120 miles to the north, a blind girl suddenly asked, "What was that?"

The thunder and blast wave spread, echoing and re-echoing between distant ranges — the Organs, the Sierra Oscuro, the Little Burros. Reflective scientists were profoundly affected. Said one: "It was the nearest to doomsday that one could possibly imagine." Another thought of Krishna: "I am become Death, the shatterer of worlds." A young scientist remarked, "Now we are all sons-of-bitches!" Gen. Thomas Farrell, Groves's deputy, saw atomic fission as "almost full grown at birth. It was a great new force to be used for good or for evil." Groves himself, as he later recalled, had no time to reflect on how world history had exploded itself into a new era. "As for me, my thoughts were now completely wrapped up with the preparation for the coming climax in Japan." It came soon, on August 6 at Hiroshima and three days later at Nagasaki.

THE TRINITY SITE can now be visited one day a year, each October. At Los Alamos, where the laboratories grow more numerous in a modern postwar city, the Science Hall and Museum, open to the public, exhibits models of the bombs that destroyed the Japanese cities—to save lives—the only such bombs ever used in warfare. A plaque says that "they represent one of the greatest scientific achievements of all time." A patio with rocks, pine trees, junipers, and fountains exhibits casings of a Little Davy Crockett ground-to-ground atomic missile, a 1955 artillery-fired atomic projectile, a 1961 thermonuclear bomb, a 1962 fission bomb, a 1969 nuclear explosive package (Plowshare—intended for

peaceful economic uses), a Kiwi-A reactor, and a Phoebus 1, the first of the nuclears with space flight capabilities. Los Alamos scientists are experimenting toward a power-producing thermonuclear reaction, a high-temperature reactor, and the use of a meson particle accelerator half a mile long to study the atomic nucleus and the potentials of curing cancer. The negative pi mesons can reach inoperable tumors deep in the body without harming nearby healthy tissue.

After the end of the war with Japan, subsequent tests of military products of the Los Alamos Scientific Laboratory were peacetime experiments on Bikini, Eniwetok, in the South Atlantic, in the Pacific near Johnston or Christmas islands, and inside the United States, especially in Nevada. The Nevada Test Site, now inside Nellis Air Force Range, became a continental site to supplement the Pacific proving grounds and speed up the assessing of test results. It has become the nation's "outdoor nuclear explosives laboratory" for both military objectives and civil uses. Since 1951 an area of approximately eight hundred fifty thousand acres, a domain of peaks, valleys, and dry lake beds, with an internal drainage system, has changed into a far-flung, intricate military-industrial-scientific complex.

During the period from 1951 to 1970 the AEC announced 381 United States weapons tests and 22 detonations in the Plowshare program. The detonations each with its own name, such as Stanley, Fawn, Wineskin, Cruet, Spider, Tijeras, or Wish Bone, took place on the towers, in the air, and underground from near the surface to several thousand feet down, in limestone, dolomite, tuff, alluvium, or rhyolite. Since 1962 all weapons tests have been underground. The tests have been designed mostly at Los Alamos or at the Lawrence Radiation Laboratory in Livermore, California. Also involved are the Sandia Laboratories at Albuquerque, which operate the Tonopah Test Range, an AEC field-test installation, north of the Nevada Test Site.

In preparing for a typical underground test, crews bore a shaft, implant the nuclear device, and connect it with diagnostic instruments at the surface above. On rare occasions these are in a steel tower mounted on tracks. After scientists have set off the device, the underground strata fracture, melt, and vaporize as concentric shock waves move out and away from the nucleus. A cavity forms, fills with hot vapor, and expands. The ground shakes. Observers in charge of the tower fire explosive bolts and cable cutters. Cut loose, the tower moves down the track and away from circles of dust puffs rising from the shock wave. In a matter of minutes, hours, or even days, the soil begins to wrinkle down, and a depression forms. Unless the chimney encounters rock strong enough to support a roof span, as the cavity far below begins to cool, radioactive material may tumble to a pool at the bottom of the hole. Above this cavity will be a sagging column of broken rock and pulverized rubble that sinks, leaving at earth's surface the saucer-shaped depression, a pockmark as wide as a quarter mile and as deep as several hundred feet—a man-made crater more significant for mankind than the glory holes of the copper companies. Later, when conditions are safe, a rig drills down into the hidden cavity to get samples of radioactive substances for the laboratory technicians, who determine how the test device performed.

On July 6, 1962, in the detonation called Sedan, a thermonuclear device was exploded 635 feet down in sand and gravel. It was in the 100-kiloton yield; that is, it equalled 100,000 tons of TNT. The detonation produced a crater about 1,300 feet across and 321 feet deep. Less than 10 percent of radioactivity escaped, to fall close by the crater. On April 26, 1969, Boxcar was 3,800 feet deep in rhyolite. It was the first United States test of a megaton or more; a megaton equals 1 million tons of TNT. Boxcar yielded 1.2 megatons, formed a depression 900 feet in diameter and 275 feet deep, produced earth tremors and thousands of small aftershocks, caught the attention of seismologists, and startled would-be carefree people in Las Vegas, more than a hundred miles away.

Though Plowshare is a minor program at the test site, the AEC sees Sedan and other detonations in this series as preliminary studies that may lead to vast ditch-digging projects, cutting railroad and highway routes through mountains, gashing a sea-level canal across an isthmus in Central America, recovering oil and natural gas from deep-lying strata, in-situ leaching of copper ore, and creation of underground chambers for water, gas, and the wastes of industrial and urban civilization.

At this site, where mortal men officially plan a deter-

rent against a nuclear attack on the United States or massive revision of the earth's surface, they also look into the means and the possibilities of human survival. Since 1960 the UCLA Laboratory of Nuclear Medicine and Radiation has worked in Rock Valley to observe the effects of low-level gamma radiation on desert animals kept in three fenced areas of twenty acres each. A herd of Hereford cattle bearing the AEC's registered brand roam the whole test site, and the Environmental Protection Agency regularly examines the herd for radionuclide uptake and radiation effect. The agency also runs an experimental dairy farm, which is probably the most meticulous, most monitored farm in the history of North American agricultural pioneering. Pumps bring up ancient water from more than a mile down, and men raise rye and especially alfalfa in irrigated soil. They irradiate the crops with various radionuclides and feed the forage to a thriving herd of Holsteins— far from the uncontaminated grass and water of their ancestral duchy. Experts then analyze the cows' milk. The end result is knowledge of protective actions that men can take to reduce the amounts of radionuclides that get into human foods.

THE HUGE NEVADA TEST SITE, almost lost in the spaces of the Southwest, easily hidden from U.S. highways *hmm* and commercial air travel routes, is one of the most guarded and deeply studied areas on earth. It is of absolute technological importance to the nation's military and foreign policy. It exemplifies a new, twentieth-century use of desert "waste" space. In the past the area was only of casual importance to prehistoric Indians and to the modern Paiutes; to cattlemen, who developed water holes and built corrals; and to miners, who extracted silver and tungsten ore.

Only plants and animals, evolved to survive in a harsh, arid climate, had steadily lived out their lives and reproduced there, maintaining an ecological balance. The site is now closed to hunting. This taboo on human predators has been a kind of boon to 43 species of mammals, notably mountain lions, antelopes, bighorn sheep, wild horses, and about twenty-five hundred mule deer, and to 188 species of birds, including chukar partridge and migrant waterfowl.

CHAPTER 21

CROWDING AROUND THE WATER HOLE

The question: how many irrigated acres, industries,
and swimming pools can the Southwest afford? ——— all

No longer true—the droughts are slowly
drying out Colorado River (21st C.)
Lower Bosque States—Calif, Nev, Ariz—soon
need cut back water use—e.g.

IN THE DESERT whoever controls the water controls everything. In 1680 the Pueblo Indians in revolt cut the *acequia* Muralla that supplied Santa Fe, and the Spanish had to leave. Twelve years later Don Diego de Vargas in his successful reconquest of the city cut the *acequia* that was supplying the interim Indian government.

As Erna Fergusson points out in *New Mexico: A Pageant of Three Peoples,* the Indians accepted the variability of water, danced for it, and moved when the water failed. The early Spanish, who knew water use and obeyed royal water laws, farmed the land sensibly and prayed when drought came. In contrast, quasi-scientific Anglos were determined to have water when and where it wasn't. They dug out springs and seepages to increase the flow. Their windmills and artesian wells brought up ground waters that turned range land into crop land but made the water table start to go down. Their dams diverted upstream water, spread it out, and left downstream users dry and furious.

In the Big Bend country, in Boot Canyon, which supports a gallery forest of Douglas-fir, southwestern white pine, and big-toothed maple, there was a bubbling spring. It was a delightful, primeval water supply older than the story of Eden. Along came an American engineer, supposedly wise in improving water flow, who inserted dynamite and blew up the spring. The water found newly made fissures deep in the rocky heart of Texas and the surface completely dried up.

The present regional push to reclaim or develop desert lands showed itself in the first Irrigation Congress, held in Salt Lake City in 1891. At succeeding congresses spokesmen more and more called on the national government to take the responsibility and make the investment. Government could spend large sums of money and wait for general returns, and it could create and enforce uniform laws. Its broad management of the western water hole would benefit all the people. President Theodore Roosevelt thumped for the idea, and in 1902 the United States Congress debated and passed the National Reclamation Act. Within a decade the new National Reclamation Service had begun to divert Colorado River water to California and Arizona.

Whether private or public, irrigation projects from 1870 on in eastern California, southern Nevada, western Sonora, Chihuahua, Arizona, and New Mexico have created patches of a new desert landscape—the varying greens of alfalfa, barley, cotton, sugar beets, wheat, beans, grain sorghum, of vegetable crops and nut or fruit orchards. Irrigation has been the making of Roswell, on the Pecos; of Delicias, near the Conchos and Aldama on the Chuvíscar; of Navojoa and Ciudad Obregón, in the Mayo and Yaqui valleys; of the attractive planned town of Chandler, near the Salt; or of Holtville, which has become the carrot capital of the world, at sea level in the Imperial Valley.

Teams of technicians in the agricultural experiment stations compare with the anonymous ancient experts who domesticated corn and beans in the Americas or wheat on the Iranian plateau. In southern New Mexico, for example, in the Mesilla Valley, experimenters at New Mexico State University have been busy and creative. They have developed a new strain of long-, strong-fibered cotton, Acala 1517, which is wilt resistant;

Colorado River water in the Coachella Canal divides desert landscape
from irrigated orchard and crop land.

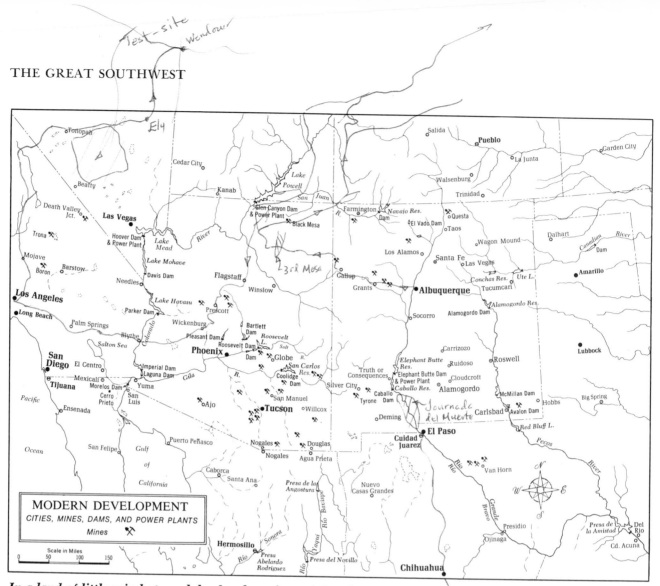

In a land of little rain but much land reclamation, mining, booming industries, and spreading cities, water is crucial and problems of water conservation and pollution command increasing attention.

superior varieties of alfalfa; an improved Hopi sweet potato; an improved chili; and a pecan tree that has a genetic resistance to aphids.

The particular pride of Arizonans is the development of the Phoenix area on Salt River in "Valley of the Sun." In the 1860s a few pioneers harvested the tall galleta grass, fine for hay, that grew along the riverbanks. Then some of them ditched out water, grubbed up groves of cottonwoods, palo verde, and mesquite, and patches of arrowweed, desert broom, and cactuses, and began to raise crops of grain. They nailed together the beginnings of the town. The settlemen grew until ten canal companies and hundreds of farmers made use of the surface water running in the Salt and once again spread sweet mountain water over the Hohokam lands, streaked with

ancient canals from Camelback Mountain on the north side of the sunstruck valley to beyond the islandlike peaks to the south. Growers experimented with varieties of citrus and dates.

In 1898 a six-year drought began. The river fell to its lowest level in memory. The valley was long on people and cultivated acreage and short on usable surface water. Tensions rose among a minority of old-timers with prior water rights, many latecomers, canal companies with large investments, traditional individualists, and engineers and city men who had new ideas for a technological solution to the problem. They proposed a storage dam, however distant or expensive, and a communal control of water. There were heated meetings, where the new ideas found listeners. Territorial

252

agents lobbied in Washington and worked out western alliances in the Capitol and the White House.

The political result was the National Reclamation Act. Since the new Reclamation Service (later the Bureau) could deal only with organizations, not with individuals, Salt River men formed the Water Users' Association, a public corporation, and 85 percent of the farmers joined. Each acre inside the boundaries of the project owned a representative interest in the association. The service set to work building the dam in a semiwilderness more than sixty miles from the nearest railroad and eighty-five miles from the land to be watered; the project cost millions of dollars. It became the world's highest masonry dam, a southwestern marvel in 1911, when speeches dedicated it in the name of Theodore Roosevelt. The dam was a sturdy regional beginning for water storage, power generation, and control of the contradictory desert problems—drought and flood. Locally it was the first of a system that now contains four more dams on the Salt and three dams on tributary streams.

From 1911 new canals fingered out over the brushy plain. Orchards of oranges, grapefruit, and dates, fields of alfalfa and cotton, and truck gardens turned the dust and the gray wild plants into eye-resting green. In the 1930s Phoenix and Tempe began to spread over prime agricultural lands in the heedless Southern California manner. The Water Users' Association assumed the activities of a municipal corporation, too. This economic and legal change enabled it to supply water and power to urban and industrial users.

Salt River has become a weedy, dry desert wash in Phoenix and Tempe. Its upstream waters less and less support crops, more and more supply luxury lawns, swimming pools, and the activities in factories, high-rise office buildings, motels, trailer parks, and suburban homes. Spokesmen who object to the fact that farming uses a disproportionate amount of water have influenced this change.

In Sonora and Chihuahua, relative newcomers to big-scale projects, despite some efforts by President Plutarco Calles and other leaders before World War II, the Secretaría de Recursos Hidráulicos and agricultural experts have strikingly transformed a once neglected region to a position of national superiority. Where there are sufficient flow and an adequate site, the gov-

ernment has built dams (presas). The Presa de la Boquilla on Río Conchos, south of Cuidad Chihuahua, supplies water for towns and farm lands, and eventually for a depleted or dried-up Rio Grande at Ojinaga. There is a dam in southern Sonora on the Río Mayo, there are three dams on the long, forked Yaqui, and there is one on Río Sonora. Mexicans have stopped in part or completely the flow of all the once permanent Sonoran rivers in order to irrigate productive fields.

The Mexican dams are on projects that are inside the nation. The Salt River project was inside a state and inside a nation, but other major projects, on the region's two longest rivers, involved interstate and international interests. The Rio Grande–Río Bravo involves Colorado, New Mexico, Texas, and five Mexican states. In 1906 a treaty guaranteed Juárez 60,000 acre-feet per year at the headgate of the old Spanish acequia. Elephant Butte Dam, completed ten years later, created a lake forty miles long and up to three miles wide that came to irrigate almost 160,000 acres along 145 miles of river in New Mexico, Texas, and Chihuahua.

FROM ANZA ON, non-Indians cast visionary eyes on the waters of the ruddy Colorado, that maker of gigantic canyons and an extraordinary delta. Of the big delta-making rivers of the world, only the Colorado has alternately discharged its fluids into the sea and into a land-locked interior basin, Salton Sink. It is the lifestream of a subregion of seven American and two Mexican states, although it ranks only twenty-third in stream flow among American rivers. Its annual flow is one-twelfth that of the Columbia, one thirty-third that of the Mississippi.

In 1849 a new Californian, Dr. Oliver M. Wozencroft, proposed the idea of reclaiming the higher lands in Salton Sink but could not get help from Congress. In the 1890s a civil engineer organized the California Development Company; its men turned Colorado water through an intake gate below Pilot Knob, near Yuma, and led it via canal to the Imperial Valley. By 1902, 14,000 people were living on former desert, most of it below sea level, and had 120,000 acres under cultivation.

In 1905 the company opened a new intake for the canal—just before a rare series of five winter floods. The river ate at the sandy banks of the new intake. Soon

Simple irrigation at Staley Ranch, New Mexico, in the 1890s. Spring water runs in hollowed branches to a collection barrel and then on to the garden.

most of the roiling waters that formerly drained into the Gulf of California started pouring into Imperial Valley and down into Salton Sink. In 1906 the whole river deflected into the interior basin, forming a gigantic pool that dissolved salt and alkali flats, covered the Southern Pacific tracks, inundated a salt company works, and began to rise toward 50,000 cultivated acres.

After the company failed in attempts to stop the break in the river, the Southern Pacific took over the task and struggled for two years, dumping in thousands of flatcar loads of rock, gravel, and clay before it plugged the mighty leak. By 1907 California had a big new lake, saline, full of river fishes, with a surface more than two hundred feet below sea level. From then on the lake rose and fell with the seasons, but mostly it rose, despite prodigious evaporation, because of irrigation water that leached down through the fields. The lake has become saltier and saltier and rich in pesticides and sewage. After salt accumulation killed the river fishes, state officials stocked the lake with ocean fishes, and fishermen and real estate operators turned this accidental Dead Sea into a bleak sports resort.

Soon after the Colorado had become the source for irrigation in Imperial Valley, it began to supply water for districts in the Gila Valley east of Yuma. Later came very big projects, the first being Hoover Dam in Black Canyon between Nevada and Arizona. The result of this marvel of engineering was water storage, flood control, and electric power for three states. With the completion of Parker Dam downstream and the Metropolitan Water System, water that first appeared as snowflakes over the glaciers of the Wind River Mountains in Wyoming

began coming out of faucets in Los Angeles, San Diego, and other Southern California communities. Imperial Dam, completed in 1938, diverts a small river westward into the All-American Canal to Coachella and Imperial valleys, and another stream eastward in the Gila Gravity Main Canal.

In fewer than seventy years the Colorado, once a dangerous mystery, has been so tamed that sometimes no water runs along its lowest miles and into the Gulf. No other major river in North America is more over-raided, overdrafted, overcommitted, and overlitigated. More than twenty tunnels through the Colorado Rockies turn some of the river's mountain waters into the Mississippi Valley; seven tunnels divert Colorado River water into alien Utah watersheds; there is one tunnel in Wyoming and engineers plan one to take water from the tributary San Juan in New Mexico to the Rio Grande at Cochití; there are four major diversions to California, Arizona, and Baja California; and there is yet another in prospect to take water to central Arizona. But estimates of Colorado River flow made before 1930 now turn out to have been too generous. Human beings have contracted for more water than the river carries.

Southwestern regional problems are national problems when they involve Mexico. After the Treaty of Guadalupe Hidalgo and the Gadsden Purchase, the natural problems of water shortages in the region were aggravated by the artificial carving up of the major watersheds. The Colorado River, cut athwart by the east-west boundary, raised problems of Mexican water rights from the 1890s on with the beginning of large-scale diversions into California. Mexico's quantitative share was worked out by treaty in 1944, when the United States guaranteed Mexico 1.5 million acre feet per year, half of which could be from a connection with the All-American Canal, but the treaty did not set clear standards for the quality of water Mexico was to receive.

The small "Great River of the North," the Rio Grande, early raised issues of international import along its course of 1,300 miles. The headwaters of the river are high in the United States but its most important tributary is the Mexican Río Conchos. From the New Mexican line to the Gulf of Mexico the river is split lengthwise down the middle of its writhing and ever-changing channel. From 1848 on, the very border itself was uncertain as the river deserted old courses and suddenly cut new ones, creating *bancos,* or islands, sometimes then creating secondary *bancos* that wrapped land of one nation completely around land of the other. Fertile alluvial bottom lands became a patchwork of *bancos* and a maze of sandy, silty, abandoned, braided riverbeds.

Between 1856 and 1970 diplomats and engineers worked at applying an old principle that a boundary moves with any slow, methodical process of erosion of one streambank and accretion to the other, but that if the new course gets suddenly cut — by avulsion — the boundary stays in the abandoned bed. An 1884 treaty reaffirmed this principle. The International Boundary Commission, established by treaty in 1889, classified changes and by the time of the Mexican Revolution had settled over a hundred cases. From 1924 to 1940 the commission was again active, granting 107 *bancos* to the United States and 65 to Mexico.

As population increased on both sides of the river, floods on the lower river lavishly destroyed houses, crops, and farm improvements. In times of low water, demand exceeded supply, or threatened to exceed it. After 1880 irrigation in the Mesilla Valley and the growth of population in El Paso and Juárez promised scarcity. A series of treaties and agreements dammed and apportioned waters. During the years from 1934 to 1938 the International Boundary Commission built floodways and levees to rectify the channel from El Paso to Fort Quitman, reducing 155 miles of tangle to 88 miles of broad bends.

A large and important *banco* with clouded title persisted very publicly for ninety years until 1963, when ambassadors under Presidents John Kennedy and López Mateos signed a treaty. It concerned the Chamizal, a tract of some 630 acres, and also Córdoba Island, a 193-acre piece, both smack in the sunglare between El Paso and Juárez, in full sight of the international bridges. The nations divided the area and made nature obey the treaty. Engineers moved the river northwards, gave it a new curve, and firmly fixed it in place in a concrete-lined channel, which cemented the fluid border of the countries. No ecologist could celebrate this arbitrary streambed. But after 111 years of troubled and even dangerous private ownership, an issue created by bloody war had been settled by diplomacy and inky signatures.

Remaining problems raised by the slim, wayward

The modern Highline Canal of the Salt River Project, south of Phoenix, carries water to citrus orchards, date gardens, and field crops.

*Theodore Roosevelt Dam and Reservoir, the initial structure of the Salt River Project.
In 1965 the Bureau of Reclamation used the spillway for the first time since 1941.*

waters apparently were solved in 1970 by agents of Richard Nixon and Gustavo Díaz, who drew up a treaty that allocated 319 *bancos* between Mexico and Texas, especially a couple thousand acres between Ojinaga and Presidio, set up plans to concretize much of the river's channel, and agreed on a simple formula for settling all future boundary problems.

To a frontiersman or a traveler dying of thirst in the desert, there is absolute importance to the immediate question, where is the water? But in the long course of events, another question is of larger import. Who owns the water in the desert streams and under the topsoil? Among the historic Indians, the Mexicans, and the Spanish, as among the Moors and Visigoths

and the ancient Mogollon-Anasazi, the custom was common rights, mutual and proportional shares. This same doctrine worked under the pioneering community discipline of the unified Mormon colonies in Utah, Arizona, and Chihuahua. In contrast, the Anglo has made the water question the single most important, most complex issue, whether the waters be exclusively personal, intrastate, interstate, international, or the all-inclusive ecological.

Anglo miners, ranchers, and farmers rejected the English common law of their tradition that made stream bank proprietors also owners of the flowing waters. Instead, the newcomers established their own ethic and legal principle. Ownership of flowing "public" water went with priority in time of appropriation for

256

Dig down:
we did

beneficial purposes. The use itself did not matter, or the location of the user, whether high or low on the stream or in another watershed. First in self-service was first in law; first in time, first in right. If the use was diligent and steady as well as beneficial, the appropriation, even if it turned the streambed below into a dusty trail, had the backing of the courts. A prior appropriator could take water even if he trespassed on another's land to get it.

This legality, which rewarded old-timers and pinched off later arrivals, applied only to running waters, not to stored ones, and the rise of big reclamation dams has superimposed new regulations for reservoir waters over the old, remaining historic allocations. Further complications came with overlapping state and federal laws, basin and interstate compacts, Spanish and Mexican land grants and grazing permits, treaties, and the inherent or implied rights of Indian tribes.

The old common law dealt only with surface waters, but ground waters went with the land. The newer western laws of beneficial use also dealt only with surface waters. Who owns the ground waters and under what conditions? Though invisible below, ground waters are now immensely valuable. Geologists and lawyers have much to learn about them. Amid contentions and lawsuits a fresh body of law and precedent is slowly growing up. Much faster, water levels are falling. Mexico has firm regulatory laws, and New Mexico has passed a ground-water law, but in flashy, booming Arizona ground-water law is particularly chaotic.

Water soaking down drop by drop into Arizona ground, as during rainfall or irrigation, belongs to the landowner. It is percolating water. But a percolating stream in a definable subsoil channel is subject to appropriation by someone other than the landowner, just as a mineral deposit is. And there is no limit to pumping. The legislature has refused to pass bills intended to establish a correlative rights principle. This would close overpumped areas and create districts to cut back local pumping.

Wild, free Arizona frontier days continue deep underground where electric motors overpump. Fast-buck "suitcase farmers" suck earth's crust dry. On the average Arizona's water level is falling ten feet a year. In some places it is down by twenty feet each year. In one area

the pumps exhaust eighteen times the annual natural replenishment of ground water. Sometimes, as the aquifers get dried out, they cave in or shrink, and fissures and depression form on the surface.

Tucson — with its population of 260,000, which appears to be healthily "growing" — is the largest city in the United States that depends entirely on ground water, on a receding supply of it. The city is beginning to reach out and try to seize the aquifers of distant farming districts instead of recycling waste water or regulating either water use or population.

Overpumping is now prevalent in the entire region. On La Costa de Hermosillo, the handsome large plain of new government-reclaimed land between Sonora's capital and the sea, there are about 475 wells, each capable of two thousand gallons a minute, and here, despite strict supervision, the water table is falling three feet a year. Las Vegas, Nevada, is pumping more water than seeps from the mountain range to the west. The populations of whole watersheds are pumping themselves into a millennium of drought.

THE LAWS THAT APPLY to water are the emptiest of abstractions if streambeds are dry, if dams fill up with silt, or if waters turn toxic. From the Pecos to the Mojave River during "the winning of the West," miners, lumbermen, and ranchers moved into stable environments and damaged or ruined them by overcutting for mine timbers and smelter fuel, and by prolonged, heavy overgrazing of range land. The total effect was massive erosion, changes in vegetation, and the intensifying of quick floods and long droughts. Fertile grasslands became wastelands of cholla cactus or tumbleweed. During its first forty years Elephant Butte Reservoir filled up one-sixth with silt. A vast subaqueous mesa of canyon silt has been building up at the head of Lake Mead. Irrigation water can dissolve subsoil deposits of alkali and bring them up into the root zone; this has ruined thousands of acres in the Mexicali, Imperial, and Pecos valleys. Land can sour and drown the roots of crops when men irrigate too much and bring a high water table to the surface, as happened in parts of the Salt River Valley before World War I, necessitating pumps to get rid of the surplusage.

Even when big governmental agencies are in control and have the advice of university experts like those in

Imperial Dam with its desilting works diverts water on the Arizona side into the Gila Gravity Main Canal, on the California side into the All-American Canal, which delivers to Imperial and Coachella valleys.

Tucson, Tempe, Ciudad, Chihuahua, Hermosillo, Reno, or Riverside, the paradoxes of progress can entrap the wise as if they were the unwary.

In the Wellton-Mohawk district on the lower Gila, for example, the solutions to old problems create new problems. After farmers had used up the surface water, they began pumping. The fifty-mile Wellton-Mohawk oasis is over a self-contained basin, and during decades of pumping, irrigating, and repumping much of the same water, minus what was evaporating at the surface, farmers produced an ever-saltier pool of ground water. By 1931 salt-encrusted soils glittered under the midday sun as if covered with hoar frost—and were going out of production.

In 1952 the United States brought in Colorado River water through the Gila Main Gravity Channel. Farmers at once expanded their acreage of citrus, cotton, and vegetables, with no worry except for an occasional winter freeze. But with the influx of Colorado water, the water table rose, bringing salts with it, and the soil turned bilious from waterlogging. So wells were installed to pump the polluting ground water to the surface, and a channel was dug to carry the briny drainwater back to the Colorado River. This water made the river three and one-half times as salty as usual, up to 2,700 parts of dissolved solids per million parts of water. Mexicans in Mexicali Valley began to suffer crop losses from the enhanced saltiness on more than one hundred thousand acres. They cried out that the Yankees were violating the 1944 treaty with a promise of "virgin

water" of no more than 750 parts of solids per million.

Acting on a proposal from Secretary of the Interior Stewart Udall, the United States quickly built the Bypass Drainage Channel, which takes the salty Wellton-Mohawk water thirteen miles farther down, to below Mexico's Morelos Dam intake for Mexicali Valley water. The United States agreed to do most of its pumping in the winter. In summer, when the Mexicans need more water and the Colorado itself is purer, they could, if they wanted, mix Wellton-Mohawk drainage with river water.

But here, too, was a growing problem. By the time the Colorado reaches Morelos Dam, its water can hardly be called "virgin." It has been used for irrigation at Grand Junction, Vernal, Blythe, Winterhaven, and many other places and then returned, loaded with leached-out chemicals. It has also been held by the big storage dams, where the waters leach out flooded earth, and the spacious surfaces of lakes like Powell and Mead, lying flat under the sun of a big, dry sky, evaporate lavishly the year around, concentrating the saline content of the giant pools that remain.

By 1966 the salinity at Imperial Dam was 850 parts per million, and farmers in the Imperial and Coachella valleys were noting a decline in crop production, especially citrus. Colorado water taken to Southern California was losing quality as a beverage and spreading alkali in soils. Unless steps were taken, said water resources officials, the average salinity would rise by the year 2000 to 1,300 parts per million. Already reclamation agents upriver were lining irrigation canals to reduce water-soil contact, sealing off natural salt springs, and selecting farm lands that were still below average in alkali content.

Scarcity, salinity, depletion—to these the achievements of chemical technology and the increase in population have added another problem: pollution. Pesticides and herbicides eventually drain into rivers and lakes. Treated in varying degrees, sewage gets into rivers —the New, the Alamo, the Rio Grande. The Health and Social Services Department of New Mexico accuses Santa Fe, for instance, of polluting the Santa Fe River so seriously that it is "not suitable for irrigation or stock watering and is a serious public health threat." The mill tailings of copper and molybdenum companies spill into rivers. In the Gila, Imperial, and Rio Grande valleys a new threat to ground waters and to runoff is the thick accumulation of urine and manure in the congested animal cities called feed lots, where there are as many as a hundred thousand beef cattle at a time. In the same region there are dairies of five hundred to a thousand cows and poultry farms with a hundred thousand or more active birds.

IF THE DESERT STATES are to live within their present water system and still try to multiply the number of swimming pools, recreational lakes, and fountains, men must find better ways to harvest, transport, and store their water, keep it clean, and use it over and over again. The region is not so much running out of water as degrading it. Flagstaff, Tucson, and other cities that face recurrent shortages may learn from Windhoek, capital of Southwest Africa, which leads the world in processing sewage back to drinking water.

Farmers could raise the crops that take little water, and they could improve irrigation practices that are only 50 percent efficient. A 10 percent such improvement throughout Arizona would supply four Tucsons. States can require water prices sufficiently high to reduce use and can put use fees on withdrawals of water or the disposal of wastes into water. In several states there are subterranean pools of boiling water that perhaps can be harnessed to distill salty waters. Men could take the advice of a desert agricultural expert: "Better a moderate area of permanent homes than a promotional development that must be shortlived."

we saw this
at San Diego, 1973

259

CHAPTER 22

LAND OF SHRINKING SPACE

*Coping with growth on both sides of the border that
brings "more of everything we need less of"*

MOST OF THE DESERT space is devoid of permanent human residents, always has been, and always should be, for lack of water, soil, or safety. The word *inhospitable,* once used by explorers, still applies to the low, labyrinthine delta of the Colorado, to walls of a thousand canyons and barrancas, to valleys of blowing sand, to playas that are occasionally sticky with saline clays, and to repetitious plains of alkaline earth. The cool highlands and the irrigated oases that men have lived in for millenia are often Edenlike if uncrowded, but choice desert spots soon reach their carrying capacity.

Rigid political lines can be good, as when they keep real estate developers out of Indian reservations and national forests. But arbitrary lines are more often bad, as when slummy border towns, or sections of border cities, grow up alongside the United States–Mexico boundary. National space reaches an absolute terminus at the cyclone fences between San Luis Río Colorado and its Arizona twin, or between Mexicali and Calexico. The nations give space and money to glorify their capital cities, but they allow crowded, soiled, tawdry entrances to their sovereign lands.

Some towns exist only because of the boundary. The two towns named Nogales exist to handle international freight. New Mexico wants a port of entry at Anapra, just west of Juárez, in order to avoid the Texas bottleneck at El Paso. After New Mexico gets the port, two paired communities will spring up.

Mexico acknowledges that its border strip—cordoned off by inspection stations—is a special part of the country. Visiting motorists there need no permits, though they need special insurance. Only there can Mexicans legally own and drive big United States and European cars.

In Mexican border towns the population grows unnaturally quickly as poor people from the back country of Sonora and Chihuahua move in, hoping to find work for the fabled high wages or somehow to get across into the great Land of Plenty. Between 1900 and 1930, 10 percent of all Mexicans moved to the border states, and nine-tenths of those stayed on. When the peasants and Indians move into the cardboard and flattened-tin slums at the bare-dirt edges of towns and along the roads, they see themselves as raising their standards of living. They are jammed together in the last mile or the last fifty feet of the most spacious Mexican states, peering through wire at the tacky, slovenly facade of the U.S.A.

Some Mexicans call the border El Paso del Mundo, the lowest hole on earth. When the Chamizal used to hold brothels as well as factories, it was termed "the hell-hole of iniquity." Each year millions of United States nationals have poured south over the line to see bullfights, buy liquor and commercial souvenirs, get a sadistic kick out of seeing the sights of poverty, and enjoy establishments of unrestricted sex diversion. For the Mexican poor and the American foolish, the local city jails are hellholes of robbery, sodomy, rape, filth, poor food, overcrowding, and arbitrary detention according to laws that go back to the Code Napoléon and Roman law. You are guilty until proven innocent. *La mordida,* "the bite"—graft, payoff, protection money—is so common and widespread at jails and prisons, as

In 1926, during Prohibition, a couple of U.S. border patrolmen in the Tucson subdistrict captured two Mexican smugglers with three packloads of the best grade of Mexican liquor.

throughout the nation, that even big campaigns like that of President Echeverría cannot stop it.

In 1961 Antonio J. Bermúdez, an important business-man and politico, inaugurated and pushed ProNaF (Programa Nacional de Reforma Fronteriza), a rehabili-tation plan to beautify the immediate border and give visitors from the north a good impression as they entered Mexico. But the whole project got strangled in state-federal politics on both sides of the border and in international complications, such as the coordination of bridges and highways. In ten years the program pro-duced only a few flashy results, such as a motel in Mexicali and a souvenir center, convention center, and Museo de Historia in Juárez. Both El Paso and Juárez want to make the Chamizal and Cordova Island into a model international area. The century may yet see it. After all, in the early 1970s the Chihuahua govern-ment outlawed quickie divorces and prostitution.

From the years of World War II on, there were in-ternational agreements that brought gangs of *braceros*, field workers, north to plant and harvest crops. The agreements ended in 1964, but legal entrance to an American border strip continues. Each working day thousands of Mexicans with green cards cross into United States cities to labor, with benefits for both nations. The twin-plant concept, though objected to by some U. S. manufacturers and labor unions, also appears to work to mutual advantage — and also to allure more thousands of Mexicans to the border. Under this concept a U. S. company, under bond, ex-ports raw materials or unfinished parts for assembly or completion. When the final product moves back to the north, the tariff regulations place a tax only on the value added by manufacturing. In Juárez industrial parks, twin plants put together electronics components, paper hospital garments, moccasins, color offset printing plates, and wooden furniture.

The border, like all national boundaries, creates the problems of smuggling. Individuals and gangs have a chance to make good money. In the past a major problem was herding rustled cattle and horses in either direction. Both countries have long tried to stop the northward smuggling of candelilla wax, made from the pencil-sized stems of a plant in canyons of the Big Bend region and valuable in several industries. While the Eighteenth Amendment was corrupting American morals, United States customs agents faced the dexterity and power of rum runners.

Smuggling into Mexico is stimulated by luxury taxes, restrictive laws, and monopolies that put a premium on illicit bringing in of such items as food, radios, watches, color television sets, rings, electrical appliances, guns and ammunition, industrial and farm machinery, automobiles, cement, or curios (for resale to tourists). To encourage Mexicans to shop in Mexico, Juárez businessmen have opened Centro Méxicano, a supermarket.

Tariffs, prohibitions, and opportunity for huge profits put a premium on sneaking into the United States things such as bullion, jewels, Mexican antiquities, illegal immigrants or field and household workers, or marijuana, heroin, and the multitudinous pills craved by drugged generations.

The weedlike hemp, marijuana, grows easily in a half dozen northern Mexican states, and the opium poppy, introduced by the Chinese in the nineteenth century, does well in the hot valleys and canyons of the Sierra Madre Occidental. The climate is right, like that in Turkey, and the necessary hand labor is ready and willing to incise the seed capsules and collect the precious juice for drying.

It was in 1904 that the United States put mounted guards to patrolling the long desert border. Twenty years later the Border Patrol was authorized to hide, watch, accost, and arrest. In 1935 the Bureau of Immigration created the Border Patrol Academy in El Paso to train its men. Nowadays Border Patrol pilots, Department of the Treasury agents, and men from eight other federal agencies keep tabs on all air traffic moving over the line. In desolate sections, as along most of the Arizona and New Mexico borders, there are special electronic sensors and other sophisticated gear for detecting smugglers and illegal entrants. Each year the

Immigration people fly thousands of wetbacks to homelands deep inside Mexico. One Mexican who kept returning to El Paso got fifty-seven free return trips. El Paso papers called him the "Champion Wetback."

The Champion, member of an ethnic minority the minute he crossed the Rio Grande, was acting to improve his status, like ethnic underdogs in both nations. Where is my space? Where do I stand in society? How can I move for the better—sideways or upwards? Or am I on the way down? Who am I? Certain individuals are driven to the withdrawal, the *nada*, the nothingness of twentieth-century disillusionment in Europe and America. This applies to some in the hippie communes near Taos. Many endure, strive as they can, and improve their lot.

Negroes, a small ethnic group in the deserts, know how they have been boxed in and are on their way into the open air of freedom. The polylingual Estévanico gives blacks a claim on desert history. Later, blacks mined, rode herd on the cattle drives, and served in army units. A black foreman on the XYZ Ranch found the prehistoric bison bones that led to the discovery of the Folsom flints and opened a new chapter in archaeology. Another black, Bill Pickett, invented the sport of bulldogging steers. At the New Mexico State Fair in 1971, Black Action had an exhibit to parallel Indian Village and Spanish Heritage Show. The Action leaders' concerns were self-determination, pride, self-respect, and control of one's destiny and community affairs.

What of the ethnic groups, a majority in many areas, called variously Spanish-Americans, Mexican-Americans, persons of Spanish surname, Hispanos, whites (but not Anglos), natives, Latinos, or Chicanos? History, kinship, community, and the ethnic mystique of "La Raza" hold them together. *Chicano* is the barrio word that came into prominence in the late 1960s, flaunted as an act of defiance and a badge of honor. Chicanos, as Ruben Salazar defined them, are Mexican-Americans with a non-Anglo image of themselves. In Calexico, which is 90 percent Mexican-American, "Chicano power" has gained new housing and a majority on the city council. All over the Southwest, Chicanos are active—in violence such as the riots in Albuquerque in June of 1971; in legal steps to end discrimination, dirty housing, and low pay; and in a burst of articles and books that reevaluate the role of the group, past and

Longwell's in El Paso when the automobile was replacing the horse and the frontier was becoming a memory called the Old West. Longwell's phone number was 1.

present. From the Chicano viewpoint, standard United States history is a biased tale that uncritically accepts "manifest destiny" — really the aggressive seizure of Mexican and Indian lands.

For thousands of Hispanos in the upper Rio Grande watershed, "forgotten Americans" with family lines that go back to Oñate and to farmers and stockmen in La Mancha and Extremadura, the central issue is the Anglo confiscation of Spanish and Mexican land grants. The Tierra Amarilla, the Casa Colorada, the Ojo del Espiritu Santo, the Mesita de Juana López, and other land grants were made to individuals and to communities. The Mexican government alone made 1,715 grants, involving perhaps four million acres.

After 1848, as also in Arizona and California, most grant holders had tradition or possession on their side but little or no documentary legal evidence that American courts would accept. Villagers began to lose their lands to the gringos, especially after the railroads came and the prices rose for beef, mutton, and wool. From 1854 to 1890, large numbers of the land claims were "settled" in favor of Anglos by the U. S. Surveyor Gen-

eral's office, and the same happened in the Court of Public Claims from 1891 to 1904. Finally the U. S. had confirmed only 1.9 million acres in New Mexico, less than 6 percent of the area the Hispanos claimed, and much of what they still hold has come within the boundaries of national forest regulations for grazing and wood-gathering that restrict local people and benefit big Anglo cattle and lumbering corporations.

A hundred and more years after Guadalupe Hidalgo, the villagers were more defeated than ever. In 1964 a judge in Albuquerque ordered the Abiquiu Corporation to dissolve. It had been trying to regain for the colonial villagers and farmers the more than half-million acres granted to José Manuel Martínez. Meanwhile, in 1963 Reies López Tijerina, fiery son of a timid Texas sharecropper, and several dozen other men had organized Alianza Federal de Mercedes to solidify "and acquaint the Heirs of all the Spanish Land Grants covered by the Guadalupe Treaty . . . thus providing unity of purpose and securing for the Heirs of Spanish Land Grants the highest advantages as provided by the aforesaid Treaty and Constitution."

Under Tijerina's heady leadership the Alliance soon made its way into regional and national news as it spoke up for the Abiquiu and the San Joaquin Town corporations. The San Joaquin spokesmen were lashing out at "the injustices and tricks of tyrants and despots, of those who insult us and seize our lands . . . tracts of land, wood, waters and minerals . . . deeded to and bequeathed by, our ancestors, the heirs and assigns of the Grant of the Corporation of San Joaquin del Rio de Chama. . . ."

The Alliance held rallies, made protest marches, broke through a roadblock to "trespass" on national forest land, put pressure on the governor, and—on June 5, 1967—raided the courthouse in Tierra Amarilla to make a "citizens' arrest" of some county officials. During two hours of shooting the raiders shot apart a state police car, wounded Eulogio Salazar, the jailer, and took as hostages a deputy sheriff and a newspaper reporter. The National Guard rounded up forty men and women, alleged sympathizers with Tijerina, and herded them all night in a cattle pen. For five days the state carried on a military manhunt until it caught Tijerina.

In 1968 among other events came the masochistic slaying of Salazar, the key witness against Tijerina. Tijerina was tried on three charges connected with the raid, but the jury acquitted him. He was later convicted on other charges and put in jail. While there, he resigned as leader of the Alliance, which continued its campaign.

On the side of the Hispanos were the Office of Economic Opportunity, Home Education Livelihood Program, sociologists, liberal lawyers and journalists, and others who saw the villagers as a deliberately neglected group of citizens entitled to lands, waters, passable roads, a decent education, and public respect. Opposed to them were the U. S. Forest Service, big lumbering and ranching outfits, the district attorney, the county sheriff, the state's attorney general, and the adjutant general.

TERRESTRIAL SPACE is a constant. However endless the North American deserts appear to be, neither minorities, the majority if any, nor human beings as a whole have anything but less space when the population keeps growing by reproduction and immigration. Wild creatures, wild plants, and even valuable agricultural crops lose out similarly. The green of fertile reclaimed land returns to dull colors, the arid whitish-gray and grayish-black of man-made deserts—highways, streets, parking lots, sidewalks, and roof tops.

The environmental desolation, lacking the self-sustaining life of natural desert, spreads outward from the cities, which are among the fastest growing on the continent. Juárez, 128,000 in 1950, was over half a million in 1970. Mexicali, 141,000 in 1950, was also over half a million twenty years later. Border towns still tiny by Hermosillo or Ciudad Chihuahua standards, are growing at an even faster rate. Quietly, as parachutists, whole suburban colonies seem to appear suddenly outside San Luis Río Colorado, Tijuana, or Nogales. Ovid Demaris quotes a Mexican joke: "We have two methods of taking the census. . . . One is to walk into a *colonia* and throw a peso in the street. The other is to count each window and multiply by twelve."

During the 1960s El Paso grew from 276,000 to 317,000, Phoenix from 439,000 to 580,000, and Las Vegas, Nevada, from 64,000 to 124,000, virtually doubling. Three satellite cities of Phoenix made phenomenal growth: Mesa doubled in population, Tempe grew two and one-half times, and elegant Scottsdale swelled a vulgar six times and began to push against the once useless land of the reservation where Yavapais and Apaches had experienced apartheid for generations.

And the growths were speeding up. Phoenix, which grew by 14,000 persons in 1968, grew by 25,000 in 1969. Such growth anywhere means inflated costs of land and everything else, increased taxes and governmental expenditures, especially for new streets and highways, while permanent problems such as pollution and urban transportation stay neglected. Public debt grows with population, but public expenditure grows faster than the population or its income.

In all the desert states there were small towns that lost population during the 1960s as small farmers gave up because of inadequate water, poor housing, lack of medical and hospital facilities, or lack of a clear title that would make possible improvements to house and land. In areas like Harding County, New Mexico, where grasslands were broken to dry farming during war years, drought and isolation were driving young and old away to Albuquerque, Los Angeles, or El Paso.

While some public officials in the capitals worried about the decline of village and rural life and the costly growth of the cities, chambers of commerce celebrated the bulging population and invited industry in to avail itself of the pool of labor—Indian, Mexican, or Anglo.

Businessmen in El Paso, the self-styled "Sun City," were proud of their Texaco and Standard Oil refineries, Phelps Dodge refinery and copper-rod mill, Peyton Packing Company, which processed meat, and factories that made garments, truck trailers, furniture, footwear, especially boots, and iron, steel, and metal products. Downtown El Paso, garlanded with freeways, on-ramps, and off-ramps, thrust upward the towers of the natural gas company, leading banks, a franchised motel, and other symbols of man's claim to dominance over the Chihuahua Desert.

In Tucson, once the tiny presidio town of Pimería Alta, now bulky with a quarter of a million human beings, a downtown core of highrise structures held savings and loan associations, construction companies, home-building corporations. Standing twenty stories was Tucson Federal Savings, a monument of glazed, bluish tile brick. A street or two away was the modernistic twelve-story Pima County administration building, which rose above the site of the original Tucson, now largely demolished.

FOR THE MEXICANS who go north to the border towns and press against the fences, the problem is jobs. Fortunately for them, in the long run the Mexican government wants to decentralize the Distrito Federal, where one-seventh of all Mexicans live and where half of Mexican industry is. That is, the government wants to distribute people, factories, and air pollution as well as reclaim and irrigate in the northern deserts. Juárez and other cities expect not only more local agricultural production but also more twin plants and new Mexican firms backed by Nacional Financiera.

Businessmen in New Mexico officially back the state's Development Credit Corporation and privately push the Industrial Development Executives Association, which urges such things as industrial growth by credit and the creation of new cities (a way to engross federal and Indian lands). Albuquerque has its Industrial Development Service and Industrial Foundation. It is glad to welcome new, relatively clean firms, like one that makes oil well equipment or a branch of a blue jeans manufacturer. A recent president of the foundation urged that Albuquerque "not ever stop selling. We have plenty to sell. . . . We have the new horizons, we have ample space, we have the climate, we have the recreation, and we have comfortable living to offer."

In Tucson, which faces a water shortage and a smog problem, the senior vice-president of a bank is professionally optimistic: "There are plenty of industrial prospects. I've never seen so many people interested in Tucson. We have room to grow, and if there is a bright place in the nation's economy, it is the Southwest, and Tucson in particular." Businessmen in three communities, Las Cruces, Alamogordo, and El Paso, were busy in the early 1970s trying to take possession of the port to outer space. A Tri-Cities Shuttle Committee wanted to have at White Sands Missile Range the national base for ferrying men and supplies, including spare parts, between earth and a manned orbiting space station.

Yet there are highly placed spokesmen who have their doubts about the industrial future, as a debate in the Arizona State Senate illustrated. Senate leaders were arguing for a tax incentive plan that would lure the headquarters of Greyhound Corporation, with its ten-million-dollar payroll, from Chicago to Phoenix. But Senator James McNulty of Bisbee criticized chambers of commerce and the State Department of Economic Planning and Development. McNulty pointed out that new industries bring not only cash but also people, children, dogs, electricity-generating plants, air pollution, cars, double sessions in schools, solid wastes, and more congestion in the streets. More off-road vehicles erode the deserts and mar the natural beauty of the mountains. Each new industry brings an apparent gain in prosperity and an actual decline in the quality of living. McNulty attacked the confident boomers like the governor and a state senator from Scottsdale, who were sure that men could overcome all obstacles through some dextrous application of technology. The Bisbee senator denied the proposition that a state such as Arizona can enjoy the best of both worlds—undiminished economic prosperity and growth, and also continued enjoyment of unique deserts and mountains, sweetwater lakes, and streams. McNulty lost; the bill passed. But he said what is being said by others in his state, by Planned Parenthood Centers, by the Nature

Conservancy, Environmental Teach-In Committees, and Arizonans for a Quality Environment. One Phoenician says, "This 'Chamber of Commerce' syndrome brings with it deepening problems in every environmental area . . . more of everything that we need less of."

Industry is not the only threat to the open spaces and the skies. Another menace to the quality of life is big-scale subdividing companies with outside money that buy up ranch land or get hold of state lands and make lavish promises in capital letters. Using any sales device that will work, from giving free trading stamps to conducting overnight free visits by plane, these hustlers sell bare lots, or "luxury model" homes, or mobile homes, or condominium apartments with club facilities. The sales pitch is a package of promises, prophecies, and picture brochures of some combination of ranch riding, haute cuisine, cookouts, a marina or a fishing pond, and a golf course.

Subdivisions along the interstate highways, the Colorado River, and the Rio Grande begin to clutter up square miles of vistas. In Baja California bulldozers rearrange beaches and cliffs so that developers can sell lots on the Gulf side and on the once-isolated stretch from the most western international marker down the Pacific coast to Ensenada. New Mexico, which in 1950 had about five thousand acres subdivided and for sale, had about forty thousand in 1960 and a million in 1970, many with inadequate water or sanitation facilities, with dusty roads and no community buildings, despite poetical names. The State Health and Social Services Department showed concern: "Proliferation of subdivisions is a No. 1 problem in the environment."

With the new premium on remaining space, real estate schemers and their allies in federal bureaus have taken a fresh look at Indian reservations. One corporation has leased land from Tesuque Pueblo for a subdivision inside Santa Fe. Another has persuaded Co-chití, one of the Rio Grande pueblos, to lease land for ninety-nine years for a recreational city alongside the reservoir the Army Corps of Engineers is building, also on Cochití land. There are only two little token state reservations, one very recent, in all the imperial square miles of the Lone Star State; but in Arizona, Indian reservations take up a greater fraction than in any other state, and the old Anglo craving to seize natives' lands now takes the subtler form of leasing, as ranchers, tourist agents, miners, water engineers, and lumbermen eye the natural resources, now precious, including space. As a problem for Indians the missionary has been replaced by the developer.

WHO OWNS THE DESERT stretches, anyhow? Before Cortes, "ownership" went to aboriginal migration, occupation, and conquest. Then came the Spanish mission, pueblo, and grazing grants, often with vague topographic boundaries. Finally came base lines, meridians, and the section lines of the U.S. public land system. In all, land tenure is now a mixture of custom, tradition, arbitrary survey lines, titles in fee simple, treaties with nations, overlaid with the complications of mineral and water law, easements, and state, Indian, and federal sovereignties.

Individuals, corporations, and tribes own whole valleys and mountains, and dominate entire counties. Public desert lands are horizons that curve around the earth's surface with huge sectors restricted to missile, bombing, and gunnery ranges, Air Force bases, to national parks, forests, and recreation areas. But the visitor who gazes out over the landscape, whether from the air, on solid earth, or afloat on one of the new reservoirs, is not aware of property lines. Instead he beholds a grandeur of space, of mountain crests, fluctuating color, and luminous, wide-open sky. Nearly all creation seems to be in sight.

CHAPTER 23

MAN AND MAÑANA

The challenge of tomorrow in the Southwest: how to enjoy, and not destroy, a glorious land

As BIG-SCALE MATERIAL progress has come to northern Mexico and the southwestern United States, it has brought a paradoxical mixture of the good and the bad. It has changed the desert scene, sometimes irreversibly. Since progress, physical or cultural, assumes endless alteration, men and women devoted to sunshine and space and all else that the deserts could permanently offer now begin to ask basic questions. Why don't we officially delineate the problems, confront them, and solve them? Watchman, what of the future?

Phoenix had its crucial moment of smoggy truth one December day in 1969, when a temperature inversion trapped fouled-up cool air near the ground. Las Vegas, Tucson, and Albuquerque now admit that they have smog. Motorists who escape from Los Angeles smog by driving to Palm Springs find that their own smog blows through San Gorgonio Pass and follows them into Coachella Valley.

Hikers who get away from it all in the Colorado River canyons find their hideaways buzzed by helicopters and planes. Anywhere desert picnickers go by car or by horse, they may well be suddenly engulfed by motorcycles zooming through the washes and over the hills, shattering the desert quiet, frightening away birds, and pounding heavy dust into the air. The desert, says a Scottsdale woman, "is being transformed into a racetrack, a testing area, a pitstop." She refers not to the annual Mila Milas de México from Ensenada southward or to the Mint 500 on a playa near Las Vegas, where racing wheels kick dust a mile into the sky, but to a daily phenomenon between the salt

lakes east of El Paso and the dry lakes west of Barstow. Not only motorcycles but jeeps, pickup trucks, homemade jalopies, dune buggies, three-wheeled jobs —almost anything that runs—drive across desert flats, over mountains, and along dunes, destroying plants, starting soil erosion, driving out animals, making scars that will last out the century—all in the name of noisy fun under a dusty sun.

The Southwest shows signs of being overdeveloped, or undercontrolled, or both. There is the lavish use of ornamental water, as in the pools and fountains of new cities, and the pollution of water in the rivers and in rare spots like Havasupai Canyon. The pools of turquoise water there, blue-green as a Navajo bracelet, in travertine basins below a dashing waterfall, are too polluted to swim in. There is the oversalty Colorado River water that Mexico objects to. Albuquerque, disturbed by the noise of jet planes warming up at Sunport, has feedlots rich in the odors of the Old West, zoo smells, and an overworked sewerage plant.

Both ordinary persons and public officials are calling for controls of dust and emissions from pumice, perlite, and mica processing; aluminum alloy plants; hot-mix asphalt batching plants; rare-earths plants, as at Henderson, Nevada; public dumps, as at Sunrise Mountain, Las Vegas; lime kilns, as near Douglas; cement factories, as at Clarkdale and Rillito, Arizona; uranium processing plants in the Four Corners region; and sulfur fumes from copper smelters at Ajo, El Paso, Hurley, Inspiration, and a dozen other places. Experts have proved that "places where there is a lot of mining and smelting have a lot of lung cancer." High

The Permanente Cement Company plant and conveyor belt in Lucerne Valley, California, on the rim of the Mojave Desert.

269

The terraced crater of the only open-pit borate mine in the world at Boron in the Mojave Desert, where in 1925 a huge oval-shaped body of pure borates was discovered.

cancer areas are central Utah, southwestern New Mexico, much of Arizona, and most of Nevada. Agricultural burning of stockpile material such as cotton waste smudges the sky. Riverside County prohibits the burning of such material in the Palm Springs–Indio area until after the Desert Golf Classic and the National Date Festival during February and March. And there are people who worry about the underground tests of the AEC. One test in 1970 leaked minimal radioactivity detected in twelve states and as far away as the Canadian border.

ONE OF THE SPECIAL GLORIES of the desert reaches has been the sense of virgin landscape, however plain, as far as eye could see in transparent air, or the sense of expanses free from all evidence of humanity. Now the scene more and more includes broad, arbitrary highways, gashing roadcuts through mountains and forests, sanitary landfills, dry creeks of mill tailings, varicolored and sterile, that blow in the wind, and a miscellaneous clutter of cans, paper, fragmentary clothing, broken bottles, cardboard boxes, and abandoned automobiles, wrecked or burned.

There is the dismantling of hillsides by quarry workers, as back of Hermosillo, and there are the hillocks and mesas of overburden and spoils at copper, uranium, coal, and molybdenum mines, often together with the terraces of tailing ponds and dikes, as at mines near Tucson and Miami, at Questa and Gallup in New Mexico, or at Cedar City and Monticello in Utah. Power lines once were welcome, since they brought modern times to countryside and city, but newspaper editors and readers now begin to see them as gigantic eyesores.

Scenic pollution in the deserts also includes ubiquitous small-scale vandalism that adds up to a general degradation of the fragile environment. Vandals chip off petroglyphs, dig up the graves of soldiers and Indians, pull down the walls of ghost-town buildings in search for souvenirs, filch prehistoric pots and tools, dig up wild plants, set fires, as to the hanging dried fronds of native palm trees, use spray paint to write on rocks, and steal signs that explain history or prohibit stealing. Vandals with guns shoot anything that runs or perches. If nothing else is around, they will shoot oranges and grapefruit from a rancher's trees.

The 2,100,000-kilowatt plant at Fruitland, producer of the smoke, gas, fly ash, and mercury emission that triggered a nationwide controversy over all the Four Corners power plants.

Subsistence hunting by pioneers and then market hunting by commercial killers wiped out the native elk in New Mexico by 1900 and in the Big Bend later. Anglos killed off the jaguar that once ranged as far north as the Grand Canyon. The last Arizona grizzly bear was shot in 1935. Nat Straw, a New Mexico hunter's hero, helped to exterminate the grizzlies in his state. The last Sonora grizzly was reported in the 1960s. Mountain lions are an endangered species, largely because of pressure from sportsmen and cattlemen, though the cost in taxes to suppress them far exceeds the value of loss in cattle and sheep. Antelope, once abundant, are now rare. Bighorn sheep are greatly threatened by rich poachers compulsive about acquiring specimen rams' heads to mount on their walls. One of Arizona's best-known hunters, a rancher near Quartzite, quit guiding hunters because of his disgust. He told of hunters who used airplanes to spot bighorns and who then planned their killing as carefully as if they were gangland murderers. Deer remain the favorite target, but with the number of guns increasing faster than the population, deer are declining in number. There are 40,000 deer hunters in Arizona; each year the number increases by 4,000.

Big two-hearted governments, federal and state, are both the bloodthirsty killer on a general rampage and the humane conservationist—in limited acreages properly called refuges. In one southwestern state in 1969, the U.S. Division of Wildlife Services trapped, snared, shot, ran down with dogs, and poisoned with cyanide some 3,125 coyotes, porcupines, black bears, and other "enemies" of mankind. The federal program cost $252,763, or $80.88 per animal, and probably nearer to $135.60 per coyote, the main quarry. The loss in livestock and other domesticated animals the same year in the same state came to $42,211.

Poison campaigns by the Bureau of Land Management and the Forest Service have sundered the entire food chain that connects Utah prairie dogs, rabbits, gray foxes, kit foxes, badgers, Texas red wolves, burrowing owls, blackfooted ferrets, woodpeckers, jays, chickadees, nuthatches, golden eagles, and bald eagles. Until 1950 one of the great sights at Carlsbad Caverns was the nightly exodus of thirty million bats, which ranged the Pecos Valley all night eating insects. Twenty years later the population was down to at most one and one quarter million. Pesticides had reduced the food supply and indirectly poisoned the bats or affected their fertility.

As desert streams are diverted or pumped to bedrock, species of rare fish become rarer yet or end their long adaptation to the deserts. A quality of human life goes when the longfin dace, the loach minnow, the spikedace, and the Sonora sucker go, however small or inedible they may be. The most extraordinary are the most vulnerable, such as the species of pupfish in tiny, lonely, isolated warm springs scattered from the base of the Chisos Mountains in Texas to the Amargosa River basin in Nevada and California. Already a moment's push from a developer's bulldozer has filled in a saline spring and wiped out an entire species.

No OTHER SINGLE EPISODE better embodies all the problems of the deserts today or tomorrow than the steam-plant controversy that began to reach prominence in early 1970. The issues are clear. The big cities in central New Mexico and at the southern ends of Arizona, Nevada, and California want power for booming populations that have more and more desire for electricity. Yet cities like Los Angeles and Phoenix no longer want to have smog-producing steam generating plants anywhere near them. Indian lands on the far-away Colorado Plateau contain large amounts of excellent, usable coal. Boosters in desert states welcome development. But friends of the tribes and environmentalists everywhere, Indians included, object to brutal blighting. Many local citizens, especially in New Mexico, see their blue sky, their long views, their sparkling sunlight as going . . . going . . .

In the early 1960s, after conservationists had killed plans for hydroelectric dams in the Grand Canyon, ten investor-owned power companies met quietly and formed Western Energy Supply Transmission Associated—WEST—an umbrella group that claimed it wanted to meet a galloping demand for power in urbanized states. WEST later grew to two dozen members, including the Nevada Power Company, the Los Angeles City Department of Water and Power, and the U.S. Bureau of Reclamation. Pooling resources, moving with careful legality, groups of companies leased Navajo land and acquired coal-mining rights, got water allocations from the bureau, and drew con-

tracts for construction, transportation, and transmission lines.

By 1970, when New Mexico conservationists raised a cry, there were several plants in operation and more being built or planned. There were six in particular, all in the Colorado River watershed. Near Farmington, at Fruitland, was the Four Corners Plant, which got its coal from Navajo Mine, the largest open-pit coal mine in the western United States.

Near Page, Arizona, on Lake Powell, the Navajo Plant was going up. This giant, intended to generate 2.3 million kilowatts, was to use coal from new surface coal mines on Black Mesa at Tsegi, near Kayenta on the Navajo Reservation. An eighty-mile railroad would bring the coal to Page. In Nevada at Davis Dam the Mohave Plant was rising to generate 1.5 million kilowatts. Its fuel would be powdered Black Mesa coal pumped as a slurry in a pipeline 275 miles long. The water for this would come from five wells 3,500 to 3,700 feet down under Black Mesa. In the original plans both the Mohave and the Navajo plants would return to the river water that had been warmed as it cooled the used steam.

Two more plants were under study, both in Utah, ~being built 1973~ one at Huntington Canyon, near Price, the other on the Kaiparowits Plateau across Lake Powell from Page. The Kaiparowits mine, deep underground, would eventually lead to the systematic caving-in of a large tract, but it would supply a plant capable of generating five or six million kilowatts—enough power to run New York City.

Peabody Coal Company contracts for Black Mesa coal guaranteed to the Navajos the highest royalties ever paid to Indians, twenty-five cents a ton. Indian families in the way of operations would be relocated at company expense. Peabody promised not to pump water from the top thousand feet, and in practice the engineers even further protected the ground waters when they used concrete to seal the wells at 2,000 feet. The company paid a firm sum for each acre-foot of water it pumped. The U.S. Geological Survey was to monitor the water supply. Towering chimneys, tall as mesas, would release smoke and fumes high in the sky, far above the people below. The railroad would run on electricity, not on the coal it carried, to avoid smudging the air in the Monument Valley Navajo

Tribal Park. After thirty-five years, when the contracts and the coal deposits reached an end, the Company would give the wells to the Indians and both reconstruct and replant Black Mesa to pines and junipers and to grass—to improved range grasses.

All WEST's actions assumed the growth of Big Population in the distant cities. Once again Big Technology would bring Surefire Progress. The clients of Arizona Public Service, Tucson Gas and Electric, Southern California Edison, Salt River Project, and other utilities could electrify day and night; the bureau could pump Colorado River water to the Central Arizona Project to reclaim more desert and entice more people. More . . . more . . .

But the rising if tardy clamor of the 1970s went up against the plan in general and certain features in particular. The big cities and the big interests were treating the plateau country as a colony, endangering the Navajo and Hopi way of life and threatening the quality of recreational areas that city people themselves seek out, such as Grand Canyon, Lake Powell, Canyonlands, and Mesa Verde. The leases stipulated jobs for Indians, but only a small fraction of the natives would get jobs, a fraction of the jobs.

In jeopardy were natural flow beneath the surface, springs on Black Mesa, and the water supply of the community of Kayenta. The plants would not only use Colorado River water but would heat it up, too, by accident or engineering design, and pollute the stream with industrial and railroad runoff, saline concentrates, and the chlorine and sulfuric acid used in cooling towers. Sulfur concentrates from the mining operations would seep toward the precious oasis of farming land at Moencopi.

The stacks of the generating plants, whether five hundred feet or taller, would contribute to discoloring and poisoning the air in half a dozen states, particularly in the Rio Grande Valley. Even though the New Mexico and Utah coals are superior to many eastern coals, the plants had a mighty potential to give off smoke, fly ash, and nitrogen and sulfur dioxides, which combine with water to form strong acids.

Already the 2.1-million-kilowatt plant at Fruitland was throwing out as much ash and smoke each day— 250 tons—as New York City and Los Angeles combined. Indeed, in 1966 the only man-made object vis-ible on earth in a photograph taken in Gemini 12, 170 miles out in space, was a vast, portentous smoke plume from the Fruitland operation. In 1971 an expert at the Southwest Research and Information Center in Albuquerque said that the mercury emission at the Four Corners plant is "possibly the greatest single health hazard in the world." The 6,000 pounds given off each year is "a staggering quantity of lethal pollution." When the San Juan Plant at nearby Waterflow and the other main plants should be completed, perhaps by 1980, a thousand tons of fly ash and smoke and transparent gas would float eastward each day to mix with natural clouds, obscure the light of the Land of Sun, and produce deadly showers of corruscating rain.

Statistics prepared by the Central Clearing House in Santa Fe got distributed. Articles on the issue appeared from coast to coast; television featured it. New Mexico and other states passed laws for air quality. The utilities began to install water devices or electronic precipitators to clean smokestack air. Engineers decided to build specially sealed evaporation ponds to "abate air pollution and eliminate any effect on Colorado River water," that is, on its temperature or its chemistry. The Department of Health, Education and Welfare took steps to set up a Four Corners Area Air Quality Control Region. Environmental groups, the governor of New Mexico, and officials in Washington asked for a moratorium on current building of steam plants, and the secretary of the interior ordered a moratorium on new plants, which stopped the Kaiparowits venture, the biggest of all.

The hit-or-miss frontier era is over, and no number of movie sets will bring it back. The promise nowadays for the people and their deserts lies in conservation and planning. These soberly involve all the physical and biological sciences, all of the social sciences, and all the arts.

Hints for a constructive future are the many tentative, piecemeal projects, public or private, such as reclamation districts in Sonora or the Rio Grande Valley, state and national parks, Sun City, rural Chandler with its planned civic center, experiments with planting native or exotic shrubs on highway cuts, or installing new and improved combustors to rid jet planes of exhaust smudge. To reduce the thunderclaps of sonic booms, Holloman Air Force Base schedules supersonic practice flights at very high altitudes in a restricted area south of Mountainair. In a search for cleaner power production, Mexico is building a plant at Cerro Prieto, south of Mexicali, to tap and use mile-deep geothermal energy, steam as hot as 500° F. Some cities and corporations are beginning to recycle water, at least for lawns and golf courses.

Leaders in Albuquerque and Phoenix are working to stop unrestricted housing developments that scar and uglify mountainsides in the Los Angeles style. Though Guadalupe National Park is being prepared for visitors to far-western Texas, they probably will have to park their cars outside and ride through the park only in special buses. There is support for expanding Grand Canyon National Park both upstream and down, for placing a quota on river travelers, and for banning motors from the river, as from the trails and the sky above.

The desert states have planning departments that serve as beginnings, though they are held so far to rhetorical and advisory functions. It takes strong government to make planning work. Centralized Mexico is proving to be more effective in some ways than the United States. It is creating a National Commission on Desert Regions, undertaking, for instance, to rehabilitate an area in Coahuila. Other programs include the Interstate Committee for Developing the Western Sierra Madre, aimed at bringing 72,000 Mexican Indians into the mainstream of modern life.

What southwestern residents and visitors can hope for and work for is a simple, strong, all-inclusive system of state, regional, and national planning. At one level or another, government can regulate the size of cities in area and population. It can institute population controls. It can zone every square inch of each state for urban, industrial, agricultural, or recreational-conservational use. It can forbid the developing of rare, choice wild areas, and it can stop the sub-

dividing of prime soils needed for crops. By changing state tax laws and the federal laws of 1954 with their capital gains provisions, and by altering Federal Housing Authority and Bureau of Land Management policies, governments can end the holding of land for speculation and the deterioration of downtown areas. It can buy key lands and lease back by agreement only for farming, recreation, or scenery. It can grant tax concessions for keeping land in its present use, or it can acquire scenic or recreational easements, as for bicycle or horse trails.

Too, government can build such superhighways as are needed around or away from cities, historical buildings and their sites, prime land, Indian reservations, and stupendous scenery. It can require automobile engines to run without polluting, and it can make all motor vehicles stay on roads. It can prohibit airplane and jet fumes and noises beyond certain levels. With a sufficient number of wardens, it can stop the killing of threatened species.

By regulating all water pumping, charging heavily for wasted or misused water, and requiring recycling of water, government can solve the water problem without further disturbing nature. It can give every encouragement to developing biological controls for pests in place of chemical poisons.

Many of these optimistic propositions have on a small scale been put into practice or law in one state or another. In a way they all aim to dethrone physics as the master science and replace it with the rising life science of ecology. They propose that Man conquer Man, not Nature. They mean revised attitudes toward money, ownership, private property, freedom, technology, growth, democracy, and physical progress. But Progress in the broad sense, which is the American faith, always calls for new ideas, new goals. The great Southwest, fascinating and beautiful still, stands open as a wonderful place to start putting Man back inside Nature, where he came from.

GLOSSARY

acequia: a ditch or channel that carries water for domestic or farm use.

acre-foot: the quantity of water required to cover one acre to the depth of one foot, or 43,560 cubic feet.

adiabatic cooling (or heating): temperature change due to altitude change. Air temperatures cool at the rate of 4° per thousand feet of ascent and increase at the same rate during descent.

algae: primitive plants, often aquatic, having neither stems, roots, true leaves, nor vascular systems.

alkali: a mixture of soluble salts found on dry lake beds in a quantity detrimental to plant growth.

alluvium: sediment deposited by flowing water.

Americans: the name United States citizens give themselves—a label that Mexicans see as presumptuous, since they consider themselves also to be "Americans," citizens of the Americas.

amphibian: a class of cold-blooded vertebrates with gilled aquatic larvae and air-breathing adults; members rank between fishes and reptiles in genealogy and include frogs and salamanders.

Anglo: a non-Indian or non-Mexican; a white person, a white American.

aquifer: a water-bearing stratum or bed of sand, gravel, or rocky material.

arriero: a muleteer.

arroyo: a steep-sided streambed or wash.

artifact: an object shaped by human workmanship.

atajo: a drove of mules.

atlatl: a throwing-stick; a dart or spear placed into position in another piece of wood, which acts as an extended arm and increases propellant force.

banco: a benchland or island formed by the shifting of a river channel; sometimes a deposit of soil and sand.

barranca: a ravine with clifflike sides, a gorge.

barrio: a district or section in a Mexican town; a Mexican section in a southwestern town.

biome: a major community of plants and animals, usually named for its characteristic vegetation; e.g., northern cone-bearing forest, tropical rainforest, etc.

biotic province: a geographic region marked by the presence of one or more ecological associations that differ from those of neighboring provinces.

bonanza: fair weather; prosperity; a rich lode or ledge of ore.

bosque: a thicket of mesquite or tamarisk.

bracero: a field worker ("one who works with his arms"); a Mexican farm worker hired through a contractor for seasonal labor in the United States.

butte: an isolated hill having steep sides but a smaller summit area than a mesa.

caldera: a large bowl-shaped crater formed either by the subsidence of the original top of a volcano or by massive eruptions.

chaparral: scrubby vegetation characterized by woody branches, small evergreen leaves, and other adaptations to harsh summer-dry climate.

Chicano: a Mexican-American with a non-Anglo image of himself.

cholla: a species of cactus, generally very prickly.

cist: a round storage pit found in cave-pithouse sites.

colonia: a land subdivision, a settlement.

conglomerate: rock composed of fragments, ranging in size from pebble to boulder, cemented together.

convection current: vertical movement of air caused by differing temperatures of two air masses.

cordillera: a long chain of mountain ranges, as in the North American Cordillera, which extends from the Brooks Range of Alaska to the Andes of South America.

corita: a mud and willow basket.

deciduous: having leaves that fall off at certain seasons.

desert pavement: ground surface strewn with flat-topped pebbles forming a mosaic pattern, resting upon finer material.

detritus: rock fragments produced by erosion.

dew point: the temperature at which air saturated with water vapor condenses to produce dew.

dike: a vein of igneous rock that has been injected while molten into a fissure in older rock.

ejido: a district of individual farm plots and larger communal plots formed by breaking up hacienda lands.

encomienda: in practice, slavery; in theory, jurisdiction granted to a lord on condition that in return he provide services such as alms, church aid, and military defense.

erosion: the wearing away of land surfaces by various natural means.

estuary: the mouth of a river where fresh and sea water mix.

fault: a fracture in the earth's crust along which movement has occurred.

fault-block mountains: highlands standing above the surrounding countryside, displaced upward along lines of fracture.

federalistas: troops of the Mexican government.

fossil: the remains or trace of an organism living in past geologic ages, embedded in a matrix rock unless exposed by erosion.

fray: short for *fraile, frater;* brother, brother monk.

gene: the hereditary unit that carries genetic information from generation to generation.

genus: a group of related organisms usually including several species (plural: genera).

gneiss: a type of metamorphic rock.

gringo: a non-Mexican, a white person or a white American; a foreigner in Mexico or in an area formerly under Mexican sovereignty (used in a pejorative sense).

habitat: the total of environmental features characterizing an area occupied by a given organism or a community.

hacendado: the owner of a hacienda; a rancher, planter, landholder.

hacienda: a ranch, a landed estate; the house or the central buildings on a ranch.

hand axe: a primitive tool crudely formed by flaking chips off a large pebble.

hibernation: a state of dormancy in which winter is spent.

Hispano: an American of Spanish ancestry.

igneous rock: rock that at one time was molten.

insurrecto: an insurgent, a rebel.

intrusion: a vein of rock that has forced its way into underground cracks while molten, then has cooled and solidified.

isohyet: a line on a map that joins places receiving the same average yearly rainfall.

jornada: a difficult, waterless tract that should be traversed in one day.

Jornada del Muerto: a day's journey of a dead man; the proper name for a difficult dry crossing north of Doña Anna, New Mexico.

kiva: an underground or partially underground chamber in Pueblo villages, ancient and modern, used chiefly for ceremonial purposes.

la mordida: "the bite"; graft, a bribe, a payoff.

La Raza: "the race" or "the lineage"; a slogan of ethnic solidarity used by Chicanos.

latitude: the distance north or south of the equator as measured in degrees.

lava: molten material coming from a volcanic crater or fissure, hardening into ropy or sharp-pointed masses of rock.

lichen: any of numerous complex plants composed of an alga and a fungus growing in a mutually supporting relationship.

life zone: a belt of distinctive plants and animals based on elevation.

magma: molten rock, some of which reaches the surface in volcanic activity. Much of it remains underground to cool slowly into igneous rock, such as granite, which is highly crystaline.

mano: a circular to semirectangular stone for grinding corn or other types of food.

matrix plant: the dominant plant within a plant community.

mesa: a flat-topped area with clifflike sides.

metamorphic rock: rock changed from its original form by heat and pressure.

metate: a large stone upon which corn and other foods were ground.

microhabitat: a segment of an area that, because of local conditions, differs from the general environment.

monsoon: wind that reverses direction seasonally, producing alternating wet and dry periods.

mutation: any inheritable change in an organism.

natural community: a group of plant and animal species in a commonly shared area.

norteamericano: the Mexican word for a United States citizen.

oasis: a green area in desert regions where surface or subsurface water is available.

ojo: "eye"; a spring of water.

osmosis: the process in which fluid passes through a certain type of membrane until the solutes in the water on both sides of the membrane are equal.

ox-bow: a crescent-shaped lake left behind when a meandering river changes its course.

paleohistory: geologic history before the advent of man.

physiographic: pertaining to the physical features of the earth, their causes and relationships to one another.

pithouse: a shelter constructed by early North American tribes before Pueblo times, having stick-and-mud walls erected over a shallow pit and covered with a flat roof supported on posts.

plateau: an elevated, level-surfaced area of land.

playa: a "beach"; dry lake, or a shallow desert lake that is intermittently dry.

presa: a dam or dike.

prestanombre: a Mexican citizen who for a price allows use of his name on land titles in Mexico.

projectile point: an arrowhead, spearhead or dart head made of rock or bone to be attached to a wooden shaft.

radiocarbon-dating: a method of dating prehistoric remnants by measuring their radioactive carbon content.

rain shadow: an area on the lee side of a mountain range that receives less rain than that on the windward side.

rancheria: an Indian camp or settlement.

reja: a lattice, railing, or series of bars over windows.

repartimiento: the practice by which representatives of the Spanish crown assigned Indians to private individuals to be used for labor in operations deemed necessary for the public welfare.

revoltosos: rebels, rioters.

riparian: relating to plants and animals living along streams or lakes, sometimes including organisms in the water itself.

scarp (escarpment): an inland cliff formed by fault action or the tilting upward of resistant rock layers.

schist: a type of metamorphic rock easily cleavable into thin layers.

Secretaria de Recursos Hidraulicos: the Mexican agency for water resources.

sedimentary rock: rock which has been formed by the consolidation of grains of minerals, broken bits of older rock, or organic material, cemented together; usually occurs in layers.

shale: a sedimentary rock composed of clays and mud cemented together.

shard: a piece of broken pottery.

soil horizons: soil layers divided according to mineral components.

species: a group of closely related organisms capable of interbreeding.

subsoil: a layer of material under topsoil, containing less organic matter than the soil above it.

substrate: the base upon which an organism grows or rests.

subtropics: the latitudes immediately north and south of the tropics.

succulent: capable of retaining fluid; a plant whose tissues have this capability as an adaptation to an arid habitat.

taiga: subarctic forest consisting mainly of willow, birch, and several cone-bearing tree species.

temperate latitudes: the region between the subtropics and the Arctic, or Antarctic Circle.

timberline: the elevation above which trees do not grow.

tinaja: a pool of rainwater caught in rocks.

trade winds: a system of tropical, one-directional winds that blow almost constantly toward the equator.

Trans-Pecos: the part of Texas west of the Pecos River.

tropics: those regions that lie between the Tropic of Cancer and the Tropic of Capricorn.

tuff: soft rock composed of volcanic ash and dust.

tundra: a treeless arctic region with permanently frozen subsoil and vegetation composed of lichens, stunted shrubs, and some perennial wildflowers.

twin plant: a factory in a Mexican border town that assembles parts made in a United States factory.

vein: a body of minerals filling a rock fissure, usually deposited by solution.

viga: an exposed ceiling beam.

volcanic plug: a mass of solidified lava filling the central vent of a volcano.

wash: the dry bed of a stream.

weather front, cold: a wedge-shaped mass of cold air pushing under a mass of warm air; rain occurs along the sharply angled line of contact.

weather front, warm: a mass of warm air rising over cold air, causing cooling; the water vapor the mass contains condenses, and rain occurs.

weathering: the distintegration of rock exposed to the atmosphere.

ACKNOWLEDGMENTS

Of the many people who have made this book possible, the authors are particularly indebted to:

Frank Anaya, Librarian, New Mexico Department of Development, Santa Fe; Guillermo Asúnsolo, *El Heraldo*, Ciudad Chihuahua; William E. Brown, Prescott; Bill Burk, Manager of Public Relations, Atchison, Topeka and Santa Fe Railway Co., Chicago; Harry Coulter, Automobile Club of Southern California, Van Nuys; Bob Crandall, entomologist and photographer, Pasadena; Departamento de Turismo, Ciudad Chihuahua, Mexico; W. A. Dinsmore, Business Manager, Kitt Peak National Observatory, Tucson; James Handley, Advertising Department, Del E. Webb Development Company, Sun City; Carle O. Hodge, Research Specialist, Environmental Research Laboratory, and Editor of *Arid Lands Research Newsletter,* Tucson; Don G. Kelley, Editor, *Oceans* Magazine, Menlo Park, California; Elmer and Evelyn LaLanne, Laguna Beach, California; Robert Lewis, Governor, Pueblo of Zuni; Richard Logan, Geography Department, UCLA; Kay Matthews, the Central Clearing House, Santa Fe; M. G. McKinney, Cdr. USN-Ret., El Paso; Arthur L. Olivas, Curatorial Assistant in Charge, Museum of New Mexico, Santa Fe; John Pastier, Los Angeles *Times;* Cal N. Peters, Acton, California; Paul Rader, New Mexico State University, University Park; C. L. Sonnichsen, Professor of English, University of Texas at El Paso; the Speakers at the Symposium on Mining and Ecology in the Arid Environment, Tucson (March 22-27, 1970); Robert Stebbins, Museum of Vertebrate Zoology, University of California, Berkeley; Editha L. Watson, Research Associate, Navajo Tribe, Window Rock, Arizona.

PICTURE CREDITS:

Gene Ahrens: Pages 66, 67, 188. Archives of the University of Texas at El Paso: Page 196. Arizona Pioneers' Historical Society: Page 181. Guillermo Asúnsolo, Chihuahua: Page 220. Otis Aultman (from El Paso Public Library): Pages 170, 183, 264. Gerhard Bakker: Pages 4-5, 8, 16, 20, 28-29, 32, 43, 45, 46-47, 69 (top), 72-73, 74 (top row, center; top row, right; third row, left; third row, right; bottom row, right), 76 (top row; second row, left; second row, center; bottom row, center; bottom row, right), 79, 80, 96, 97, 115, 116, 117, 123, 190, 191. Len Bouché: Pages 214, 215. Richard W. Brooks: Pages 41 (bottom), 44, 74 (second row, center). G. D. Brewerton (from *Harper's Magazine*): Page 168. J. Ross Browne (from *Harper's Magazine*): Pages 142, 144, 160, 176.

Dan Budnik: Page 239. Bureau of Reclamation, U. S. Department of the Interior: Pages 250, 255, 256, 258.

Harvey Caplin: Pages 14, 48, 56, 68, 76 (bottom row, left), 126, 140, 164, 185, 186 (top), 187, 192, 210-211, 238 (bottom), 243. Ernest Carter: Pages 50, 133. Center for Man and Environment, Prescott College: Pages 100, 118. William E. Connelley, from *The Journal of William H. Richardson* (New York: 1848): Page 156. Ed Cooper: Pages 2-3, 18, 22, 26, 30, 38, 54, 58, 63, 70-71, 74 (second row, right), 76 (second row, center; third row, left; third row, right), 78, 98, 212, 237 (bottom). Paul Coze: Page 124. Paul Coze (Petley Studios): Page 112. Robert Crandall: Page 74 (top row, left). Charles K. Davenport: Page 106. El Paso Public Library: Page 172. C. E. Erickson, all original maps.

C. S. Fly (from Arizona Pioneers' Historical Society): Page 179. Dick Kent: Pages 234-235. Kitt Peak National Observatory: Page 240. Jeffrey J. Kurtzeman: Pages 236 (top), 237 (top), 238 (top). Las Vegas News Bureau: Page 216. Richard G. Lillard: Page 132 (bottom). Los Alamos Scientific Laboratory, University of California: Pages 246-247. M. G. McKinney: Page 236 (bottom). David Muench: Pages 6-7, 42, 65, 69 (bottom), 77, 120, 129, 130-131, 136. Roy Murphy: Pages 41 (top), 76 (third row, center), 88. Tom Myers: Pages 74 (second row, left; bottom row, center and left), 75, 186 (bottom), 189.

National Park Service: Pages 102, 108, 110. New Mexico Department of Development: Pages 152, 182, 224. Ken Ottinger, all original drawings and diagrams. Permanente Cement Company: Page 268. Cal N. Peters (from National Park Service): Pages 134-135. Phelps-Dodge Corporation, Tyrone, New Mexico: Pages 200, 203, 206. Photography Collections, Humanities Research Center, The University of Texas at Austin: Page 262. Frederic Remington (from Arizona Pioneers' Historical Society): Page 139. Leonard Lee Rue III: Pages 19, 74 (third row, center), 90. Santa Fe Railway: Page 219. Southern California Automobile Club: Page 132 (top). Special Collections, University of Arizona Library: Page 180. Special Collections, University of New Mexico Library: Pages 162, 174, 177, 178, 254.

Texas Highway Department: Page 209. Lester Tinker: Page 213. United States Borax & Chemical Corporation: Page 270. U.S. Atomic Energy Commission: Page 233. U.S. Bureau of Indian Affairs: Pages 226, 230. U.S. Forest Service, Southwestern Region: Page 260. Utah Construction & Mining Company: Page 272. Adam Vroman (from History Division, Natural History Museum of Los Angeles County): Pages 149, 150. Del E. Webb Development Company: Page 223. Ben Wittick (from Collections in the Museum of New Mexico): Pages 146, 151, 154, 158, 194.

SOURCES AND SUGGESTED READING

Land and Climate

Arizona Climate by C. Green and W. Sellers; University of Arizona Press, 1964.

Introduction to Physical Geology by W. Miller; Van Nostrand, 1941.

Physiography of the United States by C. Hunt; W. H. Freeman, 1967.

Regional Geomorphology of the United States by W. D. Thornbury; Wiley, 1965.

Story of the Grand Canyon by N. Darton; Fred Harvey, 1962.

Desert

The Desert by A. S. Leopold; Time-Life Nature Series, 1967.

Deserts of America by P. Larson; Prentice-Hall, 1969.

Deserts of the World edited by W. McGinnies, B. J. Goldman, and P. Paylore; University of Arizona Press, 1968.

North American Deserts by E. Jaeger; Stanford University Press, 1957.

The Sonoran Desert: Its Geography, Economy, and People by Roger Dunbier; University of Arizona Press, 1968.

Ecology

The Biotic Provinces of North America by L. Dice; University of Michigan Press, 1943.

The Changing Mile by J. R. Hastings and R. M. Turner; University of Arizona Press, 1965.

Desert Biology, vol. 1, edited by G. W. Brown; Academic Press, 1968.

The Desert Grassland by R. Humphrey; University of Arizona Press, 1958.

The Life of the Desert by A. and M. Sutton; McGraw-Hill, 1966.

Range Ecology by R. Humphrey; Ronald Press, 1962.

The Study of the Plant Communities by H. Oosting; W. H. Freeman, 1956.

Plant Life

Arizona Flora (Revised Edition) by T. H. Kearney and R. H. Peebles; University of California Press, 1960.

The Cacti of Arizona (Third Edition) by L. Benson; University of Arizona Press, 1969.

California Desert Wildflowers by P. A. Munz and D. Keck; University of California Press, 1962.

Desert Wild Flowers by E. Jaeger; Stanford University Press, 1968.

Flowers of the Southwest Deserts by N. Dodge and J. Janish; Southwestern Monuments Association, 1969.

Flowers of the Southwest Mesas by P. Patraw and J. Janish; Southwestern Monuments Association, 1970.

The Genus Pinus by N. T. Mirov; Ronald Press, 1967.

Meet Flora Mexicana by M. Pesman; Dale S. King, 1962.

Natural Geography of Plants by H. Gleason and A. Cronquist; Columbia University Press, 1964.

Rocky Mountain Trees (Second Revised Edition) by R. Preston; Dover, 1968.

Trees of North America by C. F. Brockman; Golden Press, 1968.

Trees, Shrubs, and Woody Vines of the Southwest by R. H. Vines; University of Texas Press, 1960.

Vegetation and Flora of the Sonoran Desert, vols. 1 and 2, by F. Shreve and I. Wiggins; Stanford University Press, 1964.

Animal Life

The Birds of Arizona by A. Phillips, J. Marshall, and G. Monson; University of Arizona Press, 1964.

Birds of North America by C. S. Robbins, B. Bruun, and H. Zim; Golden Press, 1968.

Field Guide to Western Reptiles and Amphibians by R. C. Stebbins; Houghton Mifflin, 1966.

The Lives of Desert Animals in Joshua Tree National Monument by A. Miller and R. Stebbins; University of California Press, 1964.

Mammals of the Pacific States by L. G. Ingles; Stanford University Press, 1965.

Mammals of the Southwest Deserts by G. Olin and J. Cannon; Southwestern Monuments Association, 1970.

Poisonous Dwellers of the Desert (Revised Edition) by N. Dodge; Southwestern Monuments Association, 1970.

Vertebrates of Arizona edited by C. Lowe; University of Arizona Press, 1964.

Wildlife of Mexico by A. S. Leopold; University of California Press, 1959.

Cultures

The American Southwest: Its People and Cultures by Lynn I. Perrigo; Holt, Rinehart, and Winston, 1971.

Bordertown by Frank J. Mangan; Carl Hertzog, 1964.

The Conquest of Apacheria by Dan L. Thrapp; University of Oklahoma Press, 1967.

El Gringo, or New Mexico and Her People by W. W. H. Davis; Rio Grande Press, 1962.

Influentials in Two Border Cities: A Study in Community Decision-Making edited by William V. D'Antonio and William H. Form; University of Notre Dame Press, 1965.

New Mexico: A Pageant of Three Peoples (Second Edition) by Erna Fergusson; Knopf, 1964.

North from Mexico: The Spanish-Speaking People of the United States by Carey McWilliams; Greenwood Press, 1968.

Poso del Mundo: Inside the Mexican-American Border, from Tijuana to Matamoros by Ovid Demaris; Little, Brown, 1970.

"Potam: A Yaqui Village in Sonora," by Edward H. Spicer; *American Anthropologist* 56 (August, 1954): Memoir No. 77.

Prehistoric Indians of the Southwest by H. M. Wormington; Denver Museum of Natural History, Popular Series No. 7, 1970.

Southwestern Archaeology (Second Edition) by J. C. McGregor; University of Illinois Press, 1965.

History

Adventures in the Apache Country: A Tour Through Arizona and Sonora, with Notes on the Silver Regions of Nevada by J. Ross Browne; Harper and Brothers, 1869.

Anza's California Expeditions: Vol. 2, Opening a Land Route to California and *Vol. 4, Font's Complete Diary of the Second Anza Expedition* by Juan Bautista de Anza, translated by Herbert Eugene Bolton; Russell and Russell, 1966.

Army Exploration in the American West, 1803-1863 by William H. Goetzmann; Yale University Press, 1959.

Chihuahua: Storehouse of Storms by Florence C. Lister and Robert H. Lister; University of New Mexico Press, 1966.

The Coronado Expedition, 1540-1542 edited and translated by George Parker Winship; Rio Grande Press, 1964.

Down the Santa Fe Trail and into Mexico . . . by Susan Shelby Magoffin, edited by Stella M. Drumm; Yale University Press, 1926.

Exploration and Empire: The Explorer and the Scientist in the Winning of the American West by William H. Goetzmann; Knopf, 1966.

Filibusters and Financiers: The Story of William Walker and His Associates by William O. Scroggs; Macmillan, 1916.

The Grand Colorado: The Story of a River and Its Canyons by T. H. Watkins et al.; American West, 1969.

Great River: The Rio Grande in North American History (2 vols.) by Paul Horgan; Rinehart, 1954.

Historia del Nuevo Mejico by Don Gaspar Perez de Villagra, translated by Gilberto Espinosa; Rio Grande Press, 1962.

Kino's Historical Memoir of Pimeria Alta: A Contemporary Account of the Beginnings of California, Sonora, and Arizona . . . by Father Eusebio Francisco Kino, S.J., edited by Herbert Eugene Bolton; University of California Press, 1948.

The Life and Death of Colonel Albert Jennings Fountain by Arrel M. Gibson; University of Oklahoma Press, 1965.

Memoirs of Pancho Villa by Martín Luis Guzmán, translated by Virginia H. Taylor; University of Texas Press, 1965.

The Narrative of Alvar Nunez Cabeza de Vaca edited by Frederick W. Hodge; Scribner, 1907.

New Mexico's Royal Road: Trade and Travel on the Chihuahua Trail by Max Moorhead; University of Oklahoma Press, 1958.

New Trails in Mexico: An Account of One Year's Exploration in Northwestern Sonora, Mexico, and Southwestern Arizona, 1909-1910 by Carl Lumholtz; Scribner, 1912.

Pass of the North: Four Centuries on the Rio Grande by C. L. Sonnichsen; Texas Western Press, 1968.

Personal Narrative (2 Vols.) by John R. Bartlett; Rio Grande Press, 1965.

The Personal Narrative of James Ohio Pattie of Kentucky edited by Timothy Flint in 1831 and by Milo M. Quaife in 1930; Lakeside Press, 1930.

Western America in 1846-1847: The Original Travel Diary of Lieutenant J. W. Abert, Who Mapped New Mexico for the United States Army edited by John Galvin; John Howell, 1966.

The Year of Decision: 1846 by Bernard DeVoto; Little, Brown, 1943.

Mining

The Company Town in the American West by James B. Allen; University of Oklahoma Press, 1966.

A History of Phelps Dodge, 1834-1950 by Robert Glass Cleland; Knopf, 1952.

The Silver Magnet; Fifty Years in a Mexican Silver Mine by Grant Shepherd; E. P. Dutton, 1938.

Water Resources

Arid Lands in Perspective—Including AAAS Papers on Water Importation into Arid Lands edited by William G. McGinnies and Bram J. Goldman; American Association for the Advancement of Science and University of Arizona Press, 1969.

Aridity and Man: The Challenge of the Arid Lands of the United States edited by Carle O. Hodge; American Association for the Advancement of Science, 1963.

A Century of Disagreement: The Chamizal Conflict, 1864-1964 by Sheldon B. Liss; University Press of Washington, D.C., 1965.

Dividing the Waters: A Century of Controversy Between the United States and Mexico by Norris Hundley, Jr.; University of California Press, 1966.

International Water Law Along the Mexican Border by Clark S. Knowlton; University of Texas at El Paso, 1968.

The Politics of Water in Arizona by Dean E. Mann; University of Arizona Press, 1963.

Water and Choice in the Colorado Basin: An Example of Alternatives in Water Management; National Academy of Sciences, 1968.

Water Supplies for Arid Regions edited by J. Linton Gardner and Lloyd E. Myers; American Association for the Advancement of Science and the University of Arizona, 1967.

Miscellaneous

The Architecture of the Southwest by Trent Elwood Sanford; Norton, 1950.

Arizona Characters by Frank C. Lockwood; Times-Mirror Press, 1928.

Autobiography of a Durable Sinner by Owen White; G. P. Putnam's Sons, 1942.

The Big Bend Country of Texas by Virginia Madison; University of New Mexico Press, 1955.

Commerce of the Prairies by Josiah Gregg, edited by Max L. Moorhead; University of Oklahoma Press, 1954.

Farewell to Texas: A Vanishing Wilderness by William O. Douglas; McGraw-Hill, 1967.

Horse and Buggy West: A Boyhood on the Last Frontier by Jack O'Connor; Knopf, 1969.

"Meals by Fred Harvey": A Phenomenon of the American West by James David Henderson; Texas Christian University Press, 1969.

New Mexico Village Arts by Roland F. Dickey; University of New Mexico Press, 1970.

Sky Determines (Revised Edition) by Calvin Ross; University of New Mexico Press, 1948.

Tijerina and the Courthouse Raid by Peter Nabokov; University of New Mexico Press, 1969.

Unknown Mexico, vol. 1, by Carl Lumholtz; Scribner, 1902.

INDEX

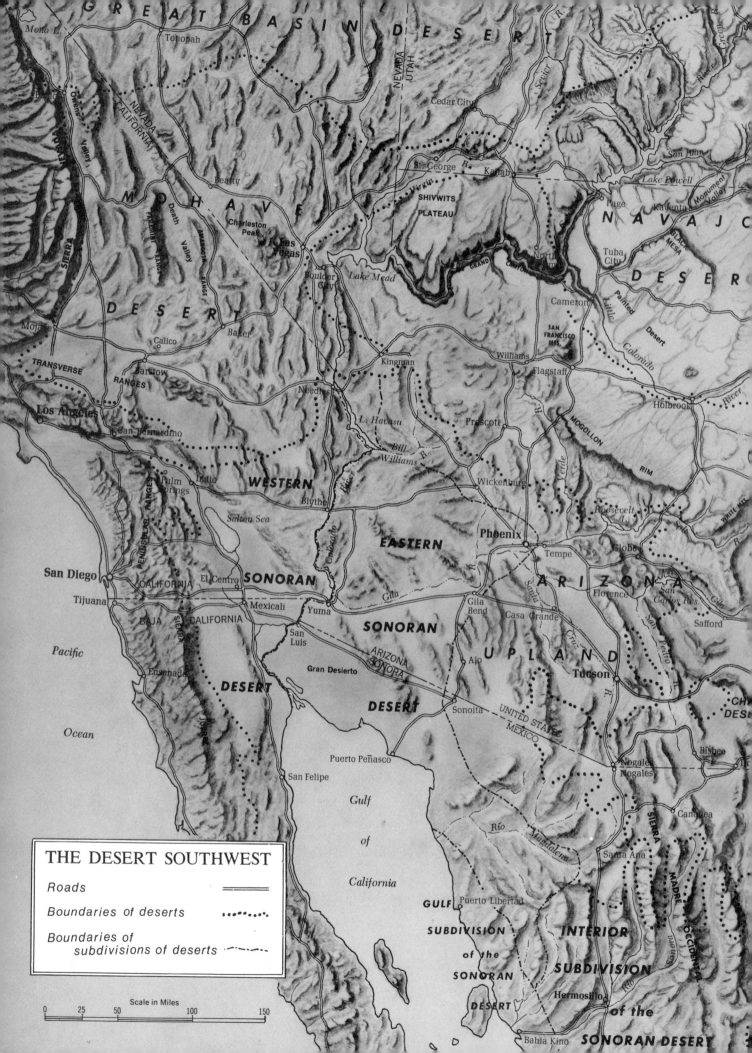

GREAT BASIN DESERT

Mono L.
Tonopah
Beatty
SIERRA
Death Valley
Charleston Peak
PANAMINT RANGE
AMARGOSA RANGE
NEVADA
CALIFORNIA
Owens Valley

M O H A V E
D E S E R T

Mojave
Calico
Barstow
TRANSVERSE RANGES
Los Angeles
San Bernardino

Las Vegas
Boulder City
Lake Mead
Baker
Needles

NEVADA
UTAH

Cedar City
St. George
Virgin R.
Kanab
SHIVWITS
PLATEAU
Sevier R.

Lake Powell
Page
Kayenta
Monument Valley
San Juan R.

N A V A J O
D E S E R T
BLACK MESA
Tuba City

GRAND CANYON
North Rim
Cameron
SAN FRANCISCO MTS.
Williams
Flagstaff
MOGOLLON
RIM
Little Colorado
Painted Desert
Holbrook
R.

Kingman
L. Havasu
Bill Williams R.
Prescott
Wickenburg
Verde R.
Roosevelt
WHITE MTS.

WESTERN
Blythe
Salton Sea
Palm Springs
Indio
PENINSULAR RANGES

EASTERN

Colorado R.
Phoenix
Tempe
Globe
Salt R.

San Diego
Tijuana
CALIFORNIA
El Centro
SONORAN
Mexicali
Yuma
San Luis
BAJA CALIFORNIA
SIERRA

SONORAN
Gila R.
Gila Bend
Casa Grande
Ajo
A R I Z O N A
Florence
San Carlos Res.
Gila R.
Safford
San Pedro R.
Santa Cruz R.

Pacific
Ocean

Gran Desierto
ARIZONA
SONORA

U P L A N D
Tucson

D E S E R T
Ensenada
JUAREZ

D E S E R T
Sonoita
UNITED STATES
MEXICO
CHI
DES

Puerto Peñasco
San Felipe

Gulf
of
California

Nogales
Nogales
Bisbee
Cananea
SIERRA
MADRE

Rio Magdalena
Santa Ana
OCCIDENTAL

GULF
SUBDIVISION
of
the
SONORAN
DESERT
Puerto Libertad

INTERIOR
SUBDIVISION
of the
SONORAN DESERT
Hermosillo
Bahia Kino

THE DESERT SOUTHWEST

Roads ————

Boundaries of deserts ••••••••

Boundaries of
subdivisions of deserts –·–·–·

Scale in Miles
0   25   50   100   150

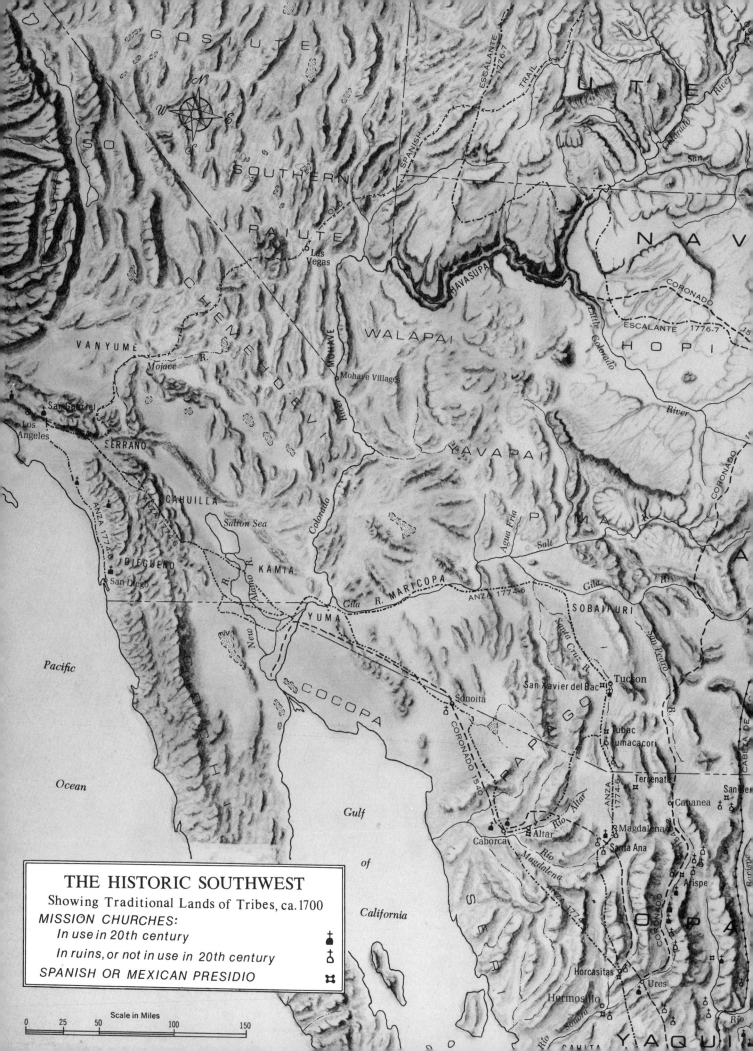

THE HISTORIC SOUTHWEST
Showing Traditional Lands of Tribes, ca. 1700
MISSION CHURCHES:
In use in 20th century
In ruins, or not in use in 20th century
SPANISH OR MEXICAN PRESIDIO

Scale in Miles
0   25   50   100   150

The type selected for this book is Baskerville, designed by English master craftsman John Baskerville in the mid-eighteenth century. Color separations are by Graphic Arts Center of Portland, Oregon; typography by Paul O. Giesey/Adcrafters, Portland; printing and binding by Kingsport Press, Kingsport, Tennessee.

Design by Arthur Andersen.